Anne Tyler as Novelist

Anne Tyler as Novelist

EDITED BY DALE SALWAK

UNIVERSITY OF IOWA PRESS  IOWA CITY

University of Iowa Press,

Iowa City 52242

Copyright © 1994 by the

University of Iowa Press

Printed in the United States of America

Design by Richard Hendel

Frontispiece photo by Diana Walker

Printed on acid-free paper

Library of Congress Cataloging-in-Publication Data

Anne Tyler as novelist / edited by Dale Salwak.

p.   cm.

Includes bibliographical references and index.

ISBN 0-87745-479-5, ISBN 0-87745-487-6 (paper)

1. Tyler, Anne—Criticism and interpretation.   I. Salwak, Dale.

PS3570.Y45Z54   1994

813'.54—dc20

[B]   94-17014

CIP

01   00   99   98   97   96   95   94   C   5   4   3   2   1

01   00   99   98   97   96   95   94   P   5   4   3   2   1

FOR GENEVIEVE CURLEY

Contents

Preface

If asked to give a general idea of Anne Tyler's novels, we would soon be talking about a steady concern with the American family; a quietly comic touch; an unobtrusive but perfectly controlled style; and a prodigious gift for bringing to life a variety of eccentric characters, their fears and concerns, their longings for meaning and understanding.

We might also be saying, along with so many of her reviewers, that each of her novels elicits from us "a deep sense of wonder—at the fundamental blindness of those with whom intimacy is greatest, at the way a chance encounter can forever change a life, and at the wrenching costs and sweet rewards of taking responsibility for others." Ordinary families with extraordinary troubles—this is her "great subject."[1]

The seventeen essays that follow concentrate on these and other distinctive features that have earned Anne Tyler, over the past thirty years, an ever-expanding body of devoted readers. Writing from a variety of critical approaches and representing some of the best among today's critics, the contributors discuss Tyler's early years and influences, development and beliefs, fictional attainments, and literary reputation stretching from her first published novel, *If Morning Ever Comes* (1964), to her twelfth, *Saint Maybe* (1991). All but two of the essays were written expressly for this volume.

The process which led to this collection began over ten years ago, and had its start with my admiration for the author and her writing and with my own search for anything at all that had been published on the subject. After she was awarded the National Book Circle Critics Award in 1985 for *The Accidental Tourist* and the Pulitzer Prize in 1988 for *Breathing Lessons*, I noticed a significant increase in the serious critical attention given to her career. Because she is heralded now as one of America's most important and accomplished writers, and because so much remains to be said of her work, it seems appropriate to bring together at last an inclusive, up-to-date study of all of her novels as a way of paying tribute to the writer herself.

Without exception, those whom I solicited responded favorably to the idea. Said one: "I admire and enjoy her work so much, and the generosity of her outlook and 'writing temperament.'" And another: "It gives me great pleasure to add my tribute, in writing, to those you will receive." And yet another: "Your invitation to write about Anne Tyler honors me, and of course I adore her and her work." I am deeply grateful to all the contributors who helped make this volume possible.

Ideally the reader of this book is someone who has already encountered the many pleasures of Anne Tyler's novels and wants to know more about them as well as their author. At the same time there may be people who have heard of her but have not yet read her works, and I hope that these essays will be useful to them as well. Altogether, may this collection perform the rightful function of all criticism in returning the reader finally to the imaginative work of the artist.

In a 1983 review of Barbara Pym's novel *No Fond Return of Love*, Anne Tyler said of Pym that she was "the rarest of treasures."[2] Certainly we may say the same of Tyler herself—and for reasons given in the essays that follow.

Acknowledgments

Grateful acknowledgment is made to the following
for permission to reprint previously published materials:
John Updike, Alfred A. Knopf, Inc., and André Deutsch,
Ltd., for "Family Ways" and "Loosened Roots" (*Hugging
the Shore*, 1983).

Every effort has been made to trace all copyright-
holders, but if any have been inadvertently overlooked
the publisher will be pleased to make the necessary
arrangement at the first opportunity.

Anne Tyler as Novelist

1 / Early Years and Influences

Nothing puts writers on their guard faster, than mention of "influence"—the suggestion, in a review or critical essay, that their work bears the mark of someone else. Small wonder, too; for when critics use the word it often has a euphemistic ring. You can just picture a schoolteacher holding up two identical test papers and accusing one student of being "influenced" by the other's answers.

Tyler begins her review of *In Praise of What Persists* (edited by Stephen Berg, the book consists of essays by twenty-four writers who spoke about what had influenced their work) with this disclaimer, warning that to suggest a particular writer indeed *influenced* another is at best risky.[1] While Tyler concedes that influence occurs, the fact remains that many writers "may strongly disagree with the critics as to who caused that effect or *what* caused it."[2] One of the contributors to this collection, Reynolds Price, recalls his resentment when reviewers declared that *A Long and Happy Life* (1962) "sprang from the side of Faulkner." Price resented being "looped into the long and crowded cow chain that stretched behind a writer" whom he admired but did not count as a conscious influence. And, Price continues, he spent much time insisting on alternative masters—"the Bible, Milton, Tolstoy, Eudora Welty."[3]

The question of "influence" is slippery and the sharply differing responses in Berg's sampling of writers "point up," as he notes, "the vanity of generalizing too far beyond the evidence of the writer's own testimony."[4] These essays show that the variety of significant influence is great and sometimes resists explanation. Berg suggests that "the mystery of the phenomenon remains and grows richer and more complex as each writer defines it in his own way."[5] Literary indebtedness in a standard sense means that one writer feels "a more or less accurate and conscious appropriation of ideas, techniques, tone of voice" from another writer.[6] Although many writers acknowledge the need of a suitable literary role model, Cynthia Ozick declares that "to be any sort of competent writer, one must keep one's psychological distance from the supreme artists. . . . Rapture and homage are not the way. Influence is perdition."[7] In a different image, Raymond Carver says that "influences are forces—circumstances, personalities, irresistible as the tide."[8] Evidence from writers themselves suggests that "influence" is a complex process and indeed a process that stems as often from the mundane as from the miraculous.

In her review, Tyler concludes that *In Praise of What Persists* explores "the struggle to find one's own voice, and to know *why* to write, as well as how and what to write."[9] And while the creative process is surely subject to many stages and many traceable influences—both from circumstances and personalities—part of that process "can only be accounted for by a notion such as inspiration."[10]

"One's influences," Gilbert Sorrentino notes, "are deeper than the 'merely' literary; are, indeed, at the core of one's life."[11] For Anne Tyler, as for most writers, "influence" reflects the chances and accidents of her individual life—her Quaker parents, her formative years living in "blessed communities," her early schooling (mostly from Baltimore's Calvert Home School Program), her major in Russian at Duke University, her marriage to an Iranian child psychiatrist and novelist, her sensitivity to *place*, her formidable reading. And Tyler has often acknowledged the influence of Eudora Welty, whose work "showed me that very small things are often really larger than the large things."[12]

The Celo Community near Burnsville, North Carolina, was the

last of a series of "blessed communities" where Anne Tyler's parents sought refuge from the traditional American life of competition. Here, near the foot of Mount Mitchell, the Tylers moved in 1948 and were secluded with the other residents of the community in the beautiful mountains of western North Carolina. Many years later an interviewer asked her, "How did your childhood or other experiences influence your work?" Tyler's answer gave a glimpse of those early days: "I think the fact that I had a fairly isolated childhood influenced me considerably. I was raised in a sort of commune arrangement, without many other children; I learned to be alone and to entertain myself by imagining, and when I left the commune (at the age of eleven) I looked at the regular world from an unusually distant vantage point." [13]

Tyler remembers that as a small child she whispered stories to herself in bed at night "in which I'd pretend to be various other people—a woman named Delores with eighteen children . . . and a girl going west in a covered wagon." [14] Although the Tyler children were educated primarily at home, their parents "sent the children to the local school briefly when we felt it was important to them to have other children as friends. In the end we just sent them for recess. . . . Celo was a perfect place for a 'home school.' The children learned arithmetic working at the Co-op Store, and other friends . . . helped teach subjects that particularly interested them. . . . I don't think it hurt the children scholastically to be taught at home. The boys all earned Ph.D.'s and Ty an M.D. after a Ph.D. in physics." [15] Phyllis Tyler (the author's mother) recalls that during the brief time when Anne Tyler did attend the two-room log schoolhouse (ironically named Harvard), her experience was singular. "Every day the teacher went to see to his farms immediately after prayers and left Anne to 'give out' (meaning stand in front of the class and call out words from the speller) until he came back to dismiss school and to pay Anne a nickel for teaching a day at Harvard."

Life at Celo centered on hard work, but it allowed some time for folk dancing and singing. Phyllis Tyler remembers that "people sat around evenings listening to symphony and opera music on records—although I can't imagine now how we ever had the time. . . . One community member was the County Bookmobile librarian; she'd drop off books she thought we'd like at each house as she walked through the community on her way home from work. We'd gather in the evenings to read aloud." Crafts were very much a part of the community's life and several residents, Mrs. Tyler notes, belonged to the Southern Appalachian Handicrafts Guild. Home gardens were very important and Anne Tyler's father always had an especially successful one. Perhaps the goat-raising phase in the lives of Duncan and Justine Peck (in *Searching for Caleb*) stems from Tyler's early years at Celo. The family kept goats because their son Seth was allergic to cow's milk. Their breeding stock came from the herd that Mrs. Carl Sandburg kept with such success on the Sandburg acres in Flat Rock, North Carolina.

When she was eleven, the family left the community and settled in Raleigh, North Carolina, where Tyler found public school a different experience. Doubtless her classmates were intrigued by the new member who "had never used a telephone and could strike a match on the soles of my bare feet." [16] The early years at Celo gave Tyler what she describes as "my sense of distance," a condition she says she has "come to cherish. Neither I nor any of my brothers can stand being out among a crowd of people for any length of time at all." [17]

That distance, the relative isolation from the bustle of urban life, the absence of many playmates, and the disciplined quiet of the Quakers are part of Tyler's formative years. And when she creates Emily in *Morgan's Passing*, Tyler draws upon the Quaker influence, presenting Emily as "reserved and quiet" around her husband's parents, perhaps because Emily "came from old Quaker stock and tended, she'd been told, to feel a little too comfortable in the face of long silence." In *Morgan's Passing* (and in *Searching for Caleb*), Tyler portrays scenes of a Quaker gathering. When Aunt Mercer dies, Emily goes home for the service at the Meetinghouse—"the only Friends Meeting in Taney County . . . small and poor as ever, a gray frame cubicle huddled in the back yard of the Savior Baptist Church; and everyone approaching it was old. . . . There was no one under fifty."

Reading (and being read to) during the early childhood years exerted an obvious influence on Anne Tyler, and a distinct experience at the age of four brought her a moment of insight that has lingered. For this birthday (in 1945) Tyler got a plaster doll, a tin suitcase, and a copy of *The Little House* by Virginia Lee Burton, a book that impressed Tyler. She felt she had "been presented with a snapshot that showed me how the world worked: how the years flowed by and people altered and nothing could ever stay the same. Then the snapshot was taken away. Everything there is to know about time was revealed in that snapshot, and I can almost name it, I very nearly have it in my grasp . . . but then it's gone again, and all that's left is a ragged green book with the binding fallen apart" (Tyler's ellipsis).[18] She may have been very young, Tyler says, but that was a moment when she acquired wisdom.

When Tyler reviewed Bruno Bettelheim's *The Uses of Enchantment: The Meaning and Importance of Fairy Tales*, she reassessed her "lifelong hatred of fairy tales."[19] She had told her two daughters for years that the implausibilities in plot and the repeated mistakes that the heroes made in fairy tales had insulted her even when she was very young. "I was furious," Tyler writes, "when what occasionally appeared to be a highly relevant problem (mean mother, unprotective father) was followed by a solution that I could not possibly hope for in real life (fairy godmother waving a magic wand)." Now, years later, Tyler accepts Bettelheim's contention that fairy tales provide valuable experience and touchstones in a child's development. Reading Bettelheim reminded Tyler, "much to my astonishment, that there really was a time in the long-distant past when fairy-tales meant something important to me. And more than that, that at least one ('Beauty and the Beast,' which I thought I'd forgotten) seems to have remained with me and become incorporated into my life in ways I had never imagined." The "influence" of fairy tales threads its way into the lives of most people who read them early; they have also provided Tyler with an allusive source, as evident particularly in *Celestial Navigation* and *Morgan's Passing*.

Another of Tyler's book reviews considers two exceptionally important "influences," conditions that certainly begin in the early childhood years: daydreaming and inactivity. In *Creativity: The Magic Synthesis*, Silvano Arieti explores the creative process of the writer. In his argument, Tyler says, Arieti becomes "positively endearing"[20] because he counts daydreaming as a necessary condition for the creative process. Daydreaming, Tyler declares, is "the most useful activity I know of, but until now it's been almost universally frowned upon." When Silvano also counts inactivity essential, Tyler applauds: "It's high time someone mentioned that. We are raised in a culture where busyness (no matter at what) is all-important. Our mothers' first recorded words to us are 'Stop staring into space.' Actually, most creative work is begun by nothing *but* staring into space, but we try not to let anyone catch us at it." Significant experiences in childhood—reading, daydreaming, pretending to be characters in made-up stories, "staring into space"—are primary forces in the writing life of Tyler.

Of course, associations with people also influence writers. In Anne Tyler's life, two teachers from Broughton High School in Raleigh, North Carolina, figure prominently—Alice Ehrlich (who taught Tyler art in grades 10, 11, and 12) and Phyllis Peacock (the highly praised English teacher whose most outstanding pupils are Reynolds Price and Anne Tyler). Phyllis Peacock (now retired and in frail health) recently recalled her teaching days and modestly insisted that her students' successes "didn't have anything to do with me. . . . It was the student being brought out by the teacher."[21] However, Peacock sensed Anne Tyler's talent very early, and that response, Tyler has said, "made a huge difference."[22] In the classroom Peacock dramatized the literature she shared with her students, even falling to her knees, Tyler remembers, to read "a dying man's speech from Shakespeare."[23] The energy Peacock brought to the classroom (she had no desk chair because she never spared the time to sit down) may at times, Tyler admits, have led some of the teenage students to smirk, "but invariably they were drawn in—maybe because they were impressed that mere words on paper could matter so much to someone."[24] Clearly, words on paper—to read and to write—mattered deeply to Anne Tyler, and Phyllis Peacock is remembered with fondness and with gratitude. In 1964 when Tyler published her first novel, *If Morning Ever Comes*, the copy she presented to her high-school English teacher bore the inscription: "To Mrs. Peacock. For everything you've done. Anne."[25] Peacock's gentle face and weak eyes brighten at the mention of Anne Tyler's name. "If only," she told me when I visited with her in February 1993, "you had come earlier when I could have told you so much."[26] The ravages of age preclude sustained conversations now.

Tyler spent her high-school years planning to be an artist, not a writer, and her art teacher, Alice Ehrlich, thought that when Anne Tyler graduated from Broughton High School "she was going to do something in art."[27] Alice Ehrlich remembers the *many* outstanding students in her classes at Broughton in the late 1950s and sensed that

Tyler "had a gift." Most of the outstanding art students were also excellent English students, and often Ehrlich joined forces with Peacock and with the music teacher for joint projects with their students. (Ehrlich remembers all four of the Tyler children—Anne, Seth, Israel, and Jonathan—and says of them all, "brilliant is the only word that comes to mind.")

In art class, Ehrlich did not try to change Tyler's style, but let her student alone, and Tyler produced "some wonderful things," paintings she was reluctant for Ehrlich to show anyone. Occasionally the students held "little art shows at Broughton," Ehrlich remembers, "and some of the teachers bought the work." Ehrlich regrets that she has none of Tyler's paintings, but a Broughton colleague who taught chemistry "has two pieces of Anne's" that she bought at one of the art shows. Ehrlich says that Tyler's paintings were "very distinctive" and generally depicted people rather than landscapes or specific scenes in nature. "Sometimes," she says, "it was a trilogy—sometimes it was like mother, father, and child. It was usually a family . . . and very stylized. Her people were very stylized." The emphasis on family members with stylized features in Tyler's early art work makes an interesting link to the major concern of her fiction: the family with all its quirky ways and eccentric members.

Like Peacock, Ehrlich proudly displays the signed copies of Tyler's novels which the author sends to her teacher. Probably because her book club in Raleigh was to discuss *Saint Maybe*, Ehrlich asked Phyllis Tyler how on earth Tyler knew about such a thing as the "Church of the Second Chance," which figures in her latest novel. The answer was that Tyler "just drove by one day and [saw] people coming out" from a store-front church. And that was enough. "You know," Ehrlich added, sensing that such a brief glimpse was quite enough for Tyler, "she's got an active imagination." And Tyler is, as Henry James would say, one upon whom nothing is lost. Ehrlich remembers with great pleasure the three years Tyler studied art with her. "I really felt very, very close to her. I think I was the one who was lucky. Anne was one of the most delightful people."

Talented in their own spheres (in February 1993, Ehrlich exhibited her own work at the Horace Williams House in nearby Chapel Hill), these two teachers were alert to the talents of their remarkable student, who in turn has honored them in her own success.

When Reynolds Price (now James B. Duke Professor of English) met his first class as a young instructor at Duke University in 1958, Anne Tyler was sitting in the front row. Price does not remember whether or not his Broughton High School English teacher, Phyllis Peacock, had alerted him to this unusual student from Raleigh, but Price was "immensely impressed with Anne Tyler right away."[28] Price taught Tyler English 1 and 2, the first two semesters of her freshman year. In the late 1950s, these classes at Duke were segregated and Tyler was among a group of eighteen women students. English 1 required ten 500-word essays; the first assignment was to write a memory of an event that took place as early as the student could remember. Tyler handed in three-fourths of a page, and Price recalled this paper in my recent interview with him. In *Clear Pictures: First Loves, First Guides*, Price also gives an account of Tyler's paper and says that, of all his students in freshman composition who attempted this assignment, only Anne Tyler went as far back into memory as he himself was able to go.[29] Thus, as he began his teaching career at Duke University, Price "was aware very fast that someone extraordinary was sitting in the front row." Eudora Welty says of Tyler and Price: "Anne Tyler was a whiz from the time she was seventeen." She laughs as she recalls that "Reynolds Price had Anne for one of his first students. He thought, 'Teaching is going to be great!' He thought *all* his students were going to be like Anne."[30]

For a later assignment, Tyler turned in an essay about life in the Celo Community (perhaps entitled "Galax Picking," Price says). Price was so impressed with Tyler's essay that he told her to ignore his future assignments and simply hand in whatever she wrote. The obligatory (and sometimes wearisome) twenty-minute conferences that professors conducted with freshmen were, in Tyler's case, always "good, and she always had a perfect paper."

During Tyler's sophomore year, Price took over a creative-writing class for a colleague. Among the students were the now prominent poet Fred Chappell and Anne Tyler. The class often met in the home of Fred and Sue Chappell, where students read and discussed their work as well as the "text" for the class—the Modern Library volume of Eudora Welty's short stories. The first story Tyler submitted, Price recalls, was about a young girl going to a dance. It was in this class that Tyler wrote and submitted to Price "The Saints in Caesar's Household," the story of Mary Robinson, who returns from New York to her hometown to find that her best school friend Laura Gates had also returned from her job in Chicago some time ago. Somehow Mary's mother could never convey the news of Laura's return in any letters to Mary. Laura's aberrant behavior has been town gossip and now she is mad, beyond Mary's reach. Some fifteen years earlier, Eudora Welty had sent Price to her agent, Diarmuid Russell, and now Price—continuing an important circle of influence—sent "The Saints in Caesar's Household" to Russell. Although Russell liked the story very much, he did not succeed in placing it.

"The Saints in Caesar's Household" did reach print, first in the Duke University literary publication *Archive* (April 1961). It was quickly reprinted in *The Young Writer at Work* (1962), edited by Jessie Rehder, and in *Under Twenty-Five* (1963), edited by William Blackburn. Price finds that the story touches a deep vein and considers it among the excellent short stories. (Every year, Price says, he reads "The Saints in Caesar's Household" for his classes, demonstrating the story that lies within the writer.) In the creative-writing class in Tyler's sophomore year, Price says she "did a lot of good fiction" and he saw that fiction as "original from the start." (Indeed, five of Tyler's stories appeared in *Archive* during her undergraduate days at Duke, 1958–61.)[31]

Price also remembers Tyler's performance of Laura in Tennessee Williams's *The Glass Menagerie*, a role that seems so compatible with many Tyler characters—a vulnerable person who cautiously perseveres in the world. Price remembers Tyler in her student days as "self-possessed, witty, communicative," traits she maintains even though she shuns the public attention many authors crave. Price describes Tyler as having an "Athena-quality," seeing her as both "wise and benign, but with the quality of deep melancholy in her work—a powerful combination that renders her work anything *but* sunny in a sentimental way."

Painting had early been Reynolds Price's medium, and he says, "In the 1950s that lone skill would have doomed me to a life of commissioned portraits—any barnacled matron or rubicund bank-president who could drum up the money."[32] For Tyler, too, art was not to be the line of creativity that she would follow. As her mother remembers it, Tyler "had trouble making the decision until she took an aptitude test at Duke which showed she'd never make it as a painter but might as a writer." (Anne Tyler's two daughters, Mitra and Tezh, are both following art-related careers. In the fall of 1993, Tyler published her first book for children, *Tumble Tower*. This winning story about Princess Molly the Messy is illustrated by Tyler's daughter Mitra Modarressi.) The early publications for Tyler in *Archive* were quickly followed by short stories in national publications—"I Play Kings" in *Seventeen* (August 1963) and "The Street of Bugles" in *Saturday Evening Post* (30 November 1963). In 1966 one of her best short stories, "As the Earth Gets Older," appeared in the coveted pages of the *New Yorker*. The success in publishing and the encouragement Reynolds Price offered played a large part in setting Tyler on her path as a fiction writer. When Tyler was his student, Price said to her, "You can write anything you want to write." And it seems she has done—and *is doing*—just that.

While Price's instruction and encouragement were of great importance, it is the influence of Eudora Welty that Tyler continues to acknowledge most frequently. In "Still Just Writing" Tyler describes her link to Welty:

> I spent my adolescence planning to be an artist, not a writer. After all, books had to be about major events, and none had ever happened to me. All I knew were tobacco workers, stringing the leaves I handed them and talking up a storm. Then I found a book of Eudora Welty's short stories in the high school library. She was writing about Edna Earle, who was so slow-witted she could sit all day just pondering how the tail of the *C* got through the *L* on the Coca-Cola sign ["The Wide Net"]. Why, I knew Edna Earle. You mean you could *write* about such people? I have always meant to send Eudora Welty a thank-you note, but I imagine she would find it a little strange.[33]

Recently I recounted this passage to Eudora Welty, who said of the thought-of-but-unsent thank-you note, "It'd be a great honor. Of course, Anne doesn't need any kind of influence. That's one thing I admire so about her."[34]

When Welty's *Collected Stories* appeared in 1980, Tyler reviewed the volume for the *Washington Star*, expressing her affinity for Welty and her world. "For me as a girl—a Northerner growing up in the South, longingly gazing over the fence at the rich, tangled lives of the Southern neighbors—Eudora Welty was a window upon the world."[35] When I mentioned this, Welty crisply replied, "Well, I think that's a two-way window. She works for me, too. She doesn't need anybody else. She doesn't need anything."

While the sublime modesty of Eudora Welty makes it difficult to discuss *her* influence on Anne Tyler, these two writers—both with northern ties by birth but with southern upbringings—express mutual admiration, and Welty's for Tyler is extreme. They even share a fear of merging into freeway traffic,[36] and, more importantly, an early interest in art as well as a reluctance to show their work in progress to anyone. (You keep such work, Welty says, "in its own pre-finished stage and just the way it is with all of its faults looking at you . . . and not *wanting* anybody to look at it.") Welty calls Tyler a "self-sufficient" writer, and when I suggested that, like Welty, Tyler had a great talent for humor, Welty replied: "Like *me*! She is the best . . . and anyway, she writes so well. I told her once if I could have written the last sentence in *Dinner at the Homesick Restaurant* I'd have been happy for the rest of my life."[37] Welty praises Tyler's latest novel, *Saint Maybe* ("I love her last novel. I'm crazy about it!"), and says of the zany character Rita diCarlo, the Clutter Consultant, "I love that, don't you? Gee, if I had her this minute!" And Rita's name, Welty says, is "so believable." When I recounted some details and the titles of Tyler's unpublished novels—*Winter Birds, Winter Apples, I Know You, Rider,* and *Panteleo*—Welty responded, "Wonderful titles! Oh, golly. Just kind of gives me gooseflesh to think about them."

Recently Eudora Welty was honored at a Washington dinner party hosted by Tim Seldes, the literary agent for both Welty and Tyler. It was a gathering of old friends of Welty's, but perhaps the guests who pleased her most were Dr. and Mrs. Taghi Modarressi: "I was especially impressed and touched and happy," Welty said, "that Anne came—all the way from Baltimore!"

Clearly Welty's fiction *has* influenced Tyler, giving her the example of humor, of *place*, of eccentric characters who baffle and charm, of dialogue that sharply defines a character, of lyric description. But Welty demurs from claiming *influence* and concedes only that the influence of one writer upon another is more a matter of absorption and sharing views of the world than anything else. "Especially," Welty adds, "with an original mind."

In *Romantic Imprisonment: Women and Other Glorified Outcasts,* Nina Auerbach discusses whether or not Jane Austen echoed the

Romantic poets in the pages of her novels. Austen's letters and her "irreverent mentions in later novels," Auerbach contends, indicate that she viewed "the poetry of her Romantic contemporaries with a certain lofty and sardonic mistrust, if she regarded it at all.... We cannot know how much she read, how much she shielded herself from, how much simply bored her, but it is safe to surmise that the 'shades of the prison-house' that close over her fiction as well as their poetry come less from mutual influence than from a *common cultural ambiance*" (my italics).[38] Much of what Anne Tyler shares with Eudora Welty (and other writers she admires) might well be described, in Auerbach's phrase, as their common cultural ambience. Both Tyler and Welty—for all their durable humor—write fiction underscored with the inevitable tragedies of life: fractious characters, strained marriages, wandering husbands and fathers,[39] the deaths of loved ones. They depict in the pages of their novels and short stories an immediate place, populated with characters whose speech, manner of dress, and daily preoccupations reveal their worlds. Both Tyler and Welty have used political issues sparingly; neither uses sex very explicitly; and the military conflicts of the 20th century remain behind a virtual scrim in their work. The fulcrum of their fiction is the family—often with its ancestors and usually with all of its current extended members—their occupations, their failed dreams, their risks, their compromises, and their view of life which is shaped so much by the local forces they experience.

Several critics have discussed precise literary echoes in Tyler's fiction, and in doing so have raised the matter of influence. In *Understanding Anne Tyler*, Alice Hall Petry stresses the connections between Tyler and Hawthorne (in *A Slipping-Down Life*, Evie Decker's mutilated forehead is her sign, as the Scarlet Letter was Hester Prynne's; and Evie lives on Hawthorne Street), between Tyler and Emerson (in *The Clock Winder*, the principal family bears the surname Emerson, ironic since they are all singularly *un*-self-reliant), and between Tyler and Thoreau (in *Celestial Navigation*, Mary Tell makes her retreat to an isolated lake cabin). Indeed, Petry says in her excellent discussion of the literary influences on Tyler, "one would do well to keep copies of Emerson, Thoreau, and Hawthorne on hand when reading Anne Tyler's novels."[40] But, as Petry demonstrates so well, overemphasizing borrowings and echoes from other authors is to skate on thin ice.[41]

Anne Tyler says that her major in Russian at Duke University played a significant part in forming her writing life—the form and technique of the great Russian writers were important to her course of study and to her development as a writer. Echoes and reflections from this study may well thread their way into Tyler's fiction in conscious and unconscious ways. The opening sentence of *Anna Karenina* provides a paradigm of sorts for all of Tyler's fiction. So familiar as to be almost a cliché, Tolstoy's line rings true: "Happy families are all alike; every unhappy family is unhappy in its own way."[42] The characters in Tyler's fiction—from the Hawkes family in *If Morning Ever Comes* (1964) to the Bedloes in *Saint Maybe* (1991)—bear out the truth of individual unhappiness within the family. Yet these same families, however strained and fractious, do somehow survive. As Petry discusses in her "Overview," Tyler's long interest in the Russian authors suggests that Chekhov and Turgenev, especially, have provided important elements for her, both in technique and in character types. Like Millicent Bell (in her review of *The Tin Can Tree*)[43] and Reynolds Price, Petry also sees an "indebtedness" to Carson McCullers. "Tyler," Petry argues, "seems receptive to McCullers's dictum that we must learn to 'connect' with one another, that love is one of the few defenses we have against a world that seems antagonistic towards a strong sense of both selfhood and freedom."[44]

Tyler's many reviews of novels and short-story collections over the past twenty-odd years (primarily in the *National Observer*, the *New York Times Book Review*, and the *New Republic*) provide evidence of the qualities she admires in fiction: plots that the author constructs so that the reader *can* follow, apt details that imbue character and place with life, and (most of all) fiction that enlarges "our view of human beings."[45] On some level Tyler is doubtless "influenced" by writers who share her views of fiction and its purpose.

When Flannery O'Connor was asked about "influence," she said that she did not "really start to read" until she entered graduate school at the University of Iowa in 1945.[46] "Then I began to read everything at once, so much so that I didn't have time I suppose to be influenced by any one writer." O'Connor's reading quickly became formidable. Yet when she was asked by a correspondent to name the authors she had read who influenced her, O'Connor found the subject "embarrassing. I hope nobody ever asks me in public. If so I intend to look dark and mutter 'Henry James, Henry James'—which will be the veriest lie, but no matter. I have not been influenced by the best people." In a more serious tone, O'Connor added that she had indeed "read almost all of Henry James—from a sense of High Duty and because when I read James I feel something is happening to me, in slow motion but happening nevertheless." Anne Tyler is not drawn to the fiction of Flannery O'Connor, but she may well agree with O'Connor's view of literary influences: *what* a writer reads does influence *what* that writer herself writes, even though the influence occurs "in slow motion."

Reviewers and critics sometimes overstate the business of influence altogether; perhaps they need to remember "the vanity of generalizing too far beyond the evidence of the writer's own testimony."[47] In a review, Tyler said that Renata Adler's novel *Speedboat* "was a wonderfully fresh and thoughtful book, written as if the author neither knew nor cared how other people wrote; she would proceed in her own remarkable way"[48]—and proceed, apparently, without benefit of influence. Anne Tyler herself needs no one else's answers to copy; like all sensitive writers, she has absorbed from listening and reading, and from observing and remembering those nuances and ideas which other writers share in a common cultural ambience.

2 / The Early Novels

A Reconsideration

Since the late 1970s, Anne Tyler has received wide critical acclaim. Most critical attention has, understandably, focused primarily on the later novels, yet it is the first three books, all of which draw heavily on Tyler's North Carolina experiences, that set the themes and concerns for her later work. It is these novels—*If Morning Ever Comes*, *The Tin Can Tree*, and *A Slipping-Down Life*—which I wish to examine.

While an undergraduate at Duke University, Tyler served for a short period as an assistant editor to the school's student literary journal, *The Archive*, probably during the 1960–61 academic year.[1] Her first story had appeared in that magazine in March 1959 and was followed by another in October of the same year.[2] "Laura" and

"The Lights on the River" represent Tyler's first attempts at fiction and her first portrayal of the subject matter that would come to dominate her work, the struggle of the individual within a family setting. Interestingly, both stories focus on the consciousness of a child—in one case, an adolescent—coming to terms with death, an important element in Tyler's first three novels. In both stories, moreover, internal conflict arises from the characters' awareness of how their responses differ from those of other family members. Both stories thus foreshadow one of Anne Tyler's major themes, the isolation of the individual within the family and the growth of self-awareness as both fostering and accompanying that isolation. As Tyler herself has noted, families offer "convenient ways of studying how people adapt and endure when forced to stay together, ... how they last, and go on loving and adjust to the absurdities of their confinement."[3] Because two early stories, "I Never Saw Morning"[4] and "Nobody Answers the Door,"[5] introduce this theme and the major characters of *If Morning Ever Comes*, they require attention.

In "I Never Saw Morning," the earlier of the two stories, the focus is Ben Joe Hawkes's girlfriend, Shelley Domer. Her family, very much alive in this tale, have been killed in an automobile accident prior to the opening of *If Morning Ever Comes*. In fact, though there are discrepancies between the early story and the novel, the story is important for its depiction of the relationship between Ben Joe and Shelley: his unconscious interest in her and her secret longing for him. Indeed, it is the furtive return of the two to the Domer residence after a date that supplies the opening scene of the story.[6] A quiet, shy teenager, Shelley frequently fantasizes about herself and Ben Joe. She likes to think of Ben Joe, two weeks older than she, lying in his crib and somehow aware of the exact moment she was born. The sudden revelation of this fantasy to her family isolates her, since they have had no inkling of her thoughts, while creating in her a sense of secret power and an experience of loss. As the girl Ben Joe takes back to New York with him at the end of *If Morning Ever Comes*, "his own little piece of Sandhill transplanted," Shelley is an important character and serves a vital role in Ben Joe's life: she offers him exactly what the Hawkes family cannot. She is more than his girlfriend; she is his bride precisely because she is something none of the Hawkes family is, a good listener.

Most of the Hawkes women, Ben Joe's six sisters and his mother, are first introduced in the story "Nobody Answers the Door." Here the theme of Ben Joe's isolation from his family is first treated. As the only male in a family of women, Ben Joe is something of an alien in his home. He is also a worrier by nature, a young man trying desperately to be understood and to understand himself and his family, to register his perception of the world on some consciousness other than his own. The title of the story suggests precisely the nature of the Hawkes women. As Ellen Hawkes, Ben Joe's mother, comments to a long-distance operator, "Go ahead, nobody in this family answers. Not the door, not the phone, not their names when I call them for supper; and *nobody* tells me anything."[7] The remark might very well be Ben Joe's. Unresponsiveness is the chief characteristic of the Hawkes women, as Ben Joe observes. Each is closed off from the others, isolated within herself and keeping her own counsel, yet somehow enduring the bickerings of family life.

In addition to introducing the Hawkes family and one of the major themes of *If Morning Ever Comes*, "Nobody Answers the Door" also provides the background for two events in the novel: Ben Joe's attempts to convey to his sister Jenny his bewilderment and curiosity about his name being the only one he recognizes in an unidentified address book and the announcement of the marriage of his eldest sister, Joanne. Although both events lead Ben Joe to realize his isolation from his family, only Joanne's marriage has a direct bearing on the plot of the novel, for it is the news of Joanne's return to Sandhill without her husband that precipitates Ben Joe's departure from Columbia University and his own journey home. Set in a period when Ben Joe is employed in a bank—we learn in the novel that there is about a three-year hiatus between Ben Joe's graduation from Sandhill College and his enrollment at Columbia University law school—"Nobody Answers the Door" serves, like Anne Tyler's other early stories, as an example of her interest in the frustration, isolation, and loneliness that are unavoidable at times in most familiar (and familial) relationships. With an irony typical of her later work, she suggests in the story a parallel between Ben Joe's relationship with his family and his being the only name he recognizes in the address book. In both cases, Ben Joe is isolated from those around him and knowledgeable only of himself. His sisters remain mysteries to him, and the address book contains, besides his own name, only what he calls "far-*away*" names and addresses.[8]

The conflict Ben Joe experiences because of his family's unresponsiveness recurs in *If Morning Ever Comes* and is extended to include not only the differences between the Hawkes women and Shelley Domer, but also between Ellen Hawkes and Lili Belle Moseley, a local working-class woman Ben Joe's deceased father had taken up with. Leaving his wife and seven children, Phillip Hawkes, a Sandhill doctor, found in Lili Belle what Ben Joe finds in Shelley: openness, understanding, warmth, and love. Moreover, the dilemma created by Phillip's choice of warmth over reticence and pride has additional repercussions for Ben Joe. Lili Belle has borne Dr. Hawkes a son and named him Phillip, after his father, a name that Ben Joe, his father's legitimate first son, was denied. After his father's death, Ben Joe had taken on the role of delivering in person each month the bequest his father had left for Lili Belle and Phillip. Unable to resign himself to his father's death and to indifference to his half brother, as his family had, Ben Joe continued these visits secretly, just as he secretly visited his father at Lili Belle's before the doctor's death. Part of Ben Joe's return trip involves visiting Lili Belle to learn of Phillip's health and coming to terms with Dr. Hawkes's death six years earlier, a memory that unsettles and disturbs Ben Joe.

In an interview with Clifford A. Ridley in 1972, Anne Tyler commented that she did not particularly like her first two novels, perhaps because "they seem so bland. Ben Joe," she commented, "is just a likable guy; that's all you can say about him."[9] But Ben Joe is not bland. The conflict he faces is one of real emotional pain and psychological turmoil. Ben Joe is dissociated from his family because of his association with Lili Belle and his continued visits to her, and he is confused and uncertain about himself and his future. The tearing he feels as family loyalty wars with the desire for human warmth is a real source of discomfort and the foundation for further growth. Ironically, when he is away from home, Ben Joe remembers only the best points about Sandhill and his family. His home appears as "a giant of a place, with children playing on the sunlit lawn and yellow flowers growing in two straight lines along the walk," unaffected by time.

In the opening chapter of the novel, Ben Joe leaves New York in November because of such a memory, a longing for what he has left behind, and a need to know how his family is managing without him. Conflict with memory causes Ben Joe to struggle, also. Unable to realize "a thing's happening or a moment's passing," Ben Joe is beset with the problem of recognizing change. Like Macon Leary in *The Accidental Tourist*, he resists change because it is too disruptive, yet he cannot deny it. Memory's ability to grant permanence to the past and his family's tendency to avoid discussing any event which disrupts the normal pattern of their daily lives serve only to exacerbate Ben Joe's condition. Yet it is only Ben Joe who expresses concern over his sister Joanne's separation from her husband. He openly protests her dating an old Sandhill beau while she is still married. "The most amazing things go on in this family," he yells, "the most *amazing* things, that no one *else* would *allow*, and this family just keeps on." Only Ben Joe challenges this family behavior and tries to "stop one more of those amazing damned things that go on . . . and [that] everyone takes for granted, pretends things are still all right and the world's still right-side up." Ben Joe's rejection of the Hawkes family pattern leads his sisters to label him "Ben Joe the worrier," but it is the same desire to break with their reticence that leads him to Shelley Domer.

Ben Joe's return to Sandhill involves several quests. As a metaphor for his psychological journey from adolescence to adulthood, this return necessarily involves a re-evaluation of himself as well as his family. But because Ben Joe has difficulty recognizing change, his journey home is rife with conflict. He at once rejects his family's acceptance of destructive events and yet clings to the security that the family offers. His response to Joanne's return offers evidence. He rejects Joanne's attempts to create a new life by breaking with her husband and returning home, yet he also recalls the warmth and security she always offered whenever fears swamped the minds of her younger brother and sisters. Ben Joe is also troubled in his relations with Shelley. He fails to commit himself, despite the longing to do so, because of the fear that maybe "time would get even more jumbled up in his head than it was already." Only when Shelley confronts him with his thoughtless treatment of her does Ben Joe recognize that in Shelley he has a chance to create what he has longed for in his family. Unlike his sisters, Shelley listens to Ben Joe, and, above all, she is dependent on him and hopeful of his attention. Because she is his "first girl," she is a part of his past that he can retain, a vivid link with his youth and his home, yet by taking her to New York with him, he can for once commit himself to someone outside his family, someone who loves him. In this struggle, Ben Joe Hawkes becomes the first of a number of Anne Tyler's characters who actively seek to fill a need their families fail to meet and who strive to reject the patterns ordained by family life.

On the surface, *If Morning Ever Comes* is a simply structured novel covering a little less than six days in the life of its hero. Five of these are spent in Sandhill, and one evening on the train ride south from New York. Yet, because memory is triggered by association with place, the book covers a lifetime of experiences, not just for Ben Joe but for his entire family. Indeed, because of the size of his family, we are reminded that his recollections are those of one individual in a family of nine people. The book's focus on him, then, is ironically deceptive. Its subject is the commonly shared experiences of the Hawkes family as well as the very different ways in which individuals respond to those experiences, some neither remembering, nor even having noticed in the first place, the very event that is paramount in the consciousness of another. A final image in the novel captures this theme. On his return trip to New York, Ben Joe fantasizes about his future, picturing Shelley and a yet-unborn son ". . . like two white dancing figures at the far end of his mind. They were suspended a minute, still and obedient, before his watching eyes and then they danced off again and he let them go; he knew he had to let them. One part of them was faraway and closed to him, as unreachable as his own sisters, as blank-faced as the white house he was born in. Even his wife and son were that way. Even Ben Joe Hawkes."

This fantasy and the realization it contains about the mystery of other human beings mark the change that Ben Joe undergoes through his journey home. Troubled by what he does not understand in others, he is nonetheless willing to let them go, accept the mysterious, hidden portion of himself and others, leave the past and his family, and move into the future. Thus Ben Joe Hawkes becomes the first Tyler character to recognize the unavoidable distance between human beings and to go on loving. Such characters, Tyler has indicated, are "the real heroes" of her books, for they "manage to endure . . . [and] somehow are able to grant other people the privacy of the space around them and still produce warmth."[10]

An awareness of the isolation of individuals in a family setting informs Anne Tyler's second novel, *The Tin Can Tree*, published in

October 1965. Unlike the earlier book, *The Tin Can Tree* focuses on the contrasts among the members of several families, most living in one house. A tri-partite dwelling with "three chimneys . . . jumbled tightly together," that house symbolizes the three disparate yet close families that live within. There are, however, more than these three families represented in the novel, mainly because several residents are refugees from other families, families that failed to provide warmth, freedom, and love. Like the house they inhabit—a strange, solitary building, rising up "among the weeds"—the individuals within are haphazardly jumbled together, isolated yet dependent on one another for all the love and understanding they seem likely to find. The one "long tin roof" which covers them parallels the one major experience of the novel that touches them all: the death and funeral of Janie Rose, the six-year-old daughter of Roy and Lou Pike.

With their ten-year-old son Simon and their niece, Joan, a refugee from her parents' home, the Pikes occupy the far right section of the house. As the novel opens, we are with them at the funeral of Janie Rose, who has been killed by a fall from a tractor two days before. The silence of this opening scene signals the dilemma each character faces individually: how to ameliorate the loss of love and the grief which Janie Rose's death has brought, how to go on living, committed to other members of the family and household community. This common grief, including, ironically, the very different ways in which the characters deal with it, offers a kind of shared fate, a common experience. Despite their various memories and impressions of Janie Rose, the characters in the novel illustrate the need that marks all families, whether blood-related or not. Families, Tyler says in *The Tin Can Tree*, as she does later in *Celestial Navigation*, are groups of people united for survival, people sharing a common experience of life, despite their differences and the essential isolation of one person from another.

Among the residents who grieve, there are, besides the Pikes and Joan, James Green, a twenty-eight-year-old photographer and bachelor, and his brother, Ansel. Like Joan, the Greens are refugees from their own family, having fled a stifling atmosphere where love could not grow. Sharing the house with the Pikes and the Greens—indeed, sandwiched in between these two families—live the Potter sisters, Miss Lucy and Miss Faye. Minor characters in the novel, these two chubby, aging, and reclusive spinsters emerge from their residence only on special occasions, for parties, and for their weekly visits to their neighbor Ansel. Tyler never gives us much background on the Potter sisters. How they are related to the Pikes, if at all, and how they came to share the same house with them, remains a mystery in keeping with the dark, tapestry-draped interior of their section of the house. Their relationships mirrored by the haphazard construction of the house in which they live, the Potter sisters, like the Greens, seem inexplicably tied to the Pikes and their lives.

The Tin Can Tree is set in Larksville, a small town of dwindling population in the tobacco-growing area of North Carolina, and reflects Tyler's experiences tying tobacco during the summers of her high-school years and listening to the other tobacco tiers talk. Like *If Morning Ever Comes*, it is chronologically compact and covers only six days. However, where the earlier novel presents Dr. Hawkes's death retrospectively, as a segment of recollected memory that Ben Joe relates to his sister, here death is an immediate experience, and paramount among the responses to it is that of Lou Pike, Janie Rose's mother. Isolated in withdrawal, Mrs. Pike has favored her son Simon over the unplanned Janie and is ridden with guilt and so depressed that she is incapable of dressing or leaving her bedroom. Simon, now ignored by his mother, grows increasingly bored and restless, illustrating the lack of comprehension children sometimes exhibit in the face of adult grief. After five days of being ignored, convinced that he is doing everything wrong and there is no longer a place for him within his own family, Simon runs away to a neighboring town and the only other family he knows about, the Greens, the very people whom Ansel and James have fled. His turning to the Greens represents an ironic comment on the nature of family relationships, for Simon accepts and affirms the Greens, whom James rejected. In turn, the Greens, who failed to fill the needs of their sons, provide shelter and attention for the runaway. The event is a means of briefly reuniting James with his family, contrasting James and Simon and their respective families, and also an effective episode for bringing Lou Pike out of her daze of grief, self-imposed guilt, and isolation.

The focus of *The Tin Can Tree* is not Simon, however, nor primarily his mother. Simon is important mainly because of his relationship with other characters, and Mrs. Pike—precisely because she has chosen withdrawal—remains somewhat in the background of the novel. Rather, the real focus is Joan Pike and her interactions with the Greens. Indeed, Joan's departure on the Thursday following the funeral precipitates Simon's leaving.

As an outsider to the immediate Pike family, Joan is seminal in illustrating the theme of the individual's isolation. The daughter of Roy Pike's older brother, Joan at twenty-six has "lived in bedrooms all her life," "the way a guest would—keeping her property strictly within the walls of her room, hanging her towel and wash cloth on the bar behind her door." Although she spends her evenings with James Green at times, and spends some time with the Pikes, Joan still lives primarily in her room, waiting for an invitation from the Pikes to come out. This failure to mingle fully and adopt the more casual way of one who feels truly at home is neither deliberate nor malicious. It is, Tyler writes, "what she was used to; that was all," a carefully learned habit and a product of the impersonal treatment she received from her parents. An only child born to middle-aged parents, Joan grew up being treated as a guest, "politely, like a visitor who had dropped in unexpectedly." Uncertain of "what they were supposed to do with her," her parents merely "gazed at her uneasily over the tops of their magazines until she retreated to her room." Years later, Joan is still retreating, still a "guest."

Governed by a strong commitment to Simon, Joan stays on after the funeral for several days to make sandwiches and to tend Simon, despite her desire to "walk off," to "go find some place to sit alone and think things out." Though she is awkward and uncertain of how to comfort her uncle, she goes on loving, like the heroes of Tyler's other books, giving her uncle space to grieve. However, Joan's staying indicates a major dilemma in her life: her longing for attachment and family and her inability to realize or actualize that dream. It is a dilemma fostered by her sense of uncertainty and impermanence as well as her isolation. Although Joan has been with her uncle and aunt for four years prior to Janie's death, she had come "planning just to stay . . . a week or two." At the Pikes' home, however, things were different from the way they were at her parents': "there was always something going on, and a full family around the supper table." There were also the children who Joan, in her walks and play, could pretend "were her own." With Janie Rose and Simon, Joan is able to live the childhood she was not allowed to have with her parents. Away from the Pikes, she is without identity, merely "another stranger." Yet as long as Joan remains with the Pikes, she removes herself from the possibilities of marriage.

This conflict centers on her love for James Green. With James, Joan remains torn between commitment and a desire to flee, between longing for a family of her own and continuing a relationship that goes nowhere. Although James appears to offer the possibility of marriage, he cannot, because of his commitment to his brother, a commitment Joan finds incomprehensible. The formality of Joan's treatment by her parents and the absence of siblings blind her to James's devotion to Ansel. Joan, like characters in other Tyler novels, remains cut off from the very dreams she seeks. The warmth and closeness, and the sense of connectedness provided by a family of her own, elude Joan even as she seeks them. At the end of *The Tin Can Tree*, Joan Pike is pictured within a circle of light that sets her apart from the other members of the Pike household. Tyler writes that Joan remains within her own "circular world . . . alone." While in reality she is sitting within this circle so that the Potter sisters can make a silhouette, symbolically she is outside the family's circle, separated from them by her single status and her alienation from the sense of family that unites the others: Roy, Lou, and Simon Pike; James and Ansel Green; and the two Potter sisters.

In the relationship between James and Ansel, Tyler captures another aspect of familial ties. James has stopped caring inwardly for his brother and has recognized that his commitment prevents growth and change. Ansel—pale, sickly, and brooding, whereas James is dark, healthy, and outgoing—represents "the one, final member of his family that he [James] hadn't yet deserted," and the one he cannot desert—for, in James's mind, Ansel is often still "that scared small brother who could sit a whole evening without saying a word or raising his eyes from the floor," a child in need of his older brother's continued attention and care. Although these features have all but vanished from Ansel, James remains bound to his original vision of his brother. This commitment negates the possibility of marriage, for James knows, despite any fantasies, that "he could never make Joan and Ansel like each other." However, his choice of brother over wife, of family member over outsider, is not comfortable. He is criticized by Joan, who is resentful because the bond between James and Ansel interferes with her own relationship, and by Maisie Hammond, a pale girl attracted to Ansel who accuses James of neglecting his brother. Ultimately, although James is deeply affected by the strength of the two women's views and the vehemence of their attacks, the relationship of the two brothers is invulnerable to change. It is deeply rooted in the past and in a shared familial experience that neither woman knows about. In a way clear only to themselves and for reasons they never express, the two brothers are bound to each other despite the differences in their natures and behavior.

Like Ben Joe Hawkes, who must confront and surrender his childhood image of his family and his fantasies of their warmth and their dependence upon him, James also makes a brief journey home, where he confronts and yields to changes in himself and in those he left behind: his father and the one brother and one sister remaining at home. Even his "dislike of his father," that "one complete and pure emotion . . . that alone could send words enough swarming to his mouth," deserts him. The confrontation between the memory of the past and the reality of the present leaves him "wordless" and tentatively redefines James's relationship with his father. As an element of plot, James's journey home is valuable for allowing the reader to see the challenge old Mr. Green posed for his children—why, in effect, James and Ansel left home in the first place. It gives the reader a closer look at the Greens themselves, apart from Ansel's and James's differing views, and a fuller understanding of the kind of relationships possible within that closed and restrictive family. But, more importantly, the scene captures the trickery of imagination and memory, the magic that only temporal and spatial distance can perform, and the deceptive ways in which these faculties combine to both glamorize and immortalize the people and places left behind. The novel leads us to the ironic and inevitable realization of the discrepancies between James's memories of his family and that family's actual condition and behavior. Indeed, as Tyler suggests in a number of her novels, family relationships, because they are the most nearly constant and fixed patterns in most lives, offer a remarkably fertile ground for studying these discrepancies and thus a way to measure change. When James leaves the Green family a second time, he has a new vision that is, though not altogether different from his childhood one, less distorted by anger. It is an adult vision that recognizes the frailty of human life. In the rearview mirror of his truck, James sees "his father . . . standing on the porch, his arms hugging his chest, his knees bagging, his small white head strained toward the truck."

In *A Slipping-Down Life*, Anne Tyler returns to the existential themes of the individual's isolation and struggle for independence and identity as well as the lack of meaningful communication among people living together. Set in the fictional towns of Pulqua and Farinia, North Carolina, *A Slipping-Down Life* is also the first of Tyler's novels to portray the barrenness of familial relationships in a culture dominated by television and rock music. But, unlike the earlier novels, *A Slipping-Down Life* chronicles one full year in the life of the heroine, a fat, dowdy, awkward teenage girl named Evie Decker. Originating in "a small newspaper story about a fifteen-year-old girl in Texas who'd slashed 'Elvis' in her forehead,"[11] the novel traces Evie's sterile interaction with her father, her only living relative, and the development and dissolution of her relationship with a local rock singer, Bertram "Drumstrings" Casey. Evie's entanglement with Casey, resulting in their eventual marriage, is initiated by her carving "Casey" in her forehead with nail scissors. The novel ends with their separation and the death of Evie's father, events that leave her more bereft than before.

At home and at school, Evie is a lonely, isolated figure. Her mother died giving birth to her only child. Her father, a mathematics teacher, is "a vague, gentle man who assumed that Evie would manage just fine wherever she was." Most often, he is unsuspecting of his daughter's loneliness and pain. One of the most telling points about his relation with Evie is that he never knows about her evenings at the Unicorn, a roadhouse where Drum plays. The fact that she has spent several weeks there before carving Casey's name in her forehead, and that later she offers to use herself as a publicity gimmick, escapes Mr. Decker. When Evie and Drum's relationship shifts from business to romance, even when Drum begins sleeping on the Deckers' front porch, Sam Decker is oblivious to it all. Drum sneaks in and out of the house, has his meals there, and spends the day watching television with Evie and Clotelia, the maid, while Sam Decker teaches high-school math and runs errands. Like Joan Pike's parents, he treats his daughter politely, giving her freedom but ignoring her pain. Only the most distressing events thrust themselves upon his attention: Evie's disfiguring her face, her failure to return to school, her elopement. The enormous psychological distance between the two is clear from the first confrontational scene, when Sam Decker is called to the hospital. Uncertain of what to say, genuinely bewildered and concerned for his daughter's welfare, Mr. Decker makes several shy efforts to cross "the years of silence" that separate him and Evie. Ironically, his one gift—a satin bedjacket clearly unsuited to Evie's chubby, drab figure—speaks to her as an admonishment, a confirmation of the regret she believes he must feel for having lost his wife in trade for his daughter. Rather than admonishing her, however, Mr. Decker tries to console and direct Evie, yet his attempts reveal his inability to face her. Seeking to be kind, he ends up being evasive. He tells her she is "a sweet-looking girl, after all, and when you lose a—when you're older, boys are going to fall all over themselves for you." Unable to point honestly to the weight Evie must lose, Mr. Decker stops himself from giving advice that might be helpful—the words that would speak straight to the issue of Evie's pain.

Tyler frequently suggests the separation of family members by vivid contrasts in physical features. Here Mr. Decker is described as "long and bony," "his hair and lashes . . . pale, his eyes set in deep shadowed sockets, his skin sprinkled with large freckles so faint that they seemed to be seeping through a white over-layer." Evie, in contrast, is dark, her hair brown and straight, while her face is "pudgy and formless." Her shape also contrasts sharply with her father's. Where his form is a "tall black angular silhouette," hers is "short and wide," shapeless and stubby. Indeed, Mr. Decker has passed on to his daughter "nothing but his awkwardness." Whether Evie's physical features might be inherited from her mother is never clear. Mr. Decker never mentions his late wife, reinforcing Evie's isolation. Moreover, his silence largely determines the nature of Evie's other relationships: with Violet Hayes, her only school friend; with Clotelia; with Drum Casey. In each case Evie seeks the intimacy and guidance lacking in her relations with her father. Ironically, she often replicates the distance between herself and her father.

As in other Tyler novels, *A Slipping-Down Life* symbolizes the characters' lives through description of the house they inhabit. The Decker house, fittingly, is "a leaden, damp-smelling" place with "flowered furniture and lacy figurines [that] had sat so long in their places . . . they seemed to have jelled there, hardening around the edges." Like Evie, the house has gone undisturbed for years, fore-shadowing the cluttered, gothic structures that characterize family relationships in Tyler's later novels. Evie, like other Tyler hero-ines—Joan Pike in *The Tin Can Tree*, Justine Peck in *Searching for Caleb*, and Charlotte Emory in *Earthly Possessions*—is an only child faced with growing up alone in a dark, stifling environment, and burdened with creating an identity without the companionship of siblings or communicative parents. Put another way, she faces silence and loneliness at home, and of the outside world she has little knowl-edge and no one from whom to gain information. Evie Decker thrusts herself painfully into this world by attempting to reach a man much colder than her father.

Evie's isolation is evident from the opening pages of the novel. Tyler writes that Evie "walked most places alone," carrying "her books clutched to her chest, rounding her shoulders" in a gesture of submission and hopelessness. Her classmates barely notice her; they never speak to her. Their conversations concern subjects Evie knows nothing about: dates with boys, rock music, and singing groups like the Beatles and the Monkeys.[12] Evie has never had a date, and she is totally unmusical. Even after her photograph with Drum Casey ap-pears in a local newspaper, Evie acquires notoriety but remains alone. Her one friend, Violet, is also isolated from her classmates. Like Evie, she is overweight, but differs from her friend in person-ality and appearance. Even the degree of their pudginess sets them apart from each other. "An enormously fat girl with teased black hair and a beautiful face," Violet is so overweight that, next to her, Evie "seemed almost thin." Where Violet dresses flamboyantly, Evie is plain, "her dowdy clothes" giving her "a matronly look." Also, where Violet is "a huge stately queen" who remains undaunted, Evie is self-conscious. Characteristically, when the two attend their first rock show, Evie wants to leave, while Violet wants to stay and enjoy the concert. Later, it is Violet who accompanies Evie to the hos-pital, calls Mr. Decker, and even remembers to get Evie a change of clothes. She takes charge of Evie's wedding, helping with most of the arrangements and investigating marriage laws. In the absence of a real mother, Violet is a partial surrogate, acting where Mr. Decker fails.

Evie has a surrogate family tie with Clotelia also, yet that relation-ship is neither affectionate nor intimate. Although Clotelia has worked in the Decker household for four years, she remains "an indifferent stranger kicking dust puffs with the toe of her cream suede high-heeled boot." Like Mr. Decker, she "continually disappointed" Evie: where "other people would have turned into members of the family," Clotelia still "carried her purse with her from room to room" and spends her time reading magazines and watching soap operas. As negligent of Evie as she is of her chores, Clotelia is concerned with the lives of fictional characters on television, not the real, troubled Evie. With Evie home and refusing to return to school, Clotelia grows increasingly annoyed. As a mother figure, she scolds Evie about her sloppiness and weight. She even nags Evie about hurting her father and threatens to tell him about Drum, but she never does. She never intercedes on Evie's behalf. Moreover, although Clotelia gives Evie the space that Tyler speaks of as essential in loving family relationships, her comments are insightful yet never compassionate, other requisites for Tyler heroes. Clotelia is often selfish; she wants Evie out of her way. She has more concern for the "relatives" she has made through television. Also, although Clotelia's remarks to Evie are honest appraisals—her assessment of Drum as "that trash" is especially astute—these comments are always scornful. They do nothing to encourage self-confidence in Evie, nor do they express tenderness. When Evie calls Clotelia the night Mr. Decker dies, Clotelia comes quickly and makes hot chocolate, yet she does not hug or pat Evie. There is no physical warmth. Indeed, Clotelia cannot resist telling Evie that she looks "like trash" and within minutes reminds her that Mr. Decker wanted to give his maid the "silver-backed mirror in the guest room." With her blunt selfishness, Clotelia remains distant, and her presence, although clearly preferable to the "deep, growing silence" of the Decker house, quickly banishes the possibility of intimacy. In effect, Clotelia, as Evie knows, is "not like . . . [a] mother at all." The fact that she, like Violet Hayes, is one of Evie's sources of support underscores the isolation in which Evie lives.

With Drum Casey, Evie establishes yet another distant relationship. Evie is totally unmusical and yet manages to align herself professionally and romantically with a rock musician. The starkly paradoxical nature of this arrangement is readily apparent. Equally evident is Evie's willingness to sacrifice herself to an empty and futile arrangement with a proud, selfish man. While Evie repeatedly attempts to identify with Drum's moods, he casually ignores her desperation and loneliness and responds with indifference and criticism. Evie's first attempts at intimacy fall flat. Later, after Evie has proposed using her scarred face as a publicity gimmick, Drum expresses open repulsion. Only after he needs a place to stay does he turn to Evie. Uneducated and poor, Drum Casey is, in Tyler's words, "the direct inheritance of all the days on the tobacco farm."[13] He believes material success alone will provide what his life lacks, and, though he is willing to give his family luxuries with any wealth he may acquire, he will not share himself. When he first appears on stage, he ushers in a cold, gloomy atmosphere. At the Unicorn, too, whenever he performs, Drum slides "onto the platform as silently and as easily as some dark fish," allusions to his mysterious and cold nature. Even as he sings, Tyler describes him as moving in his own "small circle," always isolated within a "separate, motionless circle of air." Indeed, coldness, as well as silence and separateness, recurs in the descriptions of Drum. He walks past Evie "in an envelope of cold air . . . as if he had just come in from a winter night." Even his style of playing sets him apart: frequently he stops midsong and recites words that baffle the audience. The places where he performs are also cold and isolated. The theatre in Pulqua where Evie first hears Drum has "a cavernous chill," and the Unicorn offers a picture of desolation: "a gray windowless rectangle on a lonesome highway with darkness closing in all around it." Inside, "the smell of beer . . . [gives] the place a cold feeling." Clearly, Tyler wishes to suggest the emptiness and despair that mark Evie's infatuation with Drum and the tawdry local rock scene that fosters "flimsy and temporary" relationships.

Despite the omens evident in the places where she sees Casey, Evie pursues the relationship, largely because it gives her a sense of identity, a place and role to fill her emptiness. Moreover, though Evie cannot understand Drum's music, she is attracted by his style. She hears in his voice the loneliness and despair that afflict her, and "that talking out of his" in the middle of a song makes "the difference" for Evie. She wants to answer. The words give her a sense of connectedness not only to Drum; they allow her to identify for once with those "girls who scream on the Ed Sullivan Show." Yet, in an important way, Evie is cut off from Drum still. She never understands what leads him to toss together disconnected lyrics on varied subjects to shout in the middle of his songs. This incomprehension marks the relationship throughout. The tragedy of Evie's life is that she repeatedly tries to bridge the separateness with appeals for attention. Shy and withdrawn, she is at first grateful for any notice Drum Casey gives her. Later, after she gains some self-confidence, she is capable of walking out on him, but only after his infidelity thrusts itself before her.

In a 1972 interview, Anne Tyler spoke about *A Slipping-Down Life* as the only one of her novels which she liked, possibly because "it's the one book . . . in which the characters . . . change." The other novels exhibited "an utter lack of faith in change," something, Tyler commented, "I don't think most people are capable of."[14] Confronted with insular and limited familial experience, Evie changes. She literally lashes out to find her way in the world. Though her actions are often self-destructive, Evie does take "something into . . . [her] own hands" and precipitates a cycle of change. During the brief period of marriage to Drum Casey, while his life slides downward, Evie grows more independent and determined to make her life financially solvent. When Drum is reduced to one night a week at the Unicorn and later fired, Evie continues to think of publicity gimmicks for his benefit, but, "without even planning it," she takes a part-time job at the Pulqua public library. Like later Tyler heroines—Elizabeth Abbott of *The Clock Winder* and Justine Peck of *Searching for Caleb*—Evie uses work to break free of her confinement.

A Slipping-Down Life is the first Tyler novel to trace the evolution of a romantic relationship from its beginnings to marriage and dissolution, a theme that later novels such as *Celestial Navigation* and *The Accidental Tourist* would pursue. *If Morning Ever Comes* and *The Tin Can Tree* study significant male-female involvements, yet neither looks at these relationships beyond marriage. Joan Pike and James Green never marry, and we do not see Ben Joe and Shelley after their marriage. The closest look at marriages before *A Slipping-Down Life* is a view of Roy and Lou Pike, minor characters, and a brief retrospective look at Dr. and Mrs. Hawkes. What we do see in the early novels of Anne Tyler is that marriages, like other family arrangements, are not exempt from the paradoxical contrasts and the unavoidable conflicts that mark the interactions of parents and children and of siblings. In Anne Tyler's novels, all close human relationships and alliances, whether blood-related or not, bear scars from isolating conflict. The individual is ultimately alone in Tyler's fiction, despite what comfort may come from family and friendship. Indeed, it is their uniqueness—their peculiar set of experiences and memories that form their personalities—that isolates individuals from each other.

At the end of *A Slipping-Down Life*, Evie Decker, having undergone a journey of growth similar to Ben Joe's, including the loss of a father, returns to her father's house. With no living relatives, not even a husband to comfort her, Evie is truly isolated. She notices a "smiling" photograph of her mother, a woman whom Evie never knew and who is "remembered now by no living person." Even the house in which Evie will soon live again is ominously silent. As Evie wanders through the rooms, the house itself seems to be dying: "Beneath the surface noises of clocks and motors there was a deep, growing silence that layered in from the walls, making . . . [Evie] feel clumsy and out of place."

This scene represents the first of its kind in Tyler's fiction: one in which the individual's essential isolation from others is captured in the loss of all relatives. But Anne Tyler has protested that she is "not the least bit pessimistic as a writer": "I never intended any of my characters to stagnate, certainly—it's just that I want to see how people can maneuver and grow within the small space that is the average life."[15]

Families are Tyler's way of studying how people adapt, and Evie will have a future family even as her father's generation vanishes. Evie is pregnant, although she told neither Drum nor her father about her pregnancy. Her return to her father's house at the novel's conclusion becomes a symbolic gesture indicating her reunion with the idea of family, if not with an actual family at the moment. True, it mirrors the permanent separation from her father and the mother she never knew, but the bloodline, shortened by Mr. Decker's death and endangered by Drum's refusal to live with Evie, will continue. Indeed, it seems as inevitable as the continuing need of human beings to live in some kind of family.

3 / Tyler and Feminism

In a statement published in a 1972 issue of the *National Observer*, Anne Tyler had this to say about "novels by liberated women": "I hate 'em all."[1] That's quite a remark to have made publicly at the historical moment when feminism in the twentieth century first became most visible and vocal; but Tyler never retracted it, and indeed would not comment further upon it until 1989—and even then, only through the non-public medium of a personal letter. "Certainly I don't hate liberated women as such," Tyler wrote to me in August 1989. "I assume I'm one myself, if you can call someone liberated who was never imprisoned."[2] What happens when a woman who has never personally felt "imprisoned" comes to write novels? What will happen when the next generation of American women novelists—themselves enjoying the opportunities created for them by the vanguard feminists of the 1970s, and lacking any first-hand experience of the oppression to which these reformers were reacting—begin writing their own books in the 1990s and beyond? What happens to the artist when she loses touch with the social conditions and emotional turmoil that had so shaped the writings of her mother-artists decades earlier? Perhaps the case of Anne Tyler can give some indication of the direction to be taken by American women writers in the 1990s and the new century. Perhaps it will also stand as a cautionary tale, a reminder of how easy it would be to lose the ground so painfully gained in the last twenty-five years.

At first glance, Tyler's earliest published novel, *If Morning Ever Comes*, would seem to be a protofeminist classic, the harbinger of a career devoted to reform on behalf of women. Challenging squarely the gender-based attitudes and activities of the early 1960s, *If Morning Ever Comes* delineates the myriad constraints that left women of that era disempowered, but it does so by showing them *em*powered, living in a distaff utopia which is disrupted—but only temporarily—by the return of the would-be family patriarch. For, aside from his sex, Ben Joe Hawkes possesses not one element that would qualify him for being patriarch of anything. In her first novel, Anne Tyler uses her sardonic comedy to puncture the modes of gender-based thinking that were still firmly entrenched in the American psyche at the end of the Kennedy era.

The novel opens with Ben Joe, a native of Sandhill, North Carolina, in the New York apartment where he lives while attending Columbia University Law School. To be frank, Ben Joe has no particular interest in or aptitude for the law, but it would be a lucrative career—and "practicality was a good thing when you headed a family of six women." Any delusion the reader may harbor at this juncture that Ben Joe is another Ben Cartwright is, however, undercut by the fact that he pursues this thought while cocooning himself in a "crazy quilt from home": at age twenty-five, he still needs a security blanket.

The irony is lost on him, however, as he studies the account of a golden wedding anniversary on the society page of the local newspaper—studies it, that is, literally upside down, as he learned to read when he was three years old. For everything about him is reversed: far from being the family breadwinner, Ben Joe is being supported by the Hawkes women, who are not only financing his education at Columbia but also providing him with a regular allowance—an allowance for which they demand a written receipt. Financially—and, indeed, in every other way—Ben Joe is still a child; nonetheless, he feels that he is, by simple virtue of his gender, the head of his family upon the death of his physician father. And not long after the novel opens, Ben Joe dashes back to Sandhill to insist upon the deference and respect that his androcentric mind-set maintains is his due.

His homecoming is hardly what he anticipated as a "Carolina white man." With no one to meet him at the Sandhill train station, Ben Joe must walk home, accompanied only by his allegorical double, eighty-four-year-old "Jamie" Dower—yet another male who has come home essentially to die. Jamie's status as the representative of the dying patriarchal order of the Old South is lost, however, on the myopic and childlike Ben Joe, who cannot believe that his house full of women—mother Ellen, grandmother Gram, sisters Susannah, Joanne, Jenny, Tessie, Lisa, and Jane, and niece Carol—have no need whatsoever for him, and, to be frank, no desire whatsoever to have him around. As the anonymous reviewer for *Time* put it, aptly, "The chill on Manhattan's Morningside Heights is nothing compared with that in the hearts of his family."[3] The coldness towards Ben Joe reflects the women's sense of his potential to disrupt their self-generated, self-supporting, and essentially closed system. However cold they may be with Ben Joe, the Hawkes women extend to one another an emotional warmth that runs the gamut from scorching (towards the toddler Carol) to lukewarm (towards the semi-promiscuous Joanne, estranged from her G.I. husband Gary). The Hawkes women cannot afford to subscribe, as Ben Joe does, to antiquated modes of gender-based thought which demand that women be relentlessly warm and supportive, including towards—indeed, especially towards—any males in the family. By the same token, they know only too well that no system runs without a sound understanding of economics: the adult Hawkes women are gainfully employed outside the home, supporting both themselves and family members either too old or too young to work—a role traditionally held by males. Indeed, the Hawkes family's official letter writer and bookkeeper, Jenny, tells Ben Joe of household expenditures only after the fact. And to underscore the inversion of the patriarchal economic order and Ben Joe's dismay over its implications, Tyler shows his encounter with a game token on the living room floor: "His heel crushed something; it was the flatiron from the Monopoly set. He scraped it off his shoe and kept going." The veiled violence ("crushed"), annoyance ("He scraped it off his shoe"), and myopic determination ("kept going") implicit in this encounter suggest his painful awareness that the Hawkes women (flatiron) hold the power (Monopoly) in his family, a power based on real money they themselves have earned.

Confused by his inverted world but determined to cling to outmoded values, Ben Joe does the only thing possible: he impulsively marries a high-school friend, who, having lost her family in a car accident, does not have the economic, social, and emotional network enjoyed by the Hawkes women. In her gender-specific helplessness and sweetness—qualities embodied in such popular icons as Harriet Nelson and June Cleaver—Shelley Domer is quite willing to seek security in the old patriarchal ways and be taken care of by a man—any man, but especially Ben Joe Hawkes, who can't help but notice that Shelley, too, clings to her family crazy quilt as a security blanket. It's a match made in patriarchal heaven as they run off to New York, with Ben Joe fantasizing about the child (a boy, of course) they will have someday. They'll live in a "careful little apartment where Shelley would always be waiting for him, like his own little piece of Sandhill transplanted, and asking what was wrong if he acted different from the husbands in the homemaking magazines but loving him anyway, in spite of all that." As the train conductor announces when they pull out of Sandhill station, "Won't have to change." And those words are music to Ben Joe's ears.

After reading *If Morning Ever Comes*, one might reasonably expect Tyler's subsequent novels to explore even more fully the paradigm of the weak man and the strong woman in a world where androcentric standards and values are challenged and inverted. Such is not the case. As is evidenced by a novel from her middle period, *Earthly Possessions*, Tyler instead began creating male characters who, if just as childlike as Ben Joe, nevertheless wield enormous power, while her female characters, though often troubled by their gender-based roles, are unable or unwilling to escape them.

Earthly Possessions concerns thirty-five-year-old Charlotte Ames Emory, a minister's wife in Clarion, Maryland. Charlotte is miserable without understanding why. She realizes instinctively that she must escape, but she does not know how to translate that urge into meaningful action. Unable to act on self-generated impulses, Charlotte nevertheless responds well to directives from outside sources; having found a "Keep on Truckin'" badge in her cereal box one morning, she takes it as a "sign" to run.

Whether she would actually have run away successfully is unclear; it is in fact entirely possible that she would have got no further than in her last escape attempt sixteen years earlier, in 1960, when her husband Saul had tracked her down to Clarion's Blue Moon Motel just minutes after her getaway. What is clear is that she is kidnapped at the bank by Jake Simms, who takes Charlotte on a wild ride to Florida and, in large measure, to a new acceptance of her lot in life.

Both social outcasts in "identical white shirts," the bumbling robber Jake and the bumbling housewife Charlotte are powerless: trapped together in an undependable car, they are unwilling participants in the demolition derby of life. But even that paradigm is qualified, for it is Jake the male who drives—and Charlotte the female who is forced, at phallic gunpoint, to accompany him passively wherever he goes. Her situation is an emblem of her own life. She had drifted thoughtlessly into her dead father's occupation of portrait photographer, married neighbor Saul Emory for no particular reason beyond his accessibility and her admiration for his mother Alberta, and said nothing as her husband brought home unwanted children and displaced parishioners for her to look after. Charlotte's living room is an objective correlative of her situation: residing in the very house in which she (and her mother before her) grew up, Charlotte still has in her living room the Ames family furniture, plus the furniture from the house in which Saul grew up, plus miniature versions of these pieces ("doll things") thoughtfully carved for Charlotte by her brother-in-law Linus. Even more than Nora in Ibsen's *A Doll's House*, Charlotte has been reduced to a mindless child who gamely accepts whatever life imposes upon her.

In the course of the novel, and largely at the prompting of Jake, an outsider who can see her situation more objectively than she, Charlotte comes to understand why she had the barely controllable, antisocial urge to rid her house of its contents, to achieve "the bare, polished look of a bleached skull." But more importantly, she comes to see that the urge to strip herself of all her earthly possessions had been taken too far ("after all, did we really need to write at desks, walk on rugs?"). For years a hostage of her own passivity and her misperception of her marriage and her parents, Charlotte by the end of the novel walks away from Jake Simms, despite his threats to kill her, and returns home to Saul.

She is able to do so because she is buoyed by a chipper conviction that the "Keep on Truckin'" badge was a sign not to run away, but to endure. The road ahead of her will be, like the route of the Founder's Day parade, a minefield of horse droppings, "great beehives of manure." One can either step smartly around them, like the majorettes, or slog through like the determined soldiers in the parade. Ultimately the point is to keep marching. But is this enough? Charlotte returns, after all, to a less-than-satisfying marriage in a home which, like that of the Pyncheons in *The House of the Seven Gables*, brings with it the weight of several generations of misery and guilt. Further, there is no indication that she will ever be anything more than a housekeeper who moonlights as a photographer. Although Tyler would have us believe that Charlotte has come to see the wisdom of her brother-in-law Amos's argument that tolerance is not always a virtue, there is nothing in the text to suggest that Charlotte sees endurance as being qualitatively different from tolerance. In its way, then, Charlotte's newfound capacity to endure is little more than another manifestation of her capacity to be passive. A change in attitude, after all, can indeed make a situation bearable, but it does not change the situation in the least. What was meant to be a "happy" resolution to *Earthly Possessions* is thus oddly unsettling.

Even more unsettling from a feminist perspective is Tyler's eleventh novel, *Breathing Lessons*. Its heroine, Maggie Moran, is facing all at once the kinds of life changes that at some point or other confront most middle-aged people: her daughter Daisy is leaving for college; her son Jesse is having problems with his wife Fiona; and Max Gill, the husband of her childhood friend Serena Palermo, has died unexpectedly. The novel essentially traces what happens on the day of Max's funeral, as Maggie and her husband Ira, a professional picture framer, are forced to spend several hours together during this period of extreme change and the sudden awareness of mortality.

Perhaps to counter the seriousness of the situation, Tyler engages in whimsy and slapstick to a degree never before seen in her fiction.[4] Unfortunately, virtually all of this low-level humor is at the expense of Maggie. See Maggie drive her car into a Pepsi truck! See Maggie become a "nervous wreck" over whether her odometer will pass the highway odometer test! See Maggie jump headfirst into a laundry cart! See Maggie get caught unzipping Ira's fly at Max's funeral reception! Marita Golden is quite justified in lamenting the "Lucy Ricardo quality" in Maggie Moran,[5] a response hardly defused by Tyler's insistence that "Maggie had never liked *I Love Lucy*. She thought the plots were so engineered." To be sure, Maggie "tried too hard," as Edward Hoagland argues; but that does not explain why she seems to be depicted as a buffoon.

Matters are hardly improved by the ending of the novel. When it becomes clear that Daisy will indeed be leaving for college in the morning, that Jesse will not patch things up readily with Fiona, and that Max Gill is indeed dead and gone, Maggie suddenly opens her heart to her husband Ira, an inveterate player of Solitaire who communicates with her largely by whistling appropriate popular tunes. Here is the conclusion of the novel:

> Maggie spun around and returned to the bed. "Oh, Ira," she said, dropping down beside him, "what are we two going to live for, all the rest of our lives?"
>
> She had dislodged a stack of his cards, but he kindly refrained from straightening them and instead reached out one arm and drew her in. "There, now, sweetheart," he said, and he settled her next to him. Still holding her close, he transferred a four of spades to a five, and Maggie rested her head against his chest and watched. . . . She felt a little stir of something that came over her like a flush, a sort of inner buoyancy, and she lifted her face to kiss the warm blade of his cheekbone. Then she slipped free and moved to her side of the bed, because tomorrow they had a long car trip to make and she knew she would need a good night's sleep before they started.

Even more than Charlotte Emory in *Earthly Possessions*, Maggie Moran will make no move from her present situation, although Tyler does suggest—through the medium of the card game—that Ira himself must make his next moves in life quite carefully: "He had arrived at the interesting part of the game by now. . . . He had passed that early, superficial stage when any number of moves seemed possible, and now his choices were narrower and he had to show real skill and judgment." But there is no comparable suggestion that Maggie will need to evince any "real skill and judgment" with her own life, no sense that her vague restlessness will ever be faced and resolved, no feeling that her relationship with her husband will begin anew on a different key. Her life, evidently, will continue to consist of keeping house and worrying about her children, interspersed with part-time non-professional work at a local nursing home. The most she can hope for is to get a good night's sleep before putting up with whatever else life dumps in her lap. And there is nothing to suggest that Tyler herself sees anything worrisome about this.

In looking at these representative novels from the early, middle, and late stages of Anne Tyler's career, one can only wonder what happened to the strong, independent women of the novel she wrote a quarter of a century ago. If one didn't know when they were written, one might assume *Breathing Lessons*, with its unflattering, even denigrating, caricature of a middle-aged woman, was written in 1964, the era of endless jokes about crazy women drivers on *The Ed Sullivan Show*; conversely, one might assume *If Morning Ever Comes* was released in 1988. Perhaps the answer is that as Anne Tyler ages (she is over fifty now), she is growing away from the *Weltanschauung* instilled in her during a childhood and adolescence spent in Quaker communes. In her youth, Tyler was exposed to a world which posited work as gender-specific: women did domestic tasks while men saw to more physically demanding activities. This division of labor was based on the supposition that the sexes truly were separate but equal, and women within this system consequently did not feel "imprisoned" in a male-dominated enforced-leisure or second-class citizenry. Women worked, and women mattered; and there is the clear sense in Tyler's first novel that an important corollary to this fact was that men who didn't work didn't matter in the least. So completely did the young Anne Tyler subscribe to this work-based ethic that by the time she came to write *Morgan's Passing* in the late 1970s, she was consciously looking to the Quaker paradigm to justify her husband's devoting his life to a career as a child psychiatrist while she cooked meals, cleaned house, took the car in for repairs, raised their two daughters, and wrote novels between 8:05 and 3:30—that is, during school hours.[6] The Quaker paradigm still seems to be a strong aspect of her life; what has changed over the years is her willingness to draw upon that paradigm—and the "feminist" notion of equality for women subsumed within it—in the creation of her women characters. As she has aged, and as she has continued to be exposed to daily American life outside the Quaker commune, Tyler evidently has come to question the viability of a strong woman character like Ellen Hawkes of *If Morning Ever Comes*. Far more in keeping with the unfortunate expectations of our non-Quaker society are the frequently pregnant, long-suffering Mary Tell of *Celestial Navigation*, or the shrill, relentlessly alienating Pearl Tull of *Dinner at the Homesick Restaurant*, or the immature, husband-dependent Lucy Bedloe of *Saint Maybe*. These are women strong in some respects, but essentially victims—and caricatures of the two most persistent representations of women in American culture: the Earth Mother and the termagant. Maggie Moran is essentially one more member of Anne Tyler's gallery of women who never seem to have heard of the feminist movement and who derive none of the sense of personal fulfillment from work that is enjoyed by Quaker women like Tyler. Indeed, Maggie Moran seems a throwback to the late-1950s and early-1960s conception of the middle-aged American woman as a ditzy housewife; and in creating her Tyler seems to be reflecting the idea that, after two decades of ardent feminism, our society is tending to recast American women in that non-threatening light. It was *Breathing Lessons*, after all, that received the Pulitzer Prize for fiction.

Was this award at some level intended to be a public endorsement of the seemingly antifeminist ideas increasingly evident in Tyler's fiction? If so, where will the American novel be going in the 1990s? What will happen when a new generation of American novelists, raised in that era when feminism was taken for granted, attempts to represent fictionally the status of the American woman? Lacking an experiential point of comparison, will they simply revert to earlier, more sentimental or farcical renderings of women as second-class citizens—the kind of reversion that happens so often when a once-controversial movement is absorbed into the normal rhythms of life, or—worse—when backlash becomes so politically correct that to take a giant step in reverse is suddenly deemed worthy of applause? We can only wonder what will happen to Tyler's oeuvre and to the contemporary American novel during what may well be a watershed decade in literature, society, and the feminist movement.

4 / Manacles of Fear

Emotional Affliction in Tyler's Works

In a story that is perhaps more apocryphal than historical, a Quaker farmer feeling beset by the troubles of the world once said wearily to his wife, "All the world is queer save me and thee; and sometimes I think thee is a little queer." Many of Anne Tyler's characters fit the old man's description; odd, somehow out of place, ranging somewhere outside our concept of "ordinary," they manifest the various aberrations that human beings are all prone to, more or less. With Tyler's characters, however, it is usually more, and many of her novels turn upon the ways these people adapt to their crippling emotional injuries or inadequacies.

It has been said that our somewhat tenuous definitions of "normal" and "abnormal" can be compared to a street with a university on one side and a sanitarium on the other; the two are only a shout or a glance apart, and one can turn into either gate with the same ease or difficulty. Who determines which is the real world and which the unreal? Carl Seashore writes in his *Psychology of Music* that a physician can find "all sorts of interweavings between sanity and insanity."[1] We know, for example, that for many years the world viewed Van Gogh as demented; in recent years, however, biographers have suggested that the artist may in fact have suffered from Ménière's Disease, which, in some cases, can drive its victims to strange responses to the world they live in. We view aberrant behavior, always, through a tinted glass.

Thus the characters of Tyler's fictional realm may seem both vaguely puzzling and completely comprehensible, depending upon the color of the reader's lens. Over and over, these people are driven by fear, and their adaptation to that fear is one of Tyler's central concerns. In *Celestial Navigation*, for example, Jeremy is plagued by more than his share of problems, not the least of which is a paralyzing case of agoraphobia. The youngest of three children, Jeremy was coddled and spoiled by his mother, getting a degree of attention not lost on his sister Amanda, who believes that to be the source of his troubles.

For many years now, Jeremy has refused to leave the block where he lives. A sculptor, he is able to insulate himself from the outside world by retreating to the safety of his studio. He protests any attempt to draw him from home, and he always produces some excuse for staying behind when other people take off down the sidewalk for parts unknown. One day Amanda, who holds no sympathy for his behavior and harbors resentment for his preferential treatment as a child, takes it upon herself to force him to venture into that world which so terrifies him. Suggesting that they go outside, she urges him down the steps, then onto the front walk, then onto the sidewalk, a step at a time farther and farther from the safety of his house; she steadfastly ignores his objections and heads off his attempts to turn back. The farther they walk, the more terrified he becomes. Finally, he stops and, shaking uncontrollably, collapses on the sidewalk. Frightened, Amanda calls for help, unable to comprehend how fear could crush a grown man into a quivering heap. "But what's the matter with him?" she asks her sister Laura when she comes to Jeremy's aid. "Is he ill?"

The answer is, of course, that he is not ill, but afflicted: plagued by fear and insecurity, haunted by unhappiness, overwhelmed by anxiety. When Amanda, Laura, and a boarder at the house finally get Jeremy back home where he feels secure and protected, everything settles down to his personal level of normalcy. He can cope with life here; his behavior outside is difficult for others to comprehend and even more difficult for him to face up to.

Jeremy's underlying desire is for people to allow him to move at his own pace, to deal with life from the distance at which he feels comfortable. Occasionally, he accompanies his children on walks, leaving his own yard behind for a short distance; but the inner struggle this gesture engenders always leaves him physically and emotionally exhausted. He continues to try to prove his courage despite dreadful thoughts and almost incapacitating fears.

In time, worn out by the battle, he makes one more brave try, but fails dismally through no fault of his own. Now he feels completely empty and alone. At this point, it is unclear whether Jeremy has really lost his fear; all Tyler will tell us is that he is "beyond worry" as he watches "his gray golf cap bob off across a wave and grow dark and heavy and finally sink."

Two years after this final, unsuccessful attempt, Jeremy appears to have found peace, but seems withdrawn. The question of his phobia remains unanswered, his future as indeterminate as the scene in this poem:

> She knocked on the door and pulled me out;
> She said, "Let's go for a walk."
> "Oh, no," I hedged, "you must come in
> And sit for a while and talk."
>
> Then suddenly the wind came up;
> The door slammed shut behind.
> I tried and tried to get back in,
> But the key was in my mind.
>
> "I must get in, my friend's in there;
> I have to stay with her."
> "She doesn't need you, come stay with me;
> You'll see whom you prefer."

I wanted so much to leave the house
And toss away the key;
But somehow that chain, my phobia,
Kept holding on to me.

—Frances H. Bachelder, June 1982

In *Morgan's Passing*, we find another soul in distress. The protagonist is an amusing but troubled character, who from outward appearances is a happy, well-adjusted family man. But here, as in *Celestial Navigation*, looks can be deceiving—quite literally. For unlike Jeremy, who cannot leave home, Morgan finds his home intolerable. His seven daughters, with their friends, activities, and comings and goings, cause Morgan to see the whole household as a bit of a madhouse. Jeremy copes with a threatening world by hiding from it; Morgan hides, too, but in an entirely different way: he has the strange habit of donning costumes and impersonating various characters. He poses as a tugboat captain, a doctor, a politician, a clerk at a fish market, and a priest, among others. What guise he assumes depends on his whim.

"I often find myself giving a false impression," Morgan rather aptly observes. "It's not something I intend. . . . It almost seems that other people conspire with me, push me into it." This compulsion derives, of course, from his need to escape the people around him, who serve to create a world he simply cannot deal with on his own terms, i.e., in his own identity. At home he feels useless; people who come to visit are his wife's friends, and his children deride him for his costumes and odd behavior. Even Morgan's lover, Emily, claims she understands him, but in truth has little understanding of his motivations. His fantasy life, the way he dresses, the dialects he uses, are his means of adapting to these difficult situations in Walter Mitty fashion.

Like Jeremy, Morgan has a refuge, a haven he seeks when his problems begin to close in on him. That refuge is not his home, but the world outside it. In his office at Cullen Hardware, he can lay aside the often stifling roles he must play and assume some control in his life by undertaking projects of his own making. He can, in short, be someone else. Thus Morgan seeks his disguises for the simple reason that they empower him; he creates, through them, opportunities to be wily and competent.

For Morgan, the stress of living is considerable. Like Jeremy, he is haunted; his ghosts, however, are dissatisfaction, discouragement, and distance from the people he is supposed to feel close to. The depth of his anxiety is formidable; on two occasions, for example, he has the sensation—a possible symptom of some nervous affliction or anxiety disorder—that stationary objects are moving around him. Further, he also experiences a strong sense of unreality, the feeling that he is on the outside of life looking in. Morgan tries to change that sense of observation into participation by joining the human race in the form of somebody different from who he really is.

In *Breathing Lessons*, Tyler offers the reader an amalgam of Jeremy and Morgan in the person of Ira's sister Junie. Like Jeremy, she is agoraphobic; her family cannot understand her fears because, in their view, nothing traumatic or disastrous has ever happened to her "in the outside world, at least not so far as anyone knew." They try to help her, but their empathic resources are limited, and they become discouraged. Finally, Maggie, Ira's wife, has an idea: she performs a complete make-over on the curious but cooperative Junie, from cosmetics to clothes. This symbolic change in external identity, like Morgan's disguises, somehow fortifies Junie with the courage she needs to confront her fears; Maggie tells her this new disguise protects her, while the "real" Junie remains "safe at home." With Maggie's and Ira's help, she leaves the house, step by step. She will not go with Maggie alone because Maggie is "not a blood relative." This seems to indicate that, although she is leaving the safety of home, as long as Ira accompanies her she still has a part of home with her.

Ansel in *The Tin Can Tree* also assumes a guise to deal with his inner affliction. He wants people to think he is ill. Beyond having a not-too-serious case of anemia, this hypochondriac is not in ill health, though he often complains of ailments that, whether real or imagined, cause him great psychic, if not physical, pain.

Although at first Tyler may seem to be portraying Ansel as a pathetic character, she describes his peculiarities with undeniably comic touches as well. A couch by the window where he can stretch out and pretend to be in great physical anguish is Ansel's favorite spot; he rarely allows anyone to share it, since that would put them in the way of his collapse from any possible attacks of whatever heinous syndrome might strike. Even his brother James takes

Ansel's tactics with a grain of salt. When Maisie Hammond, who loves Ansel, chastises James for not showing enough concern for Ansel's pretended ailments, James replies, "Ansel only goes so far, you notice. Only enough to worry people."

So it is difficult to take this character's afflictions very seriously. Lying on his couch—which, one might presume from Ansel's behavior, could imminently become his deathbed—Ansel pines away. When Maisie asks why he never goes anywhere, he responds, "That's *my* secret"; it's no secret, however, that he uses his bouts of "illness" to get the attention of others. Looking as though he might breathe his last at any moment, he gains a certain kind of control over Maisie and James, who cannot completely ignore his complaints. Once he has their attention, he gazes out the window, idly commenting that a jet is flying by. His mission is accomplished; he has made himself the focal point. But at times, when he has overplayed his illness, he "[fools] even himself."

Ansel is a man starving. Incapable of selflessness, only passingly acquainted with genuine affection, devoid of spiritual strength, Ansel limps through life, much more crippled emotionally than physically. In his constant quest to ensure that the warmth of the spotlight falls on his chilled soul, he remains uncertain about others and blind about himself. Even as he talks to James at extraordinary length, he complains that nobody ever listens to him. On the occasions when Ansel literally talks himself to sleep, dozing off at the end of one of his protracted solo discourses, James fights the urge to awaken him, saying, "*Now* I'll listen." He knows, however, that Ansel will start checking for more aches and pains, and then begin another monologue. And so it goes.

Emotional affliction in *Earthly Possessions* takes the form of claustrophobia, from which both Charlotte and her kidnapper, Jake Sims, suffer. Jake has escaped from prison where—quite understandably, given his phobia—the confined quarters have been getting to him. Charlotte is confined, too; tied down at home by the day-to-day care of her ailing parents, she feels there is no way out for her. Her marriage to Saul is stifling and ensnaring. Like Jake, no longer able to bear the closed-in feeling her circumstances have imposed on her, Charlotte escapes by leaving home. She stops at the bank for travel money; Jake arrives at the same time. Their fates become as intertwined as their fears; he holds up the bank, takes her hostage, and the two begin a freedom flight from suffocating lives.

Even Charlotte's two-year-old daughter, Catherine, follows the pattern of affliction and adaptation. An intelligent child with an active imagination, she invents a friend called Selinda. Over time the child assumes more and more of Selinda's characteristics, a theme that should ring familiar at this point: the child eventually takes on Selinda's identity, and Catherine ceases to exist. Whether Catherine's response to her world is the result of an inherent problem or simply a reaction to her mother's need to escape is unclear; it is impossible to know what goes on in the mind of a two-year-old. What does appear to be clear, however, is that Catherine has unwittingly rearranged reality to suit her desires or needs through a fantasy that relieves a disturbing inner pressure.

In *Psychology in Use*, Duane P. Schultz writes, "There are almost as many possible phobias as there are objects in the world to be afraid of. . . . Yet, while recognizing the absurdity of the fear, phobics are prisoners of them."[2] Tyler's prisoners attempt to break out of their cells in various ways and with varying degrees of success. Perhaps the fact that Tyler is married to a psychiatrist has no little influence on her view of humankind as essentially manacled by fear and trauma. She has said that her stories are products of her imagination; if so, it is an imagination that envisions people in general as perpetually struggling to live decent lives despite the handicaps of a tormented inner world and a troubling outer one.

5 / Breakdowns and Breakthroughs

The Hysterical Use of Language

From the Graeco-Roman medical writer Galen of Pergamum to current psychoanalytic theorists, the term hysteria has been used to define deviant female behavior. For the most part, those who have theorized about women's behavior have been men. Feminist theorists and women writers have challenged existing definitions of hysteria and reconceptualized what it means to be a hysteric. These writers lead us directly to a recognition of how definitions of women's hysteria are culturally and historically determined and relate hysteria to women's severely limited opportunities for intellectual growth. In light of a theoretical vision of the hysteric as the product of a social system which engenders conformity to a prescribed role, many of the hysteric's actions, which were construed as tinged with madness, are now reinterpreted and re-presented as clear attempts at self-preservation.

While the traditional hysteric was unconscious of her repressed desires, twentieth-century women writers such as Anne Tyler have reconceptualized the hysteric by making her conscious of her conflict. Although the contemporary hysteric acknowledges the contradictions and desires that are beginning to emerge into her consciousness, the conflict is not yet resolvable. However, she does act out her conflict by submitting to desires that carry her beyond the realm of conventional boundaries. The heroine's passion that shapes these fictions can only be released in the heroine's transgression of the laws which confine it in the first place.

When I write of the hysteric, I mean to invoke her as the embodiment of contradictions. Certain desires are expected to be repressed in favor of a feminine morality that does not accommodate the hysteric's needs. As a result, the hysteric is forced to transgress and defy convention. My critical perspective will draw on the revisionist models of the hysteric offered by feminist theorists to introduce the ways in which the hysteric, as demonstrated in Tyler's novels, subverts the traditional social structure and substitutes a structure which takes her own desires into account.

In *A Slipping-Down Life*, Evie Decker, a "plump, drab girl" who wears a "40-D bra" and has nothing to look forward to but "getting fatter" and "reading romances," attempts to transform her mundane, one-dimensional world by carving a rock singer's name on her forehead with a pair of nail scissors in the ladies' room of the concert hall: "Evie's face was rigid with vertical strands of blood. There were crimson zigzags across her forehead, dampening her hair. 'Evie, what happened?' said Violet. 'It's his name,' Evie said."

In all her novels, Tyler explores extensively how women relate to language, and sets up a motif in this early novel of Evie Decker appropriating language in her bid for attention. To that end, Evie literally externalizes her desire for the singer, Drumstrings Casey, by carving his name on her head. This scene reveals the central crisis of thought for Evie Decker, if not for all of Tyler's heroines: the very physical language Evie appropriates here is an instrument of her repression.

We meet Evie as the novel *A Slipping-Down Life* opens. A discontented seventeen-year-old, her neurotic ties to a rock singer named

Drumstrings Casey drive her to take a stance in which she demands public recognition. In the character of Evie Decker, Tyler provides us with an exaggerated representation of a young woman who has literally engraved her desire as well as her anger on her forehead for everyone to see. Some critics might choose to read this provocative scene as the hysterical reaction of a frustrated, angry woman who has no "appropriate" outlet for her sexual passion. Evie's feelings of pleasure, at this point, have been perverted into a kind of destructive rage. Moreover, it is by no means inappropriate for critics to interpret the scene as the inescapable disfiguring and scarring of Evie's body which has been inscribed literally with the male word—in this case the inscription is clear evidence of Evie's deliberate reproduction of the very discourse that has imprisoned her. And, to a certain extent, all this is true.

A feminist analysis might also focus on Evie's scars, and allegorically read them as a marker of the pain and sadness of exclusion that the woman writer must endure despite her unrelenting attempts to "get it right." When Drumstrings Casey suggests to Evie that she continue to attend his concerts as a publicity stunt until she "healed up," Evie tells him: "I'm not going to get healed up." Drumstrings then goes on to say: "Are you going to have, um—" "Scars," said Evie. At one point Evie, who realizes that the "Casey" engraved on her forehead is "uneven," says: "I know that's going to bother me. Every time I look into a mirror I'll think, why did I let the Y droop? Why did I shake on the C?" Evie carves Casey's name while looking into a mirror, and her concern with her penmanship speaks to women's overall concern with detail as well as the energy women devote to "getting it right." Luce Irigaray directly addresses the issue of woman's relation to language: Woman is always that "something else." According to Irigaray: "To play with mimesis is thus, for a woman, to try to recover the place of her exploitation by discourse, without allowing herself to be simply reduced to it. . . . It also means 'to unveil' the fact that, if women are such good mimics, it is because they are not simply resorbed in this function. *They also remain elsewhere.*"[1] Women's relation to language is radically different from men's, argues Irigaray, and women's ability to mimic patriarchal discourse situates them outside the linguistic space patrolled by men. Evie at once imitates the dominant discourse (when she writes Casey's name) and yet diverges from it (in that

"Casey" appears inversely, as "Yesac"), writing from her marginal existence.

The looking glass is a familiar trope women writers employ to examine woman's identity, and the ways in which a woman's identity is often distorted when she gazes into the mirror. Feminist critics Sandra Gilbert and Susan Gubar caution women to beware of the "trap" of the "King's" voice that resides in the mirror, as well as the ways in which women have internalized that voice—at the expense of their very own voice.[2] When a woman looks into a mirror, write Gilbert and Gubar, she does not see a reflection of her "true" self. What she sees is a sharper representation of a patriarchal construction of herself. From Gilbert and Gubar's perspective, Evie's gesture might certainly appear to be pathological or, at the very least, suspect. At the same time, Virginia Woolf's point of view in *A Room of One's Own*, is equally strong. She suggests that women become the embodiment of the mirror itself: "Women have served all these centuries as looking-glasses possessing the magic and delicious power of reflecting the figure of man at twice his natural size."[3] Woolf goes on to encourage women to resist being frozen into the static image of the male gaze.

From another perspective, Evie Decker's carving becomes, in one sense, a sexual wounding, replete with all the graphic detailing of blood and movement—the loss of virginity, the breaking of the first seal. Clearly, Tyler no less than literally "fleshes out" Evie Decker's marginal relation to language and, by extension, all women who experience themselves as scarred by the hegemony.[4] The protagonists analyzed in Tyler's novels represent the sense of fragmentation experienced by women who are prohibited by society from expressing their sexual desires, yet rebelliously seek to fulfill them in spite of the consequences. Tyler establishes a strong sense of women's isolation from language, which is directly linked to the marginal position they occupy outside the locus of power and authority, by presenting us with unconventional women who pay a high price for their unconventional lives.

Nevertheless, it seems to me that there is yet another way to read this scene which is less obvious.[5] I would suggest that the carving of Casey's name on Evie's forehead proclaims her desire in an inexorable way—metonymical of a desire that cannot be negated. For the first time in her life, Evie's body serves her *own* desires.

Evie's gesture, which is construed as a moment of madness by those around her, prepares her way into language. No longer silent, she publicly acknowledges not only her desire for Drumstrings Casey but also her desire for public significance and attention. Evie tenaciously refuses to "cut bangs," to hide the scars despite her father's (and eventually Drumstrings Casey's) frequent requests that she do so. Evie tells Drum: "I don't wear bangs because I don't back down on things I've done." Graphically imaged in her scars are the psychological underpinnings of a woman who was finally able to begin to represent her repressed desires. Tyler clearly locates the source of woman's pain in her heroines' scars, but the scars simultaneously become a fictional hallmark which symbolizes women's empowerment: Evie runs her fingers across her scar whenever she is about to contradict public authority.

Evie Decker, whose "scars shone like snail tracks," finds her counterpart in the character of Muriel Pritchett in Tyler's novel *The Accidental Tourist*. On the surface, these two characters seem antithetical. Muriel's means of expression and her outspokenness are vastly different from Evie's initial tortured attempts to speak, yet both use language as a mediating agency which enables them to challenge the dominant ideology. Consider the scene where Macon, who has gone to Muriel's apartment to leave a note declining her dinner invitation, is persuaded by Muriel to spend the night. The precise narrative moment where oppositions converge in the image of Macon's hand on Muriel's abdomen after they have made love graphically summarizes and extols the dialectic features of language which frame the scene. The following passage warrants a close examination:

> Then [Muriel] came over to the bed and lifted the quilt and slid under it. "I just want to sleep," Macon told her. But there were these folds of silk. He felt how *cool* and *fluid* the silk was. He put a hand on her hip and felt the *two layers* of her, *cool* over *warm*. He said, "Will you take this off?" She shook her head. "I'm bashful," she whispered, but immediately afterward, *as if to deny that*, she put her mouth on his mouth and wound herself around him. . . . She sighed in her sleep and lifted his hand and placed it on her stomach. The robe had fallen open; he felt her *smooth* skin, and then a *corrugated* ridge of flesh jutting across her abdomen.

[Italics mine.] And it seemed to him, as he sank back into his dreams, that she had as good as spoken aloud. About your son, she seemed to be saying: *Just put your hand here. I'm scarred, too. We're all scarred. You're not the only one.*

The key feature of the passage is the dialogic structure (sameness/difference, masculine/feminine), and Muriel, here, takes it upon herself to fuse polarities. The semantic field of the passage is explicitly polarized ("two layers of her," "cool/warm," "smooth/corrugated"), and leads to a reflection of the two gender identities at play. Figured in the binary oppositions of this "touching" collaborative moment is the possibility of creativity.

Here, Tyler plays not only with the notion of biological reproduction (Muriel's abdominal scars are the direct result of her having given birth to her son, Alexander), but also with the reproduction of a feminine discourse. Muriel's gesture of co-existence in *The Accidental Tourist*, like Evie's gesture of defiance in *A Slipping-Down Life*, becomes what Margaret Homans has described, in *Bearing the Word*, as a "literal transgression"[6] against a linguistic boundary. Underlying Homans's argument, Muriel's and Evie's scars speak for them and "bear the word" in the aphonic message of the hysteric. Muriel's gesture is doubly subversive because she makes her argument by negation. It is based on "lack" as the scene marks an auditory lack of enclosure. Moreover, the framing observation is that the scene sets up the union of the two extremes touching. In her immense capacity to love and create, Muriel succeeds in assimilating herself into Macon's experience. She cures using no sedatives or painkillers—Muriel cures by touching, in both the literal and the symbolic sense. Her silence is ambiguous: ". . . she *seemed* [italics mine] to be saying *Just put your hand here. I'm scarred, too*" (Tyler's italics), but her body—just like Evie's—speaks boldly and clearly.

On the narrative level, the still point in the text in *A Slipping-Down Life*, when Evie is incapacitated, suffering from a self-inflicted wound and being assisted to the ambulance by police officers, becomes, ironically, the epiphanic moment of movement and self-growth for Evie. The moment is illuminating for her, as she insists: "While I was walking through the crowd with the policeman, I kept thinking of my name: Evie Decker, me. Taking something into my own hands for once. I thought, if I had started acting like this a long time ago my whole life might have been different." The circumstances of Evie's life are altered dramatically by this incident. What may justifiably be perceived by some as a chilling act of self-mutilation becomes, paradoxically, the way in which Evie begins to construct her self-identity before the public. Although it was Casey's name (and not her own) that Evie chose to chisel, the action itself is groundbreaking in that Evie, for the first time in her life, usurped authority and began to write her *own* story with "letters [that] stood out clear and proud." No longer in the background, Evie deliberately places herself in the foreground: "I believe this might be the best thing I've ever done. Something out of character," says Evie, in a self-confident tone. Her transgression, which enables the creation of her own text, is underscored by her friend Violet, who reminds Evie that her action marked the difference between Evie and her other classmates: "Like when someone has crossed over where the rest of them haven't been."

The very loss of reason that supposedly motivates Evie to carve Casey's name on her forehead is immensely suggestive of the "traditional" figure of the hysteric, who is marked by her irrationality. The doctor who sutures Evie's forehead surveys "the insides of her wrists" in an attempt to assess "her state of mind," and tells Evie: "You can go home tomorrow, if you're in a normal state. Though what that would be—Help her to the nurses' station, would you, miss?" The interruption of the sentence where the doctor attempts to arrive at a definition of "normal" demonstrates how Tyler's fiction creates a fertile field for reframing what constitutes "normality"— a field where she blurs the outlines between madness and sanity. Phyllis Chesler underscores Tyler's attempt to redefine "normal" female experience, asserting that Freud's psychoanalytic theories forced women into prescribed roles—that "normal" behavior, according to Freud, consisted of female passivity and dependency.[7] Yet, how Evie "reads" herself is, at this point, profoundly at variance with how others read her. The very act of carving the word "Casey" on her body—although it is read by others as "Yesac" because Evie carved it while looking into a mirror—breaks the silence that has oppressed Evie. What might be perceived as the act of a "madwoman" at once empowers Evie.

Evie Decker's graphic spark of rebellion grows into a full-fledged revolt. Resisting her own silence that defined her previous condition and identity, she begins to engage Drumstrings Casey by asking him a welter of questions: "Questions were the only way to grab [Drum's] attentions." No longer disempowered, her questions quickly prefigure her rapid move to declarative sentences. And once Evie begins to tell her story, she cannot stop. Like Muriel in *The Accidental Tourist*, who "talked so much—almost ceaselessly," Evie begins to talk "non-stop. . . . She went against her own nature, even. She shoved down all her reserve and from her place in the front seat she drilled [Casey] with words." Evie manages to shatter that old, silent portrait of herself and create a new portrait which permits her to assert her own identity: "She told [David] the entire plot of a movie without giving him time for a single word. When the plot was finished, she analyzed it, and when that was finished she told him Clotelia's [her housekeeper's] life story." At another point, "she talked even while she was in the kitchen, freezing the three of them into silence."

Evie's struggle with words in *A Slipping-Down Life* culminates with the disclaimer she issues in the closing pages of the novel: "I didn't cut my forehead. Someone else did." Drumstrings Casey is not able to decode the subtext beneath Evie's baffling comment. He makes the mistake of taking what she says literally: "*But the letters was cut backwards. Would you explain?*," reflecting, of course, on the fact that Evie engraved her forehead while looking into a mirror. Here, Drumstrings Casey uses the wrong sensory apparatus. He looks when he should be listening. While Evie Decker has no desire to erase her physical scars (she refuses absolutely to see a plastic surgeon), she does erase the woman that she was at the outset of the novel. Clearly, Evie Decker has transformed the earlier version of herself, the one who mutilated her body in an act of self-hatred and defiance, into a woman who now possesses an ineradicable sense of affirmation—a woman who is now able, at the conclusion of the novel, to decipher the meaning of her past, and to begin to articulate her desires. In this respect she resembles other Tyler heroines who are also able to recast their moments of "madness" into moments of self-representation through language.

Tyler's women refuse to conform to traditional rules of discourse, and so they often find themselves involved in a battle of words with their male counterparts. At one point Alicia (Macon's mother) in *The Accidental Tourist* tells Julian: "All I've ever had is daughter-in-laws." Macon "automatically" corrects her and says: "*Daughters-*

in-law, Mother." But Alicia, who remains impervious to Macon's censoriousness and refuses to give Macon the satisfaction of repeating his corrective, then responds: "And didn't manage to keep them long either." Muriel, too, defies Macon's paternal attempt to encase her text (her life) by challenging his regulatory practices. Muriel, who "doesn't even speak proper English," who keeps confusing "simplistic" with "simple" and "nauseous" with "nauseated," and who "seemed [to use] words as a sort of background music," forges new texts with her frequent malapropisms, and breaks the hold of language by affirming the flexibility of linguistic constructs. Tyler presents us with women who, bound together by their remoteness from a social norm, cannot be contained in the paternal system of order and culture. Evie Decker does not copy language but embodies it; Muriel and Alicia luxuriate in language, and their disjunctive logic undercuts the dominant discourse.

Muriel's power, like Macon's, is connected to language. The locus of her power is in *her* imaginative ability to disrupt "traditional" logic.[8] Muriel's language is filled with violations—violations that play on the gap between women's language and men's language. In explaining her dissatisfaction with one of her numerous jobs, Muriel's comments mark the rupture of traditional, logical thinking:

> "I've never been so disinterested," [says Muriel].
> Macon stirred and said, "Don't you mean uninterested?"
> "Exactly. Wouldn't you be? Copies of letters, copies of exams, copies of articles on how to shop for a mortgage. . . . Finally I quit. When I got my job at Doggie Do, I said, 'I quit. I've had it!' Why don't we try the grocery?"
> Macon felt confused for a second. Then he said, "Oh, all right."

Muriel's so-called "mistake" raises interesting problems in terms of language. Which one is she? "Disinterested" or "uninterested?" "Disinterested" implies that Muriel does not have a personal investment in the situation—that she is "impartial"—and, according to the dictionary, that she might or might not be "uninterested"; "uninterested" is defined as being "indifferent." Here, Macon endows himself with the privilege of determining whether Muriel is "disinterested" or "uninterested." Muriel doesn't use language with the same precision as Macon. She probably doesn't know the difference between "disinterested" and "uninterested," nor does she care.

Moreover, Muriel's shift from a discussion centering on her job at the Meow-Bow to "Why don't we try the grocery?" leaves Macon dumbfounded. She exerts a verbal power that comes from the dismantling of accepted logic and meaning. Here, Tyler plays with the reproduction of a feminine language in that she provides us with certain patterns of discourse which she allows her female characters to violate. Muriel unconsciously subverts traditional, logical discourse and, by doing so, unselfconsciously appropriates language for her own purposes. Her perpetual displacement of meaning through her illogical sense-making operations implies the infinite possibilities of many meanings, which then threaten the hegemony of the prevailing order.

If Muriel can manipulate language, implicit in that ability is the power to create. Sandra Gilbert and Susan Gubar write: "Finally the fact that the angel woman manipulates her domestic/mystical sphere in order to ensure the well-being of those entrusted to her care reveals that she can manipulate; she can scheme; she can plot stories as well as strategies."[9] And if Muriel *can* manipulate language, she then has the "dangerous mobility" of the hysteric that Cixous and Clément describe in *The Newly Born Woman*: "Societies do not succeed in offering everyone the same way of fitting into the symbolic order; those who are, if one may say so, between symbolic systems, in the interstices, offside, are the ones afflicted with a dangerous mobility. Dangerous for them because those are the people afflicted with what we call madness, anomaly, perversion, or whom we even label, says Mauss, 'neurotics, ecstatics, outsiders, carnies, drifters, jugglers, and acrobats.' . . . And more than any others, women bizarrely embody this group of anomalies showing the cracks in the overall system."[10]

In an attempt to justify to Macon, for example, why she quit her job at the "Meow-Bow," Muriel exclaims: "Why I was coming home nights literally dead with exhaustion, Macon. . . ." "Figuratively," Macon says, to which Muriel responds, "Huh?" Macon goes on to say: "You were *figuratively* dead with exhaustion. Jesus, Muriel, you're so imprecise. You're so sloppy. . . ." Macon, by contrast, "felt he had to be terribly careful. He had to choose exactly the right words." And yet, despite Muriel's tendency to re-semanticize words—for example, to use the word *enormity* as if it referred to size—Macon remains painfully aware and certain that Muriel "could raise her chin sometimes and pierce his mind like a blade." What Tyler's heroines seem to be saying is, We have our own definitions, and we have our own grammar. Deviance is built into their subversive and transgressive gestures. Macon's need to correct Muriel's and Alicia's grammar at once recognizes and validates the inherent power in a feminine discourse, while it simultaneously marginalizes the women. Helene Cixous writes: "No matter how subversive and docile [the hysteric] may be in relation to the masculine order, she still remains the threatening possibility of savagery, the unknown quantity in the household whole."[11] Tyler's protagonists' refusal to acquiesce to the stranglehold of language becomes their subterfuge.

Language is not the only area where men attempt to set the standard in Tyler's novels. Aside from language, marriage becomes the traditional and perfect deterrent to her heroines' quest for personal freedom. It should come as no surprise that for Tyler the very structure of marriage—which often circumscribes women to the realm of domesticity—is suspect. Harley, in *Dinner at the Homesick Restaurant*, resembles Macon in his need to regulate his wife Jenny's table manners—"Twenty-five chews per bite. . . . He wouldn't want to see [Jenny] getting out of hand"—and his need to legislate her life: "He was going to run her life, arrange it perfectly, by height and by color. He was going to sit in the passenger seat with that censorious expression on his face and dictate every turn she took, and every shift of gears." However, Jenny, who "was not capable of being destroyed by love," leaves Harley—just as Muriel leaves her husband, Norman; as Evie Decker, although pregnant, leaves Drumstrings Casey; and as Charlotte Emory, the heroine in *Earthly Possessions*, begins her story: "The marriage wasn't going well and I decided to leave my husband." Tyler's men crave order with all the symptoms of addiction, and her women defy it with the same intensity. Tyler's heroines assert their successful release from marriage and manage to escape confinement in conventional scripts.

Relegated to the margins of social existence, Muriel, in *The Accidental Tourist*, is indifferent to the rules of "proper" grammar, since she has all the language she needs to convey the intensity of her feelings; and, like the hysteric, Muriel refuses to revise herself into the conformity of her social script. Nevertheless, she does not reject language entirely (by remaining silent) but deconstructs it in order to reconstruct it. She moves letters and words around, demystifying and re-contextualizing language, and thereby exposes its flexibility. For example, in expressing her desire to go to France with Macon, she leaves him a note assembled from scraps of magazines: "Don't FoRget tO BUY plANe Ticket for MuRiel." Like Cixous's and Clément's hysteric, there is no negation involved, just movement—reintegration. For the hysteric, letters and attitudes do not remain fixed. And unlike Macon, who exists in a world of facts, Muriel is counterfactual. It seems to Macon "that the world was full of equations; that there must be an answer for everything, if only he could set forth the right questions." For Muriel, on the other hand: "The news could be missed but not the lottery drawing; nor could 'Evening Magazine' or any of the *action* shows that followed" (italics mine). Muriel's life is framed by an interest in a different value system, and her interests become more and more subversive. She cares about what she enjoys doing and cannot be bothered with factual information:

> [Muriel] was inconsistent with Alexander to the point of *pure craziness*—one minute overprotective, the next callous and offhand. She was obviously intelligent, but she counteracted that with the most global case of superstition Macon had ever witnessed. . . . She believed in horoscopes and tarot cards and Ouija boards. Her magic number was seventeen. In a previous incarnation she'd been a fashion designer, and she swore she could recall at least one of her deaths. . . . She was religious in a blurry, nondenominational sort of way and had no doubt whatsoever that God was looking after her personally—ironic, it seemed to Macon, in view of how she'd had to fight for every little thing she wanted.

Refusing to allow themselves to be frozen into predictable postures, Tyler's heroines opt for the unpredictability and the suggestion of chaos associated with the supernatural world. There are resonances with Muriel in the character of Phoebe in *Dinner at the Homesick Restaurant*, Ezra's "finest cook [who] had quit because her horoscope advised it," and who "cooked by astrology." "'Nothing vinegary, the stars are wrong,'" Phoebe would say. Ezra begins to believe that there "might be something to this horoscope business. . . . Last summer the stars asked [Phoebe] to leave, and this place has never been the same." Muriel and Phoebe also have affinities with

Jenny, in *Dinner at the Homesick Restaurant*, who goes to "fortune tellers" regularly. What is it that the supernatural realm provides for Tyler's women? All Tyler's heroines consistently demonstrate a movement away from the center into "other" areas. They move into the cosmic world as well as the underground world, subverting the order they are expected to serve.

Tyler continues to explore the supernatural realm, giving us a wonderfully useful paradigm of the witch in the characters of Macon's mother, Alicia (in *The Accidental Tourist*) and Pearl (in *Dinner at the Homesick Restaurant*). The "witch figures" in Tyler's novels come to represent all that is unrepressed and, in the case of Pearl, even violent. Alicia establishes resonances with Pearl—whose "children were closed off from her in some sort of a perverse way"—as Alicia defies the prescribed maternal expectations:

> Sometimes Alicia's enthusiasm turned to her children—an unsettling experience. She took them all to the circus and bought them cotton candy that none of them enjoyed. (They liked to keep themselves tidy.) She yanked them out of school and enrolled them briefly in an experimental learning community where no one wore clothes. The four of them, chilled and miserable, sat hunched in a row in the common room with their hands pressed flat between their bare knees. She dressed as a witch and went trick-or-treating with them, the most horrifying Halloween of their lives, for she got carried away as usual and *cackled* [italics mine], croaked, scuttled up to strangers and shook her ragged broom in their faces.

Like Alicia in *The Accidental Tourist* (who "seemed to find her children comical"), Lacey Ames in *Earthly Possessions* (who doesn't believe her daughter Charlotte is really her "true daughter," leaving Charlotte to feel "dislocated and sick to her stomach"), and Elizabeth in *The Clock Winder* (who doesn't like children), Pearl in *Dinner at the Homesick Restaurant* also challenges societal prescriptions for maternal behavior. In a painful scene in which Cody (Pearl's son) recounts memories of his childhood, his harbored angst surfaces on the day of his mother's funeral:

> "You think we're a family," Cody said turning back. "You think we're some jolly, situation-comedy family when we're in

particles, torn apart, torn all over the place, and our mother was a witch." . . . "A raving, shrieking unpredictable witch," Cody told Beck [his father, who had abandoned him when he was a small child]. "She slammed us against the wall and called us scum and vipers, said she wished us dead, shook us till our teeth rattled, screamed in our faces. We never knew from one day to the next, was she alright?"

In the character of Pearl, Tyler provides us with the ultimate breakdown of the woman as m/other—showing yet another dimension of deviant female behavior. However, here Tyler is daring enough to expose the dark side that emerges from Pearl's tremendous rage and frustration and to show the destructive consequences of that rage. The sweet qualities of motherhood which are mythically perpetuated are blown apart. Tyler explodes the "apple pie" myth of motherhood and purposefully demonstrates what happens when women are ignored. In Pearl we see another aspect of the rage of the hysteric who breaks out of the conventional mode and expresses feelings that can no longer be contained to satisfy social practice.

So whether the woman is flying over culture (as the witch-like Alicia and Pearl do) or under it (as the extra-logical Muriel does), she is, according to Sherry Ortner, "both under and over (but really outside of) the culture's hegemony."[12] Gilbert and Gubar press forward Ortner's thesis: "If we define a woman . . . as indomitably earthly yet somehow supernatural, we are defining her as witch or monster, a magical creature of the lower world who is a kind of antithetic mirror image of an angel."[13] Gilbert and Gubar go on to speculate that the "witch-monster-mad-woman becomes so crucial an avatar of the [woman] writer's own self. From a male point of view, women who reject the submissive silences of domesticity have been seen as terrible objects—Gorgons, Sirens, Scylas, serpent-Lamias, Mothers of Death or Goddesses of Night. But from a female point of view the monster woman is simply a woman who seeks the power of self-articulation."[14] However, for all Alicia's, Pearl's, and Lacey's apparent rejection of their children, Tyler treats these women affectionately, understanding the tragedy in their inability to participate in the circumscribed realm of motherhood and domesticity, and their subsequent need to protect themselves from it and retreat from it. As Margaret Morganroth Gullette says, "Tyler saw that motherhood was not in every case a happy instinct, a gift of the life course. For some it comes as a curse."[15] Tyler understands that marriage and motherhood are often symbolic of structures designed to imprison women. Consequently, hysteria offers her protagonists a real way of escaping a constrained life.

The internal contradictions and juxtapositions within the hysteric are revealed in the rebellious language of women who represent different categories of marginality. Her female characters demonstrate what happens when the hysteric acts out her repression. However, Tyler takes the issue of women's hysteria and turns it around to women's advantage. In *Disorderly Conduct*, a text which explores the transgressions of Victorian women, Caroll Smith-Rosenberg observes that "hysteria may serve as one option or tactic offering peculiar women . . . a chance to redefine or restructure their place within the family."[16] And although Tyler's protagonists use language in different ways, and for different purposes, they manage to dismantle assumptions concerning the appropriate sphere of female activity without subverting the authenticity of their own voices. Anne Tyler brings an understanding to the hysteric and rescues her from the stereotype of the repressed madwoman.

6 / Crepe Soles, Boots, and Fringed Shawls

Female Dress as Signals of Femininity

ostume is important in Anne Tyler's novels, and nearly every novel has one outrageously outfitted character who stands out among more traditionally garbed family members and friends. Everyone else seems to have internalized a generally shared notion of appropriateness regarding dress, determined by class, role, occasion. But the eccentric character dresses without apparent regard for any of the shared assumptions of others. Such disregard ranges from that of Justine Peck in *Searching for Caleb* to that of Muriel Pritchett in *The Accidental Tourist*. Justine wears the same faded dress from year to year, simply turning the hem up or down to fit the current fashion. She has grown up in a tradition of ladies and gentlemen who dress formally, with attention to the most minute details of appearance, a family in which the cure for what-ever ails a woman is a shopping trip for clothes. Yet in marrying her rebellious cousin, Justine turns her back on nearly all the conventions of her family, except the customary wearing of a hat whenever she goes out. Regardless of the threadbare state of her garments and the disarray of her wiry hair, Justine never leaves home without her Breton hat. Muriel, however, revels in costume, turning her back on the conventionality of her home and dressing in ways that call attention to herself, whether in wearing skimpy shorts or the big-shouldered jackets of the 1940s. Similarly, Alberta in *Earthly Possessions*, described as gypsyish, wears flowing, sensuous garments and sometimes even goes barefoot. Tyler uses "gypsyish" to describe other characters such as Daphne in *Saint Maybe* and Serena in *Breathing Lessons* to differentiate them from conventionally clad women such as Sarah Leary or Maggie Moran. Fringed shawls, draped fabric, anything sensuous and colorful and unusual separates the free-spirited "gypsy" women from the dutiful mothers and daughters who seek to please others and not to offend.

In Tyler's novels, woman's clothing correlates with her identity. Beyond its basic task of covering the body, clothing functions quite differently for a female character than for a male and carries symbolic as well as functional importance. Tyler's characters do not meditate upon the significance of their dress as do female characters in a Doris Lessing novel, nor does the narrator analyze its importance as in Virginia Woolf's fiction. Rather, that importance is assumed, taken for granted, as it is in society, and Tyler manipulates an existing social coding of female dress as a ready-made shorthand. Through nearly thirty years of Tyler's fiction, her female characters' clothing continues to signal similar meanings: just as traffic signs indicate stop, go, and yield, and arrows point to the directions of roads, so does clothing in Tyler's novels direct the reader to a character's identity. A red light is stop. Red shoes are sexy.

Woman's association with body more than mind, with matter, with appearance, and with the external rather than the internal, is by now a cultural commonplace. Perhaps because woman has historically and metaphorically been so closely associated with nature, with the earth, with reproduction and the fleshly, her body through the ages has been understood as her primary definition of both her power and her powerlessness. Sherry B. Ortner argues that "woman's body and its functions seem to place her closer to nature than man's physiology places him. . . . Women are pan-culturally seen as being more rooted in, or having a more direct affinity to, nature than men are."[1] Because of their greater freedom from physical processes, Ortner argues, men are traditionally associated with a greater ability to transcend physical existence than women; women are viewed as being less spiritual because of their over-association with the body.

This focus on woman's body, on her materiality, has through the ages resulted in the talismanic association of woman's clothing with her sexualized body. By logical extension, a focus on the sexualized body leads to a focus on the clothed or displayed body. Female dress has emphasized, either by accentuating or by seeming to disguise, those body parts considered the most sexualized: breasts, hips, legs, throat, wrists, ankles, feet. Consider, for example, hoops, corsets, bullet bras, miniskirts, and high-heeled shoes, which all accentuate, in contrast to caftans, oversized tops, baggy pants, and sturdy boots, which disguise. If a woman has wanted to diminish her identification with her body, she has had to neutralize her body's power by her dress, hiding her shape and camouflaging her sexuality. Display and disguise may either stem from masculine insistence—from the veil to the striptease—or be a mode of defiance, as worn by Joan of Arc or Salome.

Whether calling attention to or diverting attention from her sexualized body, woman's dress has been seen as reflecting her sexual status, a status calculated in terms of her relation to men: her ability to attract a lover or husband, on the one hand, or her ability to avoid such attraction, on the other. It has generally been culturally assumed that an observer can accurately read a woman's appearance, effortlessly decoding her dress to determine whether she is sexually available or unavailable, married or unmarried, maternal or childless. In Tyler's novels, in keeping with these societal stereotypes, such decoding is automatic: fringed shawls, strappy sandals, and fingernail polish communicate a message entirely different from that of sensible cardigans, prim pumps, and plastic rain bonnets.

In Tyler's fiction, as in society, the most common assumption about a woman's appearance is that it correlates with her "self," and that the female self is identified in relation to masculinity: in search of it, avoiding it, or settled with it. The most frequent classification of female appearance in Tyler's novels is that in which a woman accepts, apparently without question, prevailing societal definitions of the feminine. She either wears clothing which accentuates and displays her femininity, applies cosmetics, especially lipstick, and styles her hair in a fashion considered attractive to men, such as Lucy in *Saint Maybe* or Joanne in *If Morning Ever Comes*, or, if a woman no longer chooses to appear sexually attractive in a generalized way but still wants to appear feminine, she may a adopt a sensible, "lady-like," already-spoken-for look, such as Mrs. Emerson in her high-heeled shoes and pearls in *The Clock Winder*. Ironically, although her body is primarily defined as sexualized before marriage and childbirth, once she bears children, she is most often considered maternal, desexualized, such as Mary Tell in her faded blue dress in *Celestial Navigation* or Pearl Tull wearing washable seersucker in *The Homesick Restaurant*. If a woman chooses to rebel against conventional codes for the feminine, regardless of her sexual orientation, she can dress to appear unfeminine, donning unisex items or those associated with male attire, such as Elizabeth's jeans and oversized shirts, emphasizing function and comfort rather than calling attention to her body.

Whatever her female character's appearance, Tyler accepts rather than qualifies or critiques the extant social coding of female dress. Her use of shoes as a readily-recognized symbol of that coding exemplifies her handling of female clothing. Shoes are the most ubiquitous item of female apparel throughout Tyler's novels. Once noticed, they walk, clomp, stomp their way into a reader's consciousness. Crepe-soled walking shoes, comfortable moccasins, heavy combat boots, oversized rubber boots, medium-heeled pumps, sandals, stiletto-heeled shoes—each alerts the reader to a female character's personality as well as to her relationship to conventional femininity. Her sensuality and the degree of her adherence to conventional dress codes are blatantly communicated by a character's footwear, regardless of her age. For example, we regard Gram at age seventy-eight as more free-spirited in her high-top black gym shoes, crazily belted denim dress, and black lace slip than Maggie Moran, in her fifties, wearing sensible crepe-soled flats. Those crepe-soled shoes, for example, are not only pragmatic and comfortable, but also, from a masculine perspective, hint accurately in the world of Tyler's novels that their wearer is dull and unsexy. Muriel Pritchett, perched on spiky heels in *The Accidental Tourist*, shares an allure and sensuality with similarly teetering Alberta in *Earthly Possessions* and Lucy in *Saint Maybe*. And all three have more sexual energy and life spirit than sensibly clad female characters in any of the novels. One can thus read Tyler as reaffirming the sexist status quo, which demands discomfort and display of the woman who would be fascinating and sexy. However, although Tyler does not redefine the existing equation between dress and sensuality, she does deviate from social stereotypes by portraying several made-up and bejeweled sexy mothers and grandmothers, including Alberta, Alicia, and Serena, whose theatrical dress puts them outside conventional standards of desexed mommies.

There is a continuum of femininity in Tyler's novels: a line from the traditional to the extreme, from the apparently ordinary, unexamined feminine to the most theatrical. In spite of some characters' attempts to avoid the continuum entirely and to simply appear neutral, feminine dress is never neutral, neither in our society nor in the world of Tyler's novels.[2] In both arenas, woman's self-presentation in whatever guise is always perceived as a way of discerning her *self*.

Mrs. Emerson and Elizabeth of *The Clock Winder* see each other as polar opposites in dress, although we may see them as simply positioned differently on the line of apparent femininity. Encountering them together in the first chapter of the novel makes the reader conscious of assumptions about female appearance that are worth examining closely. Mrs. Emerson carries to an extreme the conventions of feminine dress, giving careful attention to her appearance, regardless of her own comfort, even when she is home by herself; Elizabeth dresses primarily for comfort and function, with little awareness of how she appears to others even when they are staring at her.

Mrs. Emerson is first described as "skin and bones in a shimmery gray dress" walking on "little spiky shoes," with her face carefully made up before ten o'clock in the morning. She works to maintain the prettiness of her youth, though all she has left is "color—pink, white, blond, most of it false." She dresses up for everything, owns no slacks, and always wears ultra-sheer stockings and spike-heeled shoes. Her dress is not affected by her emotional upheavals. In fact, after her husband's death and the suicide of her son, she forces herself not to alter her dress. Fearful of frightening her children by any changes in what she considers the "reassurance" of her matched skirts and sweaters and her string of pearls, she resists the "urge to spend her days in comfortable shoes and forget her chin-strap and let herself go." She sees her polished appearance as the evidence she has not "become a broken old lady after all." Perceived by her son Matthew as someone who "still dresses every day and holds her stomach in," she not only maintains perfect physical posture, she postures emotionally even to herself about the state of her feelings and about the condition of her family and her house. However, from their initial meeting, Elizabeth sees through Mrs. Emerson's carefully maintained façade to her emotional vulnerability and need. After Mrs. Emerson has a stroke, and when her children are indeed frightened by her helplessness, Elizabeth is the one who sees her as "nothing but a small, worn-out old lady trying to gather up her lost strength." Unlike Mrs. Emerson and her children, Elizabeth never confuses the superficial façade of perfectly applied foundation and beauty-salon hairdos with personal strength.

Elizabeth, in her dungarees, white shirt, and shapeless soft-soled brown moccasins, initially strikes Mrs. Emerson as "pretty enough" if only she would wear a "nice bright lipstick." From Mrs. Emerson's perspective, Elizabeth's competent hands are "badly cared for, the nails chopped-looking and the knuckles scraped." The qualities Mrs. Emerson notices stand in contrast to her expectations of the proper look for an unmarried college-age girl. She sees only a girl who is awkward and flat-chested, with grainy textured skin and no makeup, dressed any old way. When Elizabeth varies her outfit from the ubiquitous blue jeans, white shirt, and moccasins, it is to don a helmeted cap with earflaps or a jaunty chauffeur's cap, or to replace the moccasins with huge rubber boots. Her attempts to dress up for special occasions result in unintentional comical display: for a date, she wears a bulky wool dress, wrinkled nylons, and squashed-looking black pumps; for a funeral, she has a beige linen dress, a peeling handbag, and a falling-down hairdo. For her abortive wedding, she arrives at church in a white wedding-suit. However, to the guests, "without her dungarees she seemed to lose all her style." Even the wedding veil, instead of creating an illusion, sticks out "like a peasant's kerchief." Elizabeth's manners and her dress emphasize function, not fashion. She is happiest when she is taking charge of a task, whether preparing a salad or mending the pipes. Yet, much to

Mrs. Emerson's surprise, men are attracted to Elizabeth, enjoying her sense of adventure and her competence. Elizabeth calls into question the internalized female lore of the Mrs. Emersons of the world, whose own sons prefer Elizabeth to other young women of their acquaintance.

By the novel's end, Elizabeth is Mrs. Emerson's daughter-in-law and is herself a mother, still in blue jeans, holding the household together. This second-generation Mrs. (Elizabeth) Emerson calls into question the value of adopting the feminine façade, and we can read the portrayal of the older Mrs. Emerson as a critique of the way in which women have traditionally been taught to confuse external appearance with internal worth. A more haunting critique of the danger of confusing woman's external appearance with her *self* is evident in the portrayal of Lucy in *Saint Maybe*, who, like Mrs. Emerson, buys into the feminine role but whose external façade belies the degree of actual vulnerability.

Along with Mrs. Emerson, among the conventional wives and mothers of Tyler's novels who accept the prescriptive codes of feminine appearance, are those like Sarah of *The Accidental Tourist*, Bonnie of *Morgan's Passing*, and Maggie of *Breathing Lessons*, who always wear practical clothing appropriate to the occasion, who would not stand out in a crowd, and who seem not to question the socially constructed meanings of dress. They know what is expected in their roles as wives, mothers, and daughters, as well as how to dress for the social occasions in their communities. They notice the dress of other women, differentiating themselves from the drab or ostentatious, and especially from gypsy-clad women, whom they view as less sensible than themselves. Although they may not be as extreme as Mrs. Emerson about creating an appearance, these women apply makeup and have a deep sense of propriety about their dress. Characters such as Mary Tell of *Celestial Navigation* and Jasmine of *Searching for Caleb*, who repeatedly wear their faded blue dresses regardless of the occasion, do not critique traditional femininity as extensively as does Mrs. Emerson's reliance on and overvaluation of controlled externality, but they do reveal the ways in which one's sense of self is limited by adherence to and acceptance of predefined norms and roles.

Emily of *Morgan's Passing*, unlike Elizabeth as well as these more conventionally feminine characters, actually reflects often on the difference between her own sense of self and the impression others have of her. She considers her appearance an artificial construct and dislikes "being seen from the outside . . . as someone with blond hair, someone with an old-fashioned face." In contrast to her image and the way people read her, Emily carries a Swiss Army knife in her purse, distrusts photographs of herself because they only faintly resemble her, and hates "being made to feel conscious of her physical appearance." Although Emily, like Elizabeth, dresses comfortably in clothes that are functional, usually wearing a leotard, long skirt, and ballet slippers, she appears more feminine than does Elizabeth in her jeans and moccasins. When Emily wears cloddy, stiff brown Docksiders to the beach and takes up jogging in clumsy yellow running shoes, Morgan must alter his internalized version of her, in which he has mistakenly read her ballet slippers as coded evidence of her innocence. Emily's simple wardrobe is not affected by fashion's or society's dictates any more than is Elizabeth's. Just as Elizabeth dotes on professional garb—for example, wearing a chauffeur's hat when driving Mrs. Emerson around in a Mercedes—Emily enjoys costuming herself for puppet shows.

Unlike Mrs. Emerson and Lucy, these middle-spectrum characters on the continuum of femininity—Elizabeth and Emily—do not passively accept classic roles of femininity. Nevertheless, although they are conscious of an internal/external split, they do not do very much to resist it. The action they do take is primarily a passive one, trying to appear neutral rather than traditionally feminine, whereas the most memorable characters in Tyler actively manipulate the external impressions they make and take control of them to a certain extent.

A female character who consciously recognizes the social coding of dress and of feminine display can avoid falling into the trap of assuming that her inside and her outside match, of assuming that her appearance is identical to her self. Carnival or even careless dress avoids the prescribed feminine dress. Boots as well as high-heeled shoes defy the sterility and boredom of sensible crepe-soled shoes and mid-heel pumps. There is a playfulness and costuming in the seemingly masculine as well as in the exaggeratedly feminine garb. In either outfit, the female character insists on her own creation, her choice. That insistence, on dressing as she pleases rather than merely donning a wardrobe considered appropriate to her role, marks her as someone capable of delight and surprise in the world of Tyler's novels. As readers, we tend to be captivated by her spark, by her gumption, and by her ability to care about people as people rather than to worry about what they think of her appearance. She can choose to clomp about in combat boots, as do Daphne and Rita, or to exaggerate the paraphernalia of feminine dress, as do Muriel in her stiletto shoes and Serena in her fringed shawl, but whatever she wears immediately announces a defiance of prescriptive feminine codes, projects strength rather than vulnerability, and expresses some internal pleasure.

Neither a female character nor an actual woman, accustomed to being viewed, to objectification regardless of the way she dresses, can avoid that emphasis placed by others on her appearance. Nor can she control the societal readings and interpretations of her image. She cannot, for example, change the social meanings attached to her body or her dress. However, a source of power she does possess concerning the signification of her image is to intentionally produce that image, to actively call attention to the construction of her image by costuming and exaggeration.

Among the most memorable of Tyler's female characters are those who do stand out in a crowd, those gypsy-like women who flaunt their appearance in colorful costumes and wear outrageous hairdos and bright lipstick. They share a larger-than-life vitality, an abundance, a willingness to disregard convention and the opinions of others, not only in their appearance but also in their actions. Unlike Mary, Jasmine, or even Emily and Elizabeth, these women broadcast their unconventionality by the ways in which they present themselves. And they *do* present themselves. Alberta in *Earthly Possessions* and Muriel in *The Accidental Tourist* are the most fully described, but Daphne and Rita in *Saint Maybe*, Serena in *Breathing Lessons*, and Joanne and even Gram in *If Morning Ever Comes* are cut of similar cloth. Every one of them is aware of the effect she makes on people around her. Each dresses with an eye to her appearance and takes considerable pleasure in her dress.

Alberta, the flashy mother-in-law of *Earthly Possessions*, who wears sharp, insistent colors and sequined shawls, is perceived by Charlotte as "a gypsyish type, beautiful in certain lights, and carelessly dressed, slouchy, surprisingly young." Unlike other women, she goes barefoot in the summer, reveals rather than keeps secrets, and in her lush, soft voice repeats news of scandals, disasters, miracles, and mysteries between breaths of laughter. She is the opposite of conformity, managing somehow to make her children seem remarkable, to make her many troubles appear enviable from the outside and to wear them like riches. Flying in the face of propriety, she elopes with her father-in-law, and then travels around the world with a succession of husbands. Her legacy to Charlotte, whose memories include a childhood of resistance to her own mother's attempts to entrap her in white eyelet dresses, is a hunger for adventure, and the younger woman, always expecting Alberta to return, wants the approval of the older, theatrically presented woman whom she sees as "so much braver, freer, stronger" than herself.

Alicia, Macon Leary's mother, is somewhat like Alberta, leaving her children to be raised by their paternal grandparents when she sets off around the world, and lingering in Macon's memory as "always going too far" in her enthusiasms. Her appearance—all blue-and-gold coloring, vivid makeup, and flashy print dresses—has none of the methodical care perfected by her children over the years. She shows up for her daughter Rose's wedding, where her zaniness echoes in Muriel Pritchett, the memorable dog trainer from Meow-Bow who turns around Macon's life after his son's murder and his wife's threat of divorce.

Muriel's dress receives more attention than that of any other female character in Tyler's novels; this emphasis is equaled only in descriptions of Morgan's many costumes in *Morgan's Passing*. Like Morgan, she has a zest for life and a willingness to go after whatever she wants. Unlike him, she does not impersonate others, trying on their professional identities. Muriel's outfits, as noticed by the conventional Macon Leary, include "very short red shorts," "skimpy skirts," a ruffled peasant blouse, a V-necked black dress splashed with big pink flowers, dresses and coats with thickly padded shoulders reminiscent of the 1940s in the 1970s, dark red lipstick and nails, and her ubiquitous high-heeled shoes. She costumes herself from flea markets and secondhand shops. This is part of her survival strategy, and yet one always senses that she loves theatricality and that her costuming and makeup create as much magic for her as for others. She describes her body-permed hair as looking like a fright wig, and Macon's neighbor describes her as a skinny lady with hair.

His sister Rose describes her as "a flamenco dancer with galloping consumption." Splashy shawls, a shiny black cape, a fringed skirt, a bouffant red net evening dress—every item of her clothing sets her apart from characters like Sarah, with her beige suit and matched set of luggage. Muriel's clothes, even when old, threadbare, and with darned elbows, are of shattered silk or fur or velvet—sensuous fabrics that appeal to the touch; they carry a magic that is imaginative rather than appropriate. Tiny, with spindly legs and jutting collarbones, Muriel has an appealing fierceness and incredible energy that set her apart from female characters who worry about fitting into prescribed feminine molds.

As if to emphasize their similarity, Tyler juxtaposes Muriel and Alicia at Rose's wedding, where the trim of Alicia's caftan nearly matches Muriel's shawl. Alicia blatantly disregards prescriptions for appropriate dress, even at the most formal of occasions where etiquette prohibits anyone but the bride wearing white, showing up at her daughter's wedding in a long white caftan trimmed with satin bands and wearing bangles. Her hair, like Muriel's, is flamboyant, dyed a dark tomato red.

We can critique Tyler's gypsyish, highly sexualized, exaggerated feminine characters as showing an acceptance of restrictive norms and playing into traditional genre roles, which belies another, more authentic and powerful, artifice-free femaleness. However, this conception rests upon and assumes the existence of an authentic, natural, and discernible femininity, one which is repressed by theatricality. The conscious focus on the "unnatural," or excessively theatrical, femininity of Alberta, Alicia, and Muriel suggests instead the constructed nature of femininity itself and the danger and falsity of equating femininity with female identity.[3] We can read such characters as Alberta and Muriel as inventing themselves through theatrical femininity. We can also read them as "female female impersonators"—women who imitate and impersonate the socially defined role of woman. In so doing, they exhibit some control or power over ideas of femininity, and, in not equating external appearance with internal worth, they may actually succeed in holding femininity at a distance. Thus, although we may read Tyler's portrayal of female dress as a re-inscription of societal stereotypes, we may also read not only female dress but femininity itself as constructed. Reading Tyler's female characters through the lens of the masquerade, red shoes and fringed shawls not only signal "sexy" but also hint at self-creation and suggest the possibility of a whimsical distance from the constrictions of the feminine, a space within which to celebrate with playfulness and exuberance the carnival of every-day life.

7 / Functions of (Picturing) Memory

My first memory . . . is the most important of all my memories.
If life has a base that it stands upon, if it is a bowl that one fills
and fills and fills—then my bowl without a doubt stands upon
this memory.
—*Virginia Woolf*

All the novels of Anne Tyler are about memory or, more particularly, the act of remembering. Each to one degree or another involves remembering and then coming to terms with individual and personal memories that may interfere with the business of living. One might say the same of the novels of Virginia Woolf, who believed that memories may offer "shocks" or "revelations" that ultimately free one from the emotion associated with them and engendered in the act of remembering. Speaking of the difficulties of coming to terms with a particular memory, Woolf said, "It is only by putting it into words that I can make it whole; this wholeness means that it has lost its power to hurt me; it gives me, perhaps because by doing so I take away the pain, a great delight to put the severed parts together."[1] This, she claimed in "A Sketch of the Past," which she wrote the year before her death, might have been "the strongest pleasure known to me."

What Woolf seems to say here is that it is the discrete nature of individual memories that cause pain; being able to fit them into the wider pattern of what she called here "the cotton wool of daily life" (or what she repeatedly referred to as "life itself") offers us a sense of our connection with other human beings. In regard to Anne Tyler and her novels, all of which involve in one way or another the pain caused by memory, this essay will touch on the ways that memory (or the act of remembering) serves an important role in developing a character's ability to "become" (in Matthew Arnold's sense) and to "develop" (in E. M. Forster's sense). In other words, in each of her novels, to one degree or another, Tyler shows us that the ability to connect with other human beings is related to the ability to recognize, accommodate, and integrate memory into the pattern of life itself.[2]

Anne Tyler is concerned not only with memory, but also with *how* memory is revived. To use Woolf's terms, Tyler traces the route between the "spark" and the integration. Because memory is not only elusive but abstract, it is not to be wondered that returning to a family home is the concrete representation first used by Tyler in eliciting memory. While I agree with Alice Hall Petry that Tyler's novels cannot be classified,[3] I think Tyler's first novel, *If Morning Ever Comes*, offers clues to the importance of memory and introduces motifs that are repeated in subsequent novels to explore the functions of memory.

In *If Morning Ever Comes*, we are told from the outset that Ben Joe Hawkes, the main character, although a law student, does not like his field of study: "It was all memory." That he embarks on a spur-of-the-moment trip to his home in Sandhurst, North Carolina, suggests his tentative grasp of the present and the hold that the past (in the person of his now fatherless family) has on him; but, as the novel begins, Ben Joe's consciousness of this is in doubt. That he dreams and daydreams a lot allows Tyler to show that dreaming is related to memory, although Ben Joe denies it, tellingly, in a dream within a dream:

When he got there his father was gone, and his mother had come out on the porch holding a glass of lemonade that flashed piercingly in the sun.

"You've been dreaming about your father," she said.

But Ben Joe said, "No. No, I didn't. I never did."

He awoke, and found that the sill of the train window had pressed a wide deep line into his cheekbone.

Margaret Ferry suggests that this novel illustrates "how individuals use experiences of the past and present";[4] it seems clear, however, that it is not the experiences themselves that are at issue, but rather how these same individuals remember them, sometimes—as with Ben Joe Hawkes—reluctantly. Ben Joe consciously resists remembering: "He could hear that noise still, although he always did his best to forget it." While he claims he doesn't remember, he believes (without any consciousness of contradiction) that his family and his hometown haven't changed. Even when a "spark" turns on the lights, he remains in darkness, on the outside, looking in: "When he was in high school, it had become second nature, like going downstairs in the morning for breakfast and then realizing, once he was down there, that the actual descent had been an utter blank in his memory. . . . The lights were turned on inside. The place was the same as always . . . with years of dead leaves around it." Nevertheless, as we learn in a dream he later has (one that explains the significance of the title), resistance to memory is ultimately undercut by a growing consciousness of remembering: "His father smiled, and leaned back to look around at his family. In his sleep Ben Joe smiled too. (He was proud of himself; he'd dreamed it all correctly from beginning to end.)" It seems that what Tyler is saying is that where memory is latent, dreams take over. But it is finally the willingness of Ben Joe to come to terms consciously with memory that permits his seeing beyond it.

In the novel, Ben Joe's resistance to memory is repeatedly counterbalanced by his appreciation at being remembered; he likes an old girlfriend the more for having remembered him and cannot understand that his memories are not similarly remembered by others. And he is reminded, by details in dress and demeanor, of things he thought he had forgotten. Yet, while he tries to forget what he found unpleasant, he retains his childhood memory of a secret dinner with his father and his father's mistress, Lili Belle. This childhood memory remains singularly important to him until he can see beyond the painful guilt he feels in remembering it and face a present that includes possibilities for the future. As he returns to New York, he recognizes that memories can change, that the past can alter the present, just as the present can alter one's memory of the past, and he "remembers" the future: "Behind his own eyelids the future rolled out like a long, deep rug, as real as the past or the present ever was." What is important finally is that memories of the past are related to the future, that the future, supported by memory of the past, is within our control, an ongoing theme in the novels of Anne Tyler.

Certainly Tyler, whose novels have repeatedly been praised for their sharp attention to the obvious, is keenly aware not only of the function of memory in life, but of photographs that elicit the process of memory, that may be used to serve as reminders. It is not to be wondered that photographs and photographers are used this way in her novels, most obviously in *The Tin Can Tree* and *Earthly Possessions*, where the central characters are photographers who learn the limitations and potentialities of photographs in eliciting and in relieving the pain of memory. James Pike, the central character of *The Tin Can Tree*, is a photographer who "had the idea of photographing everyone he knew in the way his mind pictured them when they weren't around," that is, as he remembered them. It is the matriarchal Miss Hattie, however, who reminds him that remembering pictures rather than people is inadequate: "I don't want Danny remembering just a picture. Remembering something flat and of one tone. What is ever all one way? . . . Photographs are the only thing. . . . Everything else is a mingling of things."

It's when memory, like a photograph, is two-dimensional and "of one tone," that it may become hurtful. If rightly seen, however, it may become a frame within which life can function and continue: "In the finder of the camera Joan could see them moving, each person making his own set of motions. But the glass of the finder seemed to hold them there, like figures in a snowflurry paperweight who would still be in their set positions when the snow settled down again. She thought whole years could pass, they could be born and die, they could leave and return, they could marry or live out their separate lives alone, and nothing in this finder would change. They were going to stay this way, she and all the rest of them, not because of anyone else but because it was what they had chosen, what they would keep a strong hold of."

In *Earthly Possessions*, Tyler shows that, if seen rightly, photographs may clarify memory. Tyler does this by exploring the character Charlotte Emory, a photographer who sees people upside down (natural for a portrait photographer looking through a viewer) and who believes (for most of the novel) she is not the "true daughter" of her parents. Finally she shows her dying mother a long-sequestered photograph: "I couldn't think what to ask next. I had lost my bearings. Oh, it wasn't that I doubted my memory; I was still sure of that. (Or almost sure.) But the picture! For now I saw that of course it was Mama. Obviously it was. . . . I slipped the picture back in my pocket, then, . . . and more gently than I'd ever done anything in my life, I laid my cheek against my mother's."

This final gesture (we are immediately told that Charlotte's mother dies the next day), suggests that photographs may serve to correct memory, not replace it, and not interfere with the rhythm of life itself: "I still wheel my camera around, recording up-side-down people in unexpected costumes. But I've come to believe that their borrowed medals may tell more truth than they hide."

Where the photographer is not developed (and photographs play a minor role in eliciting memory), as in *Celestial Navigation* and in *Morgan's Passing*, he is presented as one who freezes life and potentially distorts it (and its memory). In *Celestial Navigation*, Mary remembers that her estranged husband Guy took "artificial" photographs of their daughter Darcy, and she believes the attitude towards life this represents is why she left him for John, a professional photographer: "On the days when John can't visit, I start hating him . . . but when I see him again he does something like this, thinking up an outing and photographing Darcy, and then I remember why I came away with him in the first place. *Guy* would never do anything like that. Oh, Guy took her picture, of course . . . but he always wanted her dressed up first in artificial-looking curls and seat her on the best piece of furniture. He called her his princess. His doll baby. Darcy is no doll baby. . . ."

In *Morgan's Passing*, Tyler suggests, though in more exaggerated and indeed farcical terms, that photographs should serve only as reminders and not replacements for real life. For example, Morgan's daughter Brindle finds herself married to a man who is in love with her high-school picture, who "keeps [her] graduation photo on the television set" and while "he pretends he's watching TV, he's really watching the photo," who's "one of those people who's got to see from a distance before he knows how to feel about it—from the past or out of other people's eyes or in a frame kind of thing like a book or a photo."

Even when they are properly seen as reminders, photographs, Tyler suggests, may be of uncertain value in eliciting memory. Sometimes other senses revive memory more vividly. In the case of Pearl Tull, for example, who is near death in the first line of *Dinner at the Homesick Restaurant*, it is not visual images that help to restore memory, but smells, touches, and sounds: "She tipped her head back and recollected cousins, aunts, uncles, a grandfather whose breath had smelled of mothballs. It was peculiar how her memory seemed to be going blind with the rest of her. She didn't so much see their faces as hear their fluid voices, feel the crisp rushing of the ladies' shirtwaists, smell their pomades and lavender water and the sharp-scented bottle of crystals that sickly Cousin Bertha had carried to ward off fainting spells."

In *Breathing Lessons*, perhaps Tyler's most accomplished novel to date, it is also smells that elicit memory: "Smells could bring a person back clearer than pictures, even." In *The Clock Winder*, Elizabeth, not unlike her employer and eventual mother-in-law, Mrs. Emerson (who records letters on tape before writing them out, and who eventually relies totally on sound), claims to have an "audial memory": "Elizabeth had cut all the oranges and lemons herself, regretting it before she was halfway done; every whiff of lemon reminded her of when she and Matthew had done this job together. She had a mind like a tape recorder, an audial version of a photographic memory, and each chop of knife blade against breadboard brought her bits of things that Matthew had said." In *Searching for Caleb*, it is the discovery of an old photograph that Justine Peck, a fortune-teller, and her grandfather, Daniel, hope will ease the quest for his brother, but it does not play much of a role in remembering him or reminding others: "He [Daniel] shoved the photograph back in his pocket." By the time a sixty-one-year-old address leads to the discovery of Caleb (by a private detective), Daniel has died and Justine seeks out

Caleb as if to honor his brother's memory, only to be "exasperated." What Daniel and Justine had been seeking through memory was connection; what she finds in the person of Caleb is memory sans connection:

> "Don't you feel any *memory*?" she asked him. "Don't you feel any connection at all?"
> "Memory, yes. Connection, no."
> She believed him.

What we see here is Tyler's own understanding that it is finally not memory that establishes connection, but recalls the need for connection (perhaps, for Tyler, like reading reviews of her novels: see note 3).

This may be why Tyler finds in childhood, particularly in childhood memories, an increasingly realized motif. Childhood memories, consciously acknowledged or innate, affect one's ability to cope with the present and may leave characters feeling as outsiders, even as adults. We can see this early on, in the character of Ansel in *The Tin Can Tree*: "I know how it feels to *really* miss someone. I remember— . . . I *remember* how it feels. My memory's excellent." Childhood memories sometimes leave one unable to deal with children, as in *Searching for Caleb*: "Caleb had never been good with children. The sight of them made him wretched; he was so sorry for humans in the state of childhood that he couldn't stand to be near them. When one of the babies cried his inside knotted up and he felt bleak and hopeless. So he watched them from a distance, holding himself aloof." Sometimes childhood memories make one acutely aware of the pain of childhood (a condition not often countenanced by adults), and, in *Breathing Lessons*, leave feelings of guilt and pity: "Sometimes, deep down inside, Maggie blamed herself. . . . She saw now that there was a single theme to every decision she had made as a parent. The mere fact that her children were children, condemned for years to feel powerless and bewildered and confined, filled her with such pity that to add any further hardship to their lives seems unthinkable. She would have made a better mother, perhaps, if she hadn't remembered so well how it felt to be a child." Tyler doesn't suggest that she agrees with Maggie's harsh self-judgment, but she obviously agrees with Maggie's sense of childhood, something that can be seen in *Saint Maybe*:

It seemed that only Ian knew how these children felt: how scary they found every waking minute.

Why, being a child at all was scary! Wasn't that what grownups' nightmares so often reflected—the nightmare of running but getting nowhere, the nightmare of the test you hadn't studied for or the play you hadn't rehearsed? Powerlessness, outsiderness. Murmurs over your head about something everyone knows but you.

In *Saint Maybe*, Tyler allows the children themselves to confirm this impression, this feeling of powerlessness, of otherness. We see this as the orphaned Thomas envies his sister Agatha, who *can* remember their mother, and laments his own lack of memory, especially when shown a photograph: "It was spooky that he had no memory of that moment. It was like talking in your sleep, where they tell you in the morning what you said and you ask, 'I did? I said that?' and laugh at your own crazy words as if they'd come from someone else. In fact, he always thought of the baby in the photo as a whole other person—as 'he,' not 'I'—even though he knew better."

Sometimes, as is the case of Cody, Pearl Tull's grown son, there are bitter memories of childhood inadequately understood; these deprive Cody of the sense of connection that Thomas, the child, craves: "If only you could climb into photographs. If only you could take a running jump and land there, deep inside! The frill at his mother's neckline must have made pretzel sounds in his ear. Her bare arms must have stuck to his skin a little in the hot sunshine. His sister must have thought he was cute, back then, and interesting."

Sometimes, as is the case with Macon Lowry in *The Accidental Tourist*, it is not remembered childhood so much as the memory of his dead son Ethan that has the most telling effect. Having lived life as an outsider to avoid the pain of this memory (or any other) and to avoid having to acknowledge the need for connection, Macon has cut himself off from the past and the future; it is only when he realizes that immunity from memory is like death that he can embrace life: "And if dead people aged, wouldn't it be a comfort? To think of Ethan growing up in heaven . . . eased the grief a little. Oh, it was their immunity to time that made the dead so heartbreaking. . . . Macon gazed out the cab window, considering the notion in his mind. He felt a kind of inner rush, a racing forward. The real adventure, he thought, is the flow of time; it's as much adventure as anyone could wish. And if he pictured Ethan still part of that flow—in some other place, however unreachable—he believed he might be able to bear it after all."

In her novels Anne Tyler shows us, as Maggie says, that "The past is never past; not entirely"; no one, not even Maggie's husband Ira, is "immune" from memory: "No, he wasn't immune, and he would set eyes on Leroy and remember instantly how they were connected. People had to be reminded, that was all. The way the world was going now, it was so easy to forget." But unlike Lily Briscoe in Woolf's *To the Lighthouse*, who is able to find "the razor edge of balance" between the memory of the past and the reality of the present and declare "I have had my vision" as she completes her painting to end the novel,[5] Maggie ends *Breathing Lessons* by going to bed "because tomorrow they had a long car trip to make and she knew she would need a good night's sleep before they started."

To Anne Tyler, it isn't memory itself that is finally important, but the connections we make and what we do with discrete memories. The key to using memory wisely and well has less to do with realizing the significance of memories today than with what we do with this sense tomorrow. Ultimately, whether we remember or forget, Tyler reminds us in each of her novels and perhaps most pointedly in *Saint Maybe*, we must forgive ourselves in living as we must forgive those whose deaths have seemingly left us with memories alone. If Tyler's novels lack finality, it is because coming to terms with memory is but one step in coming to terms with life.

As Tyler continues to remind us, the revelation of memory is that however much pain it causes, we must put together the severed pieces and get on with the business of living.

8 / Marcel Proust, Involuntary Memory,

and Tyler's Novels

La vie, la Vraie vie, c'est la littérature.

Anne Tyler is an immensely popular writer. She tells lucid, swiftly readable stories about complicated emotions inside late-twentieth-century middle-class families, and contemporary readers take pleasure in recognizing the quirky ways in which these families are engagingly similar to their own. Curiously, though, there are also numerous uneventful moments in Tyler's fiction that look like citations of Marcel Proust, the creator of characters that most readers do not recognize, and the century's master of the art of *not* getting the story told. I want to begin by citing just two of them.

In her self-consciously novelistic moments, Anne Tyler likes to render states of mind without advancing the plot, the way a painter likes to paint, say, water lilies. There is the fine passage on Macon

Leary's insomnia in *The Accidental Tourist*, for instance. Or, late in *Saint Maybe*, Ian Bedloe's account of his conscience-ridden nights:

> "You know that clock downstairs that strikes the number of hours," Ian told Stuart. "And then it strikes once at every half hour. So when you hear it striking once, you can't be certain how much of the night you've used up. Is it twelve thirty, or is it one, or is it one thirty? You have to just lie there and wait, and hope with all your heart that next time it will strike two. Or what's worse, some nights it starts striking one, two, three and you say, 'Ah!' and then four, five, and you say, 'Can this be? Have I really slept through till dawn?' And then six, seven, and you say, 'Oh-oh,' because you can see it's not *that* light out. And sure enough, the clock goes on to twelve, and you brace yourself for another six hours till morning."

A very plausible guilt, not the neurasthenia of a hypersensitive artist, accounts for Ian's insomnia. Still, Ian's representation recalls with remarkable specificity the opening paragraphs of the "Overture" to *Remembrance of Things Past*, in which the narrator Marcel recounts his own nocturnal sufferings:

> I would lay my cheeks gently against the comfortable cheeks of my pillow, as plump and blooming as the cheeks of babyhood. I would strike a match to look at my watch. Nearly midnight. The hour when an invalid, who has been obliged to set out on a journey and to sleep in a strange hotel, awakened by a sudden spasm, sees with glad relief a streak of daylight showing under his door. Thank God, it is morning. The servants will be about in a minute: he can ring, and someone will come to look after him. The thought of being assuaged gives him strength to endure his pain. He is certain he heard footsteps: they come nearer, and then die away. The ray of light beneath his door is extinguished. It is midnight; someone has just turned down the gas; the last servant has gone to bed, and he must lie all night in agony with no one to bring him relief.[1]

Despite very real differences in implied audiences, in conceptions of plot, in epoch, in social class between the novels that provide their contexts, these two passages match up uncannily. They record the same psychological moment.

To take one other example: at the finale of *Dinner at the Homesick Restaurant*, Cody Tull, finally liberated from his own confining version of the past, remembers that day in his childhood when the arrow from his bow struck his mother in the shoulder:

> Through a sky so clear and blue that it brought back all the outings of his boyhood—the drives, the picnics, the autumn hikes, the wildflower walks in the spring, he remembered the archery trip, and it seemed to him now that he even remembered the arrow sailing in its graceful, fluttering path. He remembered his mother's upright form along the grasses, her hair lit gold, her small hands smoothing her bouquet while the arrow journeyed on. And high above, he seemed to recall, there had been a little brown airplane, almost motionless, droning through the sunshine like a bumblebee.

One of Tyler's most brilliant recapturings of the past, this scene is magical thanks in part to its redoubling of Pearl's own rediscovery in her diary of the happy moment of her girlhood when a bottle fly buzzed in the grass next to her as she gardened. Epiphanic in the modernist sense, it is also caught up in story, recognizable to the reader as the moment of Cody's reconciliation toward his "dysfunctional" family. Yet it also seems to be a very canny citation of the famous afternoon in *The Captive* in which Marcel took Albertine to Versailles:

> The sky consisted entirely of that radiant and slightly pale blue which the wayfarer lying in a field sees at times above his head, but so uniform and so deep that one feels that the pigment of which it is composed has been applied without the least alloy and with such an inexhaustible richness that one might delve more and more deeply into its substance without encountering an atom of anything but the same blue. . . . Suddenly I felt once again a longing for my lost freedom on hearing a noise which I did not at first recognise. . . . It was like the buzz of a wasp. "Look," said Albertine, "there's an aeroplane, high up there, very very high." I looked all over the sky but could see only, unmarred by any black spot, the unbroken pallor of the unalloyed blue. I continued nevertheless to hear the humming of the wings, which suddenly entered my field of vision. Up there, a pair of tiny wings, dark

and flashing, punctured the continuous blue of the unalterable sky, I had at last been able to attach the buzzing to its cause, to that little insect throbbing up there in the sky, probably six thousand feet above me; I could see it hum.[2]

What these matched citations suggest, I hope, is that alongside Anne Tyler's realistic power to present us with well-constructed stories that seem to mirror our own experience, there is also a poetic enterprise, an attempt to render a consciousness caught in and fascinated by the dimension of time, suffering its slow passage through a tormented night, or picking up, in a moment of heightened acuity, the very *bourdonnement*—the buzzing—of planetary existence.

It is admittedly a somewhat dated critical practice to make adjectives out of authors' names, to observe that there is this "Proustian" side to Anne Tyler's work; it is possible to be very imprecise under the guise of such impressionism. From the other side, however, one might also object that a sufficiently rich complex of values is already suggested by employing the adjective "Tylerian." A writer who is "Tylerian" portrays odd yet remarkably recognizable characters who, haunted by their past, demonstrate over an expanse of time the curious mix of freedom and compulsion of people molded in the heat and pressure of family life. One could call Larry Woiwode a "Tylerian" writer, or Alice Hoffman. There is plenty of critical work to do close to home; why seek far-fetched comparisons?

At the very least, then, it is necessary to be as explicit as possible about the meaning of the word "Proustian," and then see what light it sheds. The adjective has come to describe the work of a solitary, aesthetically susceptible writer in retreat from daily experience; one who seeks a solitude where, in the absence of other stimuli, involuntary memory will have occasion to carry him past the illusions of surface realism to the poetic recapturing of reality. Finally (and inconveniently), there is one great "Proustian" theme, which all of *Remembrance of Things Past* pursues in widening concentric circles—erotic obsession, the mad, self-conscious need to possess the beloved, a personage apprehended and appreciated in coldly aesthetic terms, in human terms as often hated as loved.

It is perhaps best to acknowledge the problem of Proust's great theme early. For, while Proust's theory of memory is most hospitable to the novelistic treatment of erotic obsession, recording its pained intensities, its searing contradictions and shifts of mood, Tyler's, of course, is not. In fact, John Updike, a longtime admirer of Anne Tyler, has lamented the absence of obsession in her work, and has worried that it deprives her of a necessary passion.[3] In terms of obsession, Tyler's work can be called "Proustian" in reverse. While *Remembrance of Things Past* re-paints, on ever grander canvasses, the story of an obsessive love—first Marcel's for his mother, then Swann's for Odette, then Marcel's for Gilberte, and finally Marcel's for Albertine—Tyler's protagonists never fall in love at all, or at least never *à folie*. They are, in fact, most pronouncedly un-Gallic. (Just to recall Macon Leary in Paris makes for delightful irony.) Tyler protagonists reflect at interminable length on the possibility of their performing a spontaneous act. *Un crime passionnel* is not a possibility. But while they don't fall in love, they are fallen in love with. They are not pursuers but the pursued, and they negotiate the hurdles that that condition puts upon them. Elizabeth Abbot in *The Clock Winder* finds herself the obsessional love-object of the entire Emerson family. When they get done with her, there is little that is left. Even her name has been altered by an invalid to "Gillespie." Charlotte Emory in *Earthly Possessions* is a chronic kidnap victim. As a child, she suspected her parents had kidnapped her. Then a refugee woman did. Then she is kidnapped by the bank robber Jake, who can't seem to get on without her. And she is the emotional hostage of her husband Saul, who begins every appeal, "I know you love me, Charlotte." Jeremy Pauling in *Celestial Navigation*, Tyler's most Proustian protagonist in that he ends up agoraphobically confined to an attic, is ultimately overwhelmed by his own loved ones; they fill his house like rising water, and he retreats up the stairs. A Tyler novel is the Proustian predicament told from the point of view of Marcel's *maman*, tortured by her child's dependency. Not becoming the object of the obsession of others is the constant—but most often futile—work of the Tyler protagonist.

But if we are willing to invert this troublesome issue of erotic obsession, the other definitively Proustian attributes seem highly visible in Tyler's compositional method, and in the fictions that mirror it. Certainly, Anne Tyler maintains a privacy and a solitude that are tightly bound to the way she says she works. In acknowledging her affinities with her artist-figure Jeremy Pauling, a sculptor of found objects, she offers a glimpse of her method. Like Proust, she testifies

(a) that she has to be alone, and (b) that her sources are largely involuntary, issuing from an imagination that operates outside her conscious will:

> I need to protect myself from experiences. I find in fact that I really don't want to see people, although it always seems to me that surely I should want to if I'm writing about them. But I just don't want to be influenced in any way by the outside and I think . . . part of a reason for writing is to put out on paper some of your own privacy that you've kept bounded in. . . . And also I share with him [Jeremy] the feeling that whatever you produce is like olives out of a bottle, that you don't have any choice. If someone were to say, Well I don't like this novel and we won't publish it, I still wouldn't feel that it had been wasted because I had no choice. It had to come before the next came. It seems to be a progression that's expected.[4]

Tyler invokes a sense of magical space when she describes her study, a silence and solitude reminiscent of Proust's cork-lined bedroom: "Also, there is only one room I can work in—a stern white cubicle. Most of the pictures on its walls (I realized one day) have to do with isolation: uninhabited houses, deserted courtrooms, stark old men staring into space. I hate to travel away from here, I hate even to rearrange the furniture, or start writing at an unaccustomed time. All these magic spells to get me going."[5] And the degree of her passivity before the involuntary aspect of invention is quite startling. She admits to listening to her characters' voices with her right ear,[6] to not being able to type her books because the clacking keys would destroy the silence required to hear them. She avows that creative tangles are automatically ironed out during her sleeping hours. She observes that her work comes to her in a kind of stream, that if she's interrupted, it flows without her, but that, with maturity, she has learned to enter and leave it in full confidence that what she needs will be provided.[7]

It may be just here that we can find the explanation for Anne Tyler's often-remarked-upon apoliticality. The reified creative mind, and the isolation it demands of its artist-possessor, result in a necessary distance from and indifference to political causes, social concerns, human involvements. It was Proust who said that the absolute priority of involuntary memory in the artist's life extricated him from the more mundane effort of realistically recording the known world, of writing with a historical eye, or of engaging himself politically. Below, he compares the world revealed through the imagination to a book of hieroglyphics, and he says of his realist contemporaries:

> Every public event, be it the Dreyfus case, be it the war, furnishes the writer with a fresh excuse for not attempting to decipher this book: he wants to ensure the triumph of justice, he wants to restore the moral unity of the nation, he has no time to think of literature. But these are mere excuses, the truth being that he has not or no longer genius, that is to say instinct. For instinct dictates our duty and the intellect supplies us with pretexts for evading it. But excuses have no place in art and intentions count for nothing; at every moment the artist has to listen to his instinct; and it is this that makes art the most real of all things, the most austere school of life and the true last judgment.[8]

As with Proust, the operative myth behind Anne Tyler's creative procedure is that of the authority of the powerful, subjective impression, which shapes and dictates the work.

A second, more profound sense in which Anne Tyler is a "Proustian" writer lies in the way her fable invariably recapitulates the act of its composition. The deeper pattern that her characters insist upon fulfilling is the same in every novel—the uncovering of the personal past, the reading of a preexistent hieroglyph of the self. The Tyler hero experiences a sequence of uncoverings, a sequence which reenacts the compositional process of the novelist. In other words, Anne Tyler's novels are autobiographical in the way Proust's are—they are correlatives for the adventure of composition. The mystery of artistic discovery is redoubled in the adventure of the character, and is figuratively represented as memory.

It is interesting in this context to consider just how remarkably successful Tyler is as a realist, a novelist of character. If we take those terms to mean a writer whose genius lies primarily in the canny observation of individual human beings in the external social world and their reproduction in fiction, a kind of higher journalism, then in fact her range is rather narrow. While memorable Tyler characters are black as well as white, lower- as well as upper-middle class, rural as well as urban, and certainly female as well as male, they are nevertheless constructed out of a preexistent set of terms, pro-grammed to negotiate the problems that their personal past imposes: of freedom or entrapment, drifting or agoraphobia, nurturing or anorexia. In fact, Tyler's characters seem to come from a common source deep within their creator. Herein may lie the explanation for what she considers their recalcitrance:

> What's hard is that there are times when your characters simply won't obey you. Nearly every writer I've heard of says that; not one has satisfactorily explained it. Where did those little paper people get so much power?
>
> I'll have in mind an event for them—a departure, a wedding, a happy ending. I write steadily toward that event, but when I reach it everything stops. I can't go on. Sentences come out stilted, dialogue doesn't sound real. Every new attempt ends up in the wastebasket. I try again from another angle and then another, until I'm forced to admit it: the characters just won't allow this. I'll have to let the plot go their way. And when I do, everything falls into place.
>
> No wonder I often feel, sitting alone in my study, that the room is overpopulated.[9]

Late in *Remembrance of Things Past*, Proust distinguishes the par-tial and relative "realistic" truths of the conscious observation of the external world from the bedrock validity of "subjective impression":

> For the truths which the intellect apprehends directly in the world of full and unimpeded light have something less profound, less necessary than those which life communicates to us against our will in an impression which is material because it enters us through the senses but yet has a spiritual meaning which it is possible for us to extract. In fact, both in the one case and in the other . . . the task was to interpret the given sensations as signs of so many laws and ideas, by trying to think—that is to say, to draw forth from the shadow—what I had merely felt, by trying to convert it into its spiritual equivalent. And this method, which seemed to me the sole method, what was it but the creation of a work of art? Already the consequences came flooding into my mind: first, whether I considered reminiscences of the kind evoked by the noise of the spoon or the taste of the madelaine, or

those truths written with the aid of shapes for whose meaning I searched in my brain, where . . . they composed a magical scrawl, complex and elaborate, their essential character was that I was not free to choose them, that such as they were they were given to me. And I realised that this must be the mark of their authenticity. I had not gone in search of the two uneven paving-stones of the courtyard upon which I had stumbled. But it was precisely the fortuitous and inevitable fashion in which this and the other sensations had been encountered that proved the trueness of the past which they brought back to life, of the images which they released, since we feel, with these sensations, the effort that they make to climb back towards the light, feel in ourselves the joy of rediscovering what is real.[10]

Precisely this form of anamnesis constitutes the plot of Anne Tyler's novels as well as the central mystery of their conception. The character seeks a formative story that lies in the family past; the author seeks a book that preexists her scrivening. In *Dinner at the Homesick Restaurant*, Pearl Tull has Ezra search her journals for something that she cannot identify until she finds it—the day some seventy years before when she was gardening and heard the Bedloe girls' piano and thought, "I have had this moment. It belongs to me." Daniel Peck devotes his last years to the search for his lost brother Caleb, saying, "If they could just give me back one little scrap of time, that's all I ask!" In *Breathing Lessons*, Serena Gill sardonically requires the attendance of her friends at the replaying of her wedding home-movies made some twenty-five years before. These impositions of a powerful past are not mere incidents in their respective novels, they are their central predicament, that which organizes all other events around it.

And it is fair to say that memory in a Tyler novel is often precisely Proustian in its dynamic: it is triggered by an apparently trivial sensory phenomenon in the present that brings the past rushing back, it is significant only if entirely involuntary, it overwhelms those whom it visits by changing, in Justine Peck's words, not what happened, but what effect it has on you. I want to cite four of Anne Tyler's moments of subjective memory to suggest the extent to which they define the character whom they visit, marking him or her as a receptor of subjective truths, an autobiographical figure.

In *The Clock Winder*, Margaret Emerson, married now for the second time, suffers a disturbance that takes her out of her life:

1963

The trouble began on a Sunday morning in June. Margaret woke early, before her husband. She lay in bed feeling pleasantly hungry but too lazy to do anything about it, and she spent some time making pictures out of a complicated crack in the ceiling while she tried to remember a dream she had had. None of it came back to her. Only vague sensations—the smell of parsley in a brown paper bag, the feel of some rough fabric against her cheek. Then the crack in the ceiling dimmed, and she found herself looking directly into the face of her first husband. He was laughing at something she had just said. His black eyes were narrowed and sparkling; his mouth was open, lengthening his pointed chin. He had the carelessly put together look that is often found in young boys. While she watched he stopped laughing and grew serious, but deliberately, exaggerating the effort, making a mockery of it, as if the laughter were still bubbling within him. He pretended to frown. All she saw in his eyes was love.

This is a relatively early use of the trope in Anne Tyler's work, and it approaches hallucination. As with Ben Joe Hawkes in Tyler's first novel, *If Morning Ever Comes*, memory in Margaret's case does not so much disturb as bludgeon. In later novels, the psychology turns more subtle, but the phenomenon abides. Nevertheless, Margaret does illustrate a principle in Tyler novels—she drifts off her bearings. In most instances, the quirky or eccentric behavior we celebrate as Tylerian is the consequence of the past's imposing.

Mary Tell in *Celestial Navigation* stands at a greater distance and contemplates, like a Proustian narrator, the persistence in her own mind of a memory trigger:

Is Dewbridge Lake still there? Well, it must be. But after that one Summer I have never been back. It's as if the lake had fulfilled its purpose and then vanished from the face of the earth. . . . Now I imagine that the entire forest has fallen, giving off no sound, like that tree they always bring up in science classes. All that will remain of it is a little golden dust floating upwards in the sunlight. Yet there is a thirty-nine-cent strawberry-flavored lipstick in the dimestore whose smell can still, to this day, carry me back to the ladies' changing room at Dewbridge Lake. Hot pine needles will always make me feel pleasantly endangered and out of my depth. The trashy taste of orange Nehi fills me even now with a longing to break loose, to go to foreign places, to try some adventure undreamed of by my father in his baggy plaid trunks and my mother in her black rayon bathing suit with the pleated skirt.

This is no incidental tic of Mary Tell's; it signals that she bases her life's decisions on subjective impression. Tyler heroes are moved by springs too deep for comprehension, but which surface in ways that to more practically minded people seem trivial. Because these characters understand the profundity of such impulses, they grant freedom to others. The ethical principle of Mary's life is never to intrude: her predicament is that she must.

Searching for Caleb (or, *A la Recherche d'un Frère Perdu*) is overtly Proustian in plot. It also contains Proustian moments of sudden, involuntary recollection. Here Justine recalls her first day of kindergarten, when her grandfather led her to the school:

> They went down streets that were bitterly familiar, where she had shopped with her mother in the dear, safer days before school was ever thought of. At a square brick building her grandfather stopped. He pointed out where Claudia would meet her in the afternoon. He cupped her head briefly and then, after some fumbling and rustling, pushed a sack of horehound drops at her and gave her a little nudge in the direction of the brick building. When she had climbed the steps she looked back and found him still waiting there, squinting against the sunlight. Forever after that, the dark, homely, virtuous taste of horehound drops reminded her of the love and sorrow that ached in the back of her throat on that first day in the outside world.

Here, of course, Tyler rather deliberately reconstructs the moment of the *petite madelaine* dipped in tea, which brought back to Proust the anguished dependency of his childhood, suddenly swept away by the sensation of parental love.

Finally, there is Pearl Tull's search through her girlhood diaries, perhaps the most deservedly famous passage in all Anne Tyler's prose, the moment in which the past provides Pearl with that sense of tranquil completeness that subsequently evaded her. It is the author's gift to her dying heroine, a moment in which she experiences *Le Temps Retrouvé*. Ezra reads:

> *"I went out behind the house to weed. Was kneeling in the dirt by the stable with my pinafore a mess and the perspiration rolling down my back, wiped my face on my sleeve, reached for the trowel, and all at once thought, Why I believe that at just this moment I am absolutely happy."*

His mother stopped rocking and grew very still.

> *"The Bedloe girl's piano scales were floating out her window,"* he read, *"and a bottle fly was buzzing in the grass, and I saw that I was kneeling on such a beautiful green little planet. I don't care what else might come about. I have had this moment. It belongs to me."*

That was the end of the entry. He fell silent.

"Thank you, Ezra," his mother said. "There's no need to read any more."

These moments of profound recollection serve as emblems of the novel's subject and also as keys to its protagonists. Margaret's hallucination condenses the novel's lengthy discourses on the impossibility of choice, the central predicament of its heroine, Elizabeth. Dewbridge Lake is the signifier of Mary Tell's erotic restlessness; horehound drops evoke Justine Peck's ambivalent love for her time-encapsulated family. Pearl's journal records her lifelong hunger for a happiness that eludes her.

Nostalgia and the past's partial recapturability are the poetic center of Tyler's finest novel, *Dinner at the Homesick Restaurant*. (It is appropriate that the novel's French translation is titled *Le Déjeuner de la Nostalgie*.) Jenny, recuperating from nervous collapse, listens to her mother read *The Little House* to her own daughter Becky:

> Jenny had forgotten about *The Little House*. Why, she had loved that book! She'd requested it every evening, she remembered now. She'd sat on that homely old sofa and listened while her mother, with endless patience, read it three times, four times, five . . . Now Becky said, "Read it again," and Pearl returned to page one, and Jenny listened just as closely as Becky did.

The scene possesses autobiographical importance. In 1986, Anne Tyler wrote an article for the *New York Times Book Review* entitled

"Why I Still Treasure 'The Little House,'" in which she identifies time and memory as the central concern of her imagination and this children's book as her personal *madelaine*. "The Little House," given to her on her fourth birthday and still in her possession, concerns a house in the country that is slowly surrounded by the city, but is rediscovered (*retrouvée*) by the great-granddaughter of its first owner and moved to a new situation, back in the country again.

> Like a child, the Little House has her periods of restlessness. And like a child, she finds even longed for changes both exciting and saddening. Alone at night in the city that has always seemed to beckon, "she missed the field of daisies and the apple trees dancing in the moonlight."
>
> When I see those words now (and when I hear them, murmuring across the decades in my mother's voice), I recall the feeling of elderly sorrow that came over me at age 4. At age 4, listening to "The Little House," I had a sudden spell of . . . wisdom, I guess you could say. It seemed I'd been presented with a snapshot that showed me how the world worked: how the years flowed by and people altered and nothing could ever stay the same. Then the snapshot was taken away. Everything there is to know about time was revealed in that snapshot, and I can almost name it, I very nearly have it in my grasp . . . but then it's gone again, and all that's left is a ragged green book with the binding falling apart.[11]

Tyler speaks of her reading of the book, when she was four, as her introduction to the experience of "nostalgia—the realization of the losses that the passage of time can bring."

The characters Tyler seems to value most in her fiction are especially vulnerable to the allure of the mysteriousness of the past. They all undertake its recapture. For Tyler, novel-writing is analogous work—the fabling of memory—the means, if not to solve, then to stay in the presence of, that mystery. Her work implies that it is memory that makes us human, that brings us the integrity of a life built upon our subjective impressions, for it is these—rather than adherence to ethical doctrine or political party or religious dogma— that forms the bedrock of our half-discovered, half-invented selves.

9 / Forgetting and Remembering

In Praise of Tyler's Older Women

There is a moment late in Anne Tyler's *Celestial Navigation* which in retrospect helps me understand the unexpected sadness I felt when I finished it, a sadness all the more surprising because I had not found myself, I thought, particularly engaged by this novel. Jeremy Pauling, a reclusive forty-nine-year-old man who makes art with all the childish absorption of a *bricoleur*—it is his life—finally resolves to ask his estranged wife and children to come back home. He takes the bus from Baltimore to the Maryland shore (with his obsessive aversion to travel, it is an act of momentous proportions). Miscellaneous thoughts can come to us while traveling, as we are lulled by the movement of a train or a car, detached from the distractions and pressures of everyday life. Such thoughts come to him, his random reflections forming a chain of associations which concludes in a sudden insight:

> He thought of things that had not occurred to him for years, some of them sad. He thought of his grandmother Amory, whom he had loved very much, and of the gilt-framed picture that hung in her parlour. A crowd of people in a jaded forest. "See that forest?" his grandmother said. "Every bit of it is real. It is made of dried plants, the pines are dried ferns and the flowers are dried violets." "How about the people?" Jeremy had asked, not thinking. "Are they dried too?" He thought of Mrs. Jarrett, his mother's old boarder. Why, he had never properly mourned Mrs. Jarrett's passing! Grief flashed through him like a sharp white light. How elegant she had been, with her plumed hats and her white gloves! How hard she must have worked to keep up her appearance!

Dried . . . died. Jeremy had never "properly" noticed, never mind mourned, this scrupulously groomed widow who had in fact lived in *his* house as a boarder for years and presumably had died there as well. Only belatedly does he imagine, in an act of empathy rare for him, a small measure of what her life must have been like.

Mourning is a theme and a strategy central to Anne Tyler's fiction. Novels open with characters on their deathbeds or with funerals. Parents grieve for a lost child, children for their parents. What interests me in this small scene, however, is that the character of Mrs. Jarrett is not a member of the family. She is a minor stock character, somehow inanimate, a piece of furniture almost. Indeed, as a reader at this late point in the novel I only vaguely remembered who Mrs. Jarrett was (*Mrs.* Jarrett? we know nothing about her earlier years). Tyler has given us no particular reason to develop an imaginative attachment to her.

But I certainly did remember Amanda Pauling, the character from whose point of view Tyler opens the novel. She is Jeremy's older sister by eight years, a brisk, bossy Latin teacher who hates to be touched and who refers to herself dryly as a spinster. An unyielding, unlikable character, she struck me as irritating. When she disappeared from the plot, I scarcely noticed (indeed, if anything, I felt relief). But here lies Tyler's skill in structuring *Celestial Navigation*. As readers we are placed in the same relation to Amanda Pauling as

Jeremy is to Mrs. Jarrett. In the course of the novel we are informed offhandedly that Amanda Pauling has died—and that's all we learn. We don't know what had become of her, or even how old she was when she died (a small detail that carries so much significance). Like Jeremy's feeling about Mrs. Jarrett, then, I had the sudden feeling I had not taken sufficient interest in Amanda Pauling. And this accounts in part for the poignancy of the novel. Middle-aged women are suddenly old women, gone without our noticing until it is too late. It is, surely, more than improper.

At the same time, however, the novel closes with a certain triumph for an older woman of indeterminate age. Miss Vinton, also a spinster—and a boarder in Jeremy's house—achieves her long-held dream of privacy and attachment. Bookish and responsible for others (she took care of her mother until she died), Miss Vinton is a nononsense woman, uninterested in romance and skeptical of familial sentiment. She flatly believes, for example, that we would all be better off living in boarding houses. At the novel's end she forms a loosely linked couple with Jeremy, who has failed (disastrously) to convince his wife to return home. Jeremy has suddenly grown old; Miss Vinton takes pleasure in looking after him. They shop together. An elderly couple, both of whom are perfectly at ease in the boarding house, they close the novel, and why not?

Mrs. Jarrett, Amanda Pauling, Miss Vinton: I evoke these characters as a way of introducing the subject of older women in Tyler's fiction. By older women, however, I mean in this essay primarily women in their middle years.[1] How older women are represented should be of concern to us all in a culture where aging, especially for women, is either a scandal or a matter of indifference (it amounts, of course, to the same thing). For me it is also a matter of natural curiosity as my mother and I, my friends, my colleagues, all grow older. I am interested in particular in three of Tyler's women in their middle years: the forty-eight-year-old Maggie in *Breathing Lessons* and Bonnie and Brindle in *Morgan's Passing*. These are women—the first a central character, the next two much more "marginal" to the novels—whom I want to remember, properly. I will devote, however, my final words to Pearl Tull, the central character of *Dinner at the Homesick Restaurant*, whose imagined life stretches into her eighty-fifth year and whose death is mourned, albeit in a madcap

Tyler way, by her immediate family, immediately. With Pearl Tull, Tyler gives us an indelible, compelling portrait of a woman in her last years.

In *Breathing Lessons*, a novel that is as hilarious as it is moving, the funeral that sets the narrative in motion doubles as an unexpected thirtieth (or so) high-school reunion. The husband of Maggie's best friend from girlhood has died abruptly of cancer. Tyler, with her deft comic touch for the conversations and details of everyday life, brings the characters together in this breezy way: "The Barley twins told Maggie she hadn't changed a bit. JoAnn Dermott announced that everyone had changed, but only for the better. Wasn't it odd, she said, how much younger they were than their parents had been at the very same age." What a wonderfully quirky formulation of a psychic truth. For what *is* odd is that our perception of age is so skewed by our age in relation to others. Age, it strikes me forcibly, is the most unreliable of variables: age shifts, like mercurial weather, depending upon whom we are with and how we feel. When we are ten, our parents (at whatever age) seem inscrutably old. Yet in middle age some sort of psychic insulation, developed in response to our culture's insistence on youth, protects us from similar views of those younger, like an umbrella protects us from the rain. We know we are older, of course, but not *old*. Perhaps, in fact, *better*.

The unconscious counterpart of the denial of aging is an obsession with it, although in the context of *Breathing Lessons* "obsession" is too strong a word. At forty-eight, Maggie is preoccupied with—how does our culture put it?—*growing* older (a formulation which seems a contradiction in terms for people in their middle years and older). She *doesn't* feel better. It's not so much the changes in her appearance or her body that bother her (she's always been a bit overweight and continues to worry about it daily—as do I, it occurs to me; what a waste of our attention), although she does inventory physical changes: "Lately," Tyler tells us, "when she took a pinch of skin from the back of a hand and released it, she noticed that the skin would stay pleated for moments afterward."

Rather, it's the changes in her life that bother Maggie. In *Celestial Navigation*, a young mother, contemplating two women in their fifties (they seem to her so unfathomably, so stereotypically old), wonders, *is it events which age people?* It can be, certainly. But in Maggie's world, this is definitely not the case, at least not in the sense of events as catastrophic or disruptive occurrences, as tragedies. Instead, what is important is "just an ordinary life development," as the admirable Bonnie puts it in *Morgan's Passing*. What drives the irrepressible and impetuous Maggie throughout *Breathing Lessons* is one of the most ordinary of maternal fantasies: she wants her children at home. Her daughter is leaving for college, and Maggie concocts schemes to throw her divorced son and former daughter-in-law together, to win them (along with her granddaughter) back. Naturally all of these *I Love Lucy*–like plots of hers are bound to fail.

The distinction I am making here between an "ordinary life development" and a catastrophic event is crucial in terms of aging. Neither ordinary life developments nor catastrophic events need necessarily be linked with a sense of aging, but ordinary life developments in the middle years need never be. I would suggest too that an ordinary life development such as Maggie's is accompanied by moods, by feelings more diffuse than, say, the strong emotions occasioned by catastrophic events (like the sharp pangs of grief, for example, in the case of her friend's husband's death). Maggie's feelings of loss color the smallest and seemingly most inconsequential happenings of everyday life. She explicitly and incorrectly links them to growing old, as if such feelings—and hence aging—were a pathology and not in fact quite ordinary. Tyler conveys Maggie's wacky tremulous mood marvelously. As Maggie appraises her improbable reactions to domestic change, she finds them peculiar in the extreme. First her daughter-in-law and granddaughter leave home. Then her kitten dies. Then the sounds of autumn silence leave her bereft: "Here was something even stupider: A month or so later, when cold weather set in, Maggie switched off the basement dehumidifier as she did every year and even *that* absence had struck her. She had mourned in the most personal way the silencing of the steady, faithful whir that used to thrum the floorboards, what on earth was wrong with her? she had wondered. Would she spend the rest of her days grieving for every loss equally—a daughter-in-law, a baby, a machine that dries the air out? Was this how it felt to grow old?"

No, it is not how it *must* feel to grow old, but it *is* how Maggie feels with her children gone (her daughter-in-law and granddaughter had lived with her until the baby was seven months old). It has been so long, Maggie sighs, since she "herself was so central to anyone's world." For her, then, the feeling of growing old is not connected with the loss of male attention, so often and overly attributed to be so important to women, but rather with the loss of her role as a mother to dependent children (Maggie is deeply secure in a companionable marriage characterized in great part by constant, genial bickering). Her sense of loss expands to fill every corner of her life, even the basement. As Maggie muses to herself, why does our commercial culture focus so excessively on romantic love when, as Tyler puts it, "life was also full of children's births and trips to the shore and longtime jokes with friends?" In my middle years, I could not agree with Tyler more.

But Tyler's vision in *Breathing Lessons*, though sad, is ultimately recuperative. In the last chapter Tyler proposes a brilliant antidote to assuage Maggie's grieving mood. She invents a kind of thought experiment, one similar to imagining the three books you would want to have with you on a desert island. Actually it is not so much a thought experiment as a stretching, an exercising of remembered affections. It is the opposite of mourning (although displaced), a conscious reattachment to bits and pieces of her past rather than a giving up of them. Maggie does not work to relinquish what she lost, as Freud would counsel her to do. Instead, she rummages through her past, much like going through boxes of stuff long stored in the attic, to renew old psychic ties. That she has borrowed this experiment of sorts from an old man I take to be significant. It is an old man who "believed that once he reached heaven, all he had lost in a lifetime would be given back to him. . . . At the Pearly Gates, he said, Saint Peter would hand him everything in a gunny sack." What a consoling notion! Maggie turns this little fantasy into a form of conscious psychic play. Leisurely she leafs through her past as she cooks dinner. She grows absorbed in imagining what things she would want to find in that sack, objects "freely given up, even, which later she wished back again": a green dress that she had loved for the way it moved, a trinket of a keychain given to her by her first boyfriend. And then, as her mind moves, it begins to race: "And the summer evenings as well, why not—the children smelling of sweat and fireflies, the warm porch floorboards sticking slightly to your chair rockers," and also "one of those looming moonlit clouds that used to float overhead like dirigibles as Ira"—her husband—"walked her home from choir practice."

A scene such as this invites us to pause, to take the time to ask ourselves the same question: what lost objects would we conjure up? How different this process is from that of filling out a prefabricated questionnaire, the kind you find in *Redbook* or *Woman's Day*, where you total up your score to find out if you are happy enough, too controlling, and so on. Here Tyler asks us to take a meditative (if enthusiastic) pleasure in our lives, to breathe between her lines. And so, taken by this passage in *Breathing Lessons*, I stopped thinking about Maggie and Anne Tyler and thought about myself, at first keying my memories to Maggie's. Her mind conjured up a green dress, and I thought of the heliotrope-blue skirt my mother had made for me in high school. I want to wear this exact purple-shaded blue again. And I would want the pendant necklace of three pearls given to me by my first "real" boyfriend, whom I later married. And my kitten Couscous, who was found dead, my former neighbor Quan Soo told me, in the street around the corner where she had been run over by a car.

As Maggie warms to her memories—some of them are more than that: discoveries, actually, about people in her past—she warms to her life, bringing her children imaginatively closer to herself. She remembers, for example, the way her daughter Daisy would always borrow a necklace she herself had treasured. The point of course is that, in imagining what she would want to find in that hypothetical sack, Maggie does find the little things that meant so much. What's more, she brings herself back to life.[2]

In this wonderful scene Tyler has staged a "festival of remembrance." I take this convivial phrase from Freud, who used it somewhat differently in *Studies in Hysteria* to describe the almost-ritual-like behavior of a woman to exorcise herself of painful affect.[3] Freud's patient, "a highly-gifted woman," had devoted herself to nursing three (maybe even four) people whom she loved through their illnesses to their deaths. These were extended periods of care during which she was required to suppress her own emotions and divert her attention from her own "impressions," as Freud calls them. Some time later, after their deaths, she would rehearse in her mind the scenes of illness and passing—Freud uses the theatrical metaphor advisedly—and only then would she allow herself to experience her own emotions, appropriate to suffering and bereavement. "Every day," Freud writes, "she would go through each impression once more, would weep over it and console herself—at her leisure, one might say."[4] This woman, Freud continues, "also celebrated annual festivals of remembrance at the period of her various catastrophes, and on these occasions her vivid visual reproductions and expressions of feeling kept to the date precisely."[5] What a dramatic scene. What a strange "celebration." The woman postponed the performance of grief and pain until later, until after the fact, in anniversary timing. Freud's theoretical point is that such emotions only lie buried, waiting to be revived. But this is open to question. Perhaps the emotions are themselves produced with the imaginative rehearsal of these scenes during which this woman only played the role of a witness at the time. And so too, perhaps, the healing emotions of remembrance are only produced through a rehearsal of the past, as we see in Maggie's festival of remembrance, staged Tyler-fashion in a cluttered kitchen.

At any rate, what is important if not altogether remarkable in the Freud canon is that his female patient, this "highly-gifted woman," is not a hysteric, although her symptoms are similar to those exhibited by a hysteric. She is, Freud insists, not ill. The process of settling emotional accounts, or what he calls an "abreaction of arrears," is altogether a normal one. Thus the term "festival of remembrance," with its celebratory overtones so uncharacteristic of Freud, is appropriate for Maggie's reinvention of the past. But Maggie is not purging herself of painful affect. Instead, she is storing up binding emotions, replacing a despondent mood with another one, with hope. She is kindling her past into emotional life through memories of (primarily) objects of her everyday life. It is an imaginative act of modest proportions that gives her, for an extended moment, comfort that will, paradoxically, take her out of the past and into the future. (In a wonderful touch, Tyler adds that Maggie's daughter Daisy is at this moment packing her stuffed animals to take along with her to college, literally taking her objects with her into the next part of her life.) And thus Maggie's grieving mood is alleviated by an appreciation for her past—no, it's warmer than that, closer, a kind of nestling into her past. Yet it is not a nostalgic longing for her past but rather a repossession of a feeling for it.

What does this figure of a forty-eight-year-old woman have to do with me? As I write this at age forty-seven I think: not much, not very much at all really. Maggie's sense of loss as aging, as something wrong with her, is connected to the crisis of her children's leaving home. It is traditionally a woman's crisis for all the reasons we know. I'm near Maggie's age, but my daughter Jessamyn is nine and a half. It seems to me that I am much younger than Maggie. (Do we not often think of ourselves as younger, or older, than those our own age, and always to our advantage?) I often calculate that I could be my daughter's grandmother (if I had had my daughter at twenty, as my mother had me, then . . .). But I am fully aware that I would be offended if anyone took me for my daughter's grandmother. This may not be so much a sensitivity to age as the desire for narcissistic identification (*I'm* her mother). But no doubt it's both.

Do young children, then, keep us from feeling old (and isn't this different from the banality that children keep us young)? My friend Kathleen Hulley has said as much. She is about my age and does not have children. But all her friends have children who are not yet even sixteen. We'll start feeling old, she tells me, when these kids go off to college. The clear separation of one generation from another, I would agree, is a powerful subjective marker of age. But is this not, as I've been suggesting, the wrong way to conceive of an "ordinary life development"? Maggie is older, yes. But how she feels is not necessarily how it feels to grow old. Or perhaps I'm being pious. I have no idea how I'll react when my daughter leaves home. We still hold hands as we cross the street together, and we still sleep together in the same bed when her father is not at home. Perhaps I will feel a terrible loss. And perhaps I will feel old—even though it will be one of life's ordinary developments.

What happens, you might wonder, to the fictional Maggie? At the novel's end she settles down into marriage with her husband.

Still I value Tyler's common-sense wisdom voiced by Bonnie in *Morgan's Passing*, that the growing up of children is "just an ordinary life development," not worth grieving over passionately, as we would the death of a child (it is not unusual to find Tyler's mothers imagining with anticipatory horror the death of their young children). So it is ironic that what befalls the unsuspecting Bonnie at fifty-three is a totally unpredictable event. Bonnie's husband is the improbable, unreliable, lovable eccentric Morgan of the novel's title. One day Morgan walks out of his rambling life with her (their life together is like their house—genial, cluttered, accommodating). A remarkably unflappable woman—she manages with distracted aplomb to hold together a household of seven daughters plus Morgan's spinsterish sister Brindle *and* his mother—Bonnie is caught genuinely unawares.

Any reader of *Morgan's Passing* could argue that this novel is really Morgan's story or Emily's story (she is the young woman with whom Morgan entangles himself). Morgan and Emily are the central characters. Bonnie is peripheral, seemingly incidental, a middle-aged woman from whom we do not expect anything unusual: she is so comfortable, like an overstuffed chair! So it came as a surprise to me—one of Tyler's wonderful surprises for women—to discover that it is Bonnie who gives this pleasurable novel its title. What does she do? I will come back to this after what may seem to be a detour but is really not.

Popular music, someone once told me, does not so much draw attention to itself as it prompts us to remember where we were in our lives when a particular song or album first made an impression on us. And reading? I won't hazard a generalization for all literature, but some writing lends itself to daydreaming in our life. I find this to be true of much of Anne Tyler's fiction. For me one of the pleasures of reading her novels comes from the wandering of my thoughts through a kind of imaginative space created by the permeability of her fictional world with my own experience. The British psychoanalyst D. W. Winnicott would call this potential space, a psychic space where things can be invented. Hence, for example, my pleasure in following the middle-aged Maggie's listing of the lost objects of her life by musing on my own inventory of objects. So too my pleasure in reading *Morgan's Passing*, where something I imagined as I made my way through the story came uncannily to be found later in it, reinforcing my own little fantasy.

One of the first things I loved about Morgan (and thus about Tyler, who invented him) was the way he is drawn to the personals in the newspapers. He will read them at the breakfast table, moving from the lost-and-founds to the obituaries. "I love the classified ads," he declares, adding, in a wonderful formulation, "They're so full of private lives." Why, so do I, I thought. And then, while reading

Morgan's Passing in preparation for this essay, it occurred to me to structure my piece on Tyler around the personals. My "research" would consist of selecting classifieds and obituaries that spoke to the subject of mourning and older women. That would be fun, to the point, and in the madcap spirit of many of Tyler's characters as well. Being a dutiful scholar I would cull them from Tyler's fictional part of the United States, from Baltimore and its surroundings. Perhaps the *Washington Post*. But the *Post* is too urbane for Tyler's world and too difficult to come by in Paris, where I was writing this essay. Well then, why not invent the personals? After all, that's what I'm sure Tyler did. Tyler wrote, and Morgan reads, "Lost. *White wedding dress size 10. No questions asked.*" I found this hilarious and tried to make one up too. Nothing came to my mind. But the obituaries: now that was instantly easy. I would compose the obituary of my first husband, the one who gave me the pearl necklace (we've been divorced for twenty years). I was now halfway through the novel and, over coffee, told a friend about my idea. You can't do that, she said unequivocally. Absolutely not. Out of the question. And then she confided to me that every morning she looked in the newspaper for the obituary of her former lover's father. I imagined her motive to be revenge, one for which she would not be responsible (instead, she told me later, she wanted to maintain contact, to know about the events which would profoundly affect her former lover's life, a motive more generous than mine). So why can't you write the obituary, another friend, a fifty-year-old man, urged me (he is a philosopher and couldn't see any compelling ethical objections). And so did Anne Tyler's novel itself, I came to conclude.

Where did that odd title of *Morgan's Passing* come from, I wondered as I read. At the breakfast table, early in the novel, the commonsensical Bonnie sighs to Morgan, "Why do you always take the papers so personally?" and "Morgan, I wish you wouldn't put so much stock in obituaries." Seven years later, after they are divorced and the novel is winding to a close, Bonnie has the inventive gesture of mind to place Morgan's concocted obituary in a newspaper where he is bound to read it. What a brilliant idea. What a harmless revenge, for it has the intended effect—it really bothers him. When Morgan confronts her with it, Bonnie explains endearingly (at least to me) that it was only an impulse, like the purchase of a pair of wildly dangly earrings. It was just a passing thought, she insists. She had meant to cancel it all along. And most importantly—for here the narrative swerves toward her future—the obituary "was meant to be an announcement." It was her way of declaring to both him and herself that he was dead to her and that she was involved with another man. Mourning, it has been said, is the process of killing the dead. How much more difficult it is in many cases—perhaps especially in the case of divorce—to kill, psychically, those who are still alive.

Thus I admire this small but marvelously renegade act of a middle-aged woman whose competence, although it never had been of the bankerly sort, takes such an unexpected turn. And I concluded that if Bonnie could do it, so could I. Actually I had the idea first, in a way. I would be sure to include Bob Woodward's middle name, one he hates; I would have him die, like Morgan, of a lengthy illness, but I would specify it as leukemia. (By the way, my friend Joan DeJean, a professor of French literature at the University of Pennsylvania, has since told me that composing and publishing people's obituaries before they died, for just such reasons of delicious revenge, was often done in seventeenth-century France.) I would not be able to publish it in Bob Woodward's newspaper, the *Washington Post*, of course. But I would place it in a small Maryland weekly. I would declare that long-term bond broken.

Is it peculiar to feel oneself authorized by a fictional character, as one of my friends suggested to me. Not at all, it seems to me. I live in great part by literature—as parable, as touchstone, as gesture. Tyler's (often-exasperated) affection for everyday life, evident particularly since the publication of *Earthly Possessions* in 1977, when her work took on a more comic tone, instills a sense of imaginative complicity between her readers and her characters. This has to do in great part with the quality of dailiness in her fictional world. Even though the implausible, if not downright bizarre, often happens, peculiar lives seem somehow sensible. When the thirty-five-year-old Charlotte, for example, is taken hostage in *Earthly Possessions*, flight is transformed into everyday travel, complete with car breakdowns and difficulties with directions.

Tyler's middle-aged women are a resourceful if daffy lot. They have lively interior lives. They can improvise. They can turn sharp corners in their middle years. They can also recognize when it's time to go home (as does Charlotte at the conclusion of *Earthly Posses-sions*). I want to call attention to just one more of these female char-acters, to Brindle, who, like Bonnie, is a minor personage in *Morgan's Passing*. Brindle is an aggravatingly morose widow-turned-spinster who doesn't even have a job, who yet compels my admiration when she walks out on her new husband, an old childhood sweetheart. Why? Because she knows what age she is, and he doesn't. Tyler conveys this marvelously by literalizing the situation. It is hilarious.

Who of us in middle age does not occasionally have the fantasy of meeting up with our childhood sweetheart (how powerful is the attraction of a first love)? Brindle's high-school sweetheart, absurdly named Robert Roberts, comes back to sweep her off her feet—she is thirty-eight, I calculate—after his wife dies. This time it is not the woman who is in a grieving mood but the man. The signature Tyler twist is that he is not mourning his first wife but Brindle—as she was. Tyler puts these words into Brindle's fictional mouth after two years of marriage: "He keeps my graduation photo on the television set. Half the time that he pretends he's watching TV, he's really watching my photo. I see him clicking his eyes back in focus when I walk into the room. When he thinks I'm busy with something else, he'll go over to the photo and pick it up and study it. Then he'll shake his head and set it down again." When Brindle finds Robert Roberts sleeping on the couch with her graduation photo tucked under his arm, she leaves him definitively—good for her! The scene is, of course, preposterous. Within this slapstick moment is contained a truth about women and aging. Our culture clings to younger women at the expense of older women. Brindle refuses to accept that system of values; she refuses to be what he wants her to be. She insists that she is no longer that girl in the photograph. Importantly, she has no regrets. She does not grieve for her youth. Tyler pushes the scene further, showing us the absurdity of conform-ing to (society's, men's) demands that we somehow be (act, look) younger than we are. A lovers' triangle, doomed by jealousy, has been created by Robert Roberts. It is both ridiculous and sad. "'I'm getting so I'm jealous of my own self,' Brindle said, muffled. 'I'm jealous of my photograph and the silver-plated ID bracelet I gave him when I was thirteen. He never takes that bracelet off. He sleeps with it; he bathes with it. Let it go, I feel like saying. Can't you ever forget her?'" (How admirably different the determined Brindle is from the weakish middle-aged Sarah in Tyler's *The Accidental Tourist*, a novel which I find does not go as deep as many of her others. Reunited with her husband—but only for a short time—she confides to him, "I think that after a certain age people just don't have a choice . . . you're who I'm with. It's too late now for me to change. I've used up too much of my life now." Bonnie and Brindle put the lie to that. They are two fictional women in their middle years who take decisive action.)

Thinking of Brindle—momentarily setting aside the sitcom flavor of the scene—I wonder to what extent in our age of the photographic portrait (snapshot or formal) we think of ourselves in relation to photographs. When do we say, like Brindle, that's no longer me, I no longer identify with being a younger woman? As the acerbic, elderly Miss Hattie says in Tyler's *The Tin Can Tree* to the photographer James (she objects to having her picture taken), "Pictures are merely one way, Mr. Green. . . . Remembering something flat and of one tone. What is ever all one way?"

Tyler is fascinated by photography as portraiture (she is not interested in photography as art or as documentary practice). Several of her characters are portrait photographers by ramshackle profession (James in *The Tin Can Tree* and Charlotte and her father before her in *Earthly Possessions*; even the silent Ira in *Breathing Lessons* is a picture framer). To a certain extent, Tyler's writing is itself a kind of photography of the everyday. She presents us with portraits of the unnoticed and overlooked—and many of them are of older women. But the practice of photography, as it is represented in her work, is not overburdened with the rhetoric of tragic loss, as it is in much contemporary writing on photography. The French cultural critic Roland Barthes has insisted that in every photograph is a "terrible thing . . . the return of the dead."[6] For Barthes, photography evokes—or, more precisely, certain photographs evoke—feelings of persisting pity; gazing at such photographs, he tells us, he enters the theater of the image, "taking into my arms what is dead, what is going to die."[7] Similarly, for Susan Sontag, photography is preeminently "an elegiac art, a twilight art. Most subjects photographed are, just by virtue of being photographed, touched with pathos."[8]

I would not deny that in Tyler's fictional world, poignancy is at times associated with photograph portraiture. Indeed I opened this essay celebrating the subtle power of Tyler's fiction to suggest—and more importantly, to evoke—the grief felt when someone (it was Jeremy in *Celestial Navigation*) understands belatedly that an older woman is not just one-dimensionally that—an older woman. Thus, as I come to the end of this essay, I want to consider in this context the flinty-willed, fiercely independent Pearl Tull, the major character of *Dinner at the Homesick Restaurant*. Tyler traces her life from young adulthood to very old age and death when she is eighty-five. (It is important that Tyler opens *Dinner at the Homesick Restaurant* with Pearl Tull dying—we are introduced to her as an older woman—and that Tyler imagines for us what Pearl Tull was thinking, wishing, imagining at that moment. As readers we are presented first with a portrait of this older woman's personal feelings rather than with what younger characters think and feel about her.) Much later in the book, yet somewhat earlier in the chronology of events, Pearl Tull complains in exasperation to one of her middle-aged children that they don't pay enough attention to her now, that once she was special in their eyes but that now "I'm old and I walk along unnoticed, just like anyone else"—meaning, I take it, that she is, like any other old woman, overlooked. "It strikes me as unjust," she declares. I agree. It is not so much that she longs to replace the present with the past, however. Rather she wants a better here and now.

I read Tyler's narrative as providing that better place and time and wished-for ending for the frail and blind Pearl Tull. She is cared for by one of her children, the middle-aged, unmarried Ezra who lives with her (and she with him), and she is loved by her grandson Luke. In one of the last scenes in the book of her life, Pearl Tull asks Ezra to sift through with her the drawers of her desk, presumably to lend some organizing principle to the photographs and the predictable, odd mementos (her fourth-grade report card, a dried corsage), to sort and straighten. Tyler writes this affecting scene from both of their points of view, points of view which differ. Ezra thinks that his mother is looking for her self, as if "she" could be found in the old photographs. Actually it is Ezra who "finds" his mother in them. Like Jeremy in *Celestial Navigation*, who abruptly remembers Mrs. Jarrett with a rush of grieving feeling, Ezra just as suddenly "sees" his mother through time. As he reads to her from her girlhood diary, he "all at once had the feeling that the ground had rushed away beneath his feet. Why, that perky young girl was this old woman sitting next to him. She has once been a whole different person, had a whole different life separate from his." What Ezra feels, though, is not grief, but wonder. He properly sees his mother as not just an old woman, as not just his mother, but as a woman who has lived a long life, a woman whose "interior self" is "still enormous, larger than life, powerful."

And Pearl Tull herself? What was she searching for? As Tyler characterizes her, she "had never been the type to gaze backward . . . she didn't use these photos as an excuse for reminiscing." For Pearl Tull, Tyler dismisses the photograph as a nostalgic touchstone (I think too of the wonderful scene in *Earthly Possessions* where an old woman, dying of cancer, tears up a photograph of herself as a young girl, an act initially inexplicable to her daughter who does not at first have the remotest sense of her mother's thoughts and feelings). The last glimpse which Tyler gives us of Pearl Tull has the quality of a still life—full of life, not, pace Barthes, the "return of the dead." Again, Ezra is reading to her from her girlhood diary, a commonplace enough recitation of everyday life—what she bought, what she did. Unexpectedly in the midst of the ordinariness of it all, the dailiness of life is suspended—in the here and now, in a moment still and spatial. I understand this scene as a festival of remembrance, to echo Freud's phrase. The diary entry reads: *"I went out behind the house to weed. Was kneeling in the dirt by the stable with my pinafore a mess and the perspiration rolling down my back, wiped my face on my sleeve, reached for the trowel, and all at once thought, why I believe that at just this moment I am absolutely happy."*

Remembering this feeling, Pearl Tull grows still: it is not conjuring up a visual image of herself in a past time that is important, but rather the memory of an emotion itself—here of happiness—which brings the narrative of this life to a conclusion, novelistically, with her subjectivity—and then her death. Far from being unnoticed and overlooked, Pearl Tull, an older woman, is one of Anne Tyler's most memorable characters, one who prompts me to wonder about the interior lives of the women in my family who have gone before me.

10 / Family Ways

Out of her fascination with families—with brotherly men and auntly women, with weak sisters and mama's boys, with stay-at-homes and runaways—Anne Tyler has fashioned, in *Searching for Caleb*, a dandy novel, funny and lyric and true-seeming, exquisite in its details and ambitious in its design. She here construes the family as a vessel of Time. The Pecks, who live (as her families tend to) in Baltimore, are known for longevity. Great-Grandma Laura, the second wife of the clan's founder, Justin Montague Peck, lived to be ninety-seven, and at the age of ninety-three Daniel Peck, Justin's first son, is lively enough to be riding trains and buses in search of his half-brother, Caleb, who disappeared from Baltimore back in 1912. It is 1973, and Daniel is living with two of his grandchildren, Justine and Duncan, who, though first cousins, have married. The minister who officiated at the wedding remembers "the bride's and groom's joint family" occupying the front pews: "There was something dreamlike in the fact that almost everyone in the front section had the same fair, rather expressionless face—over and over again, exactly the same face, distinguished only a little by age or sex." The intensely blue Peck eyes— "those clear, level eyes that tended to squint a little as if dazzled by their own blueness"—run through the layers of this saga like a trickle of icy-pure spring water; the motif is distilled in the marriage of Justine and Duncan, "their blue eyes opening simultaneously to stare at each other across the pillow." In Miss Tyler's vision, heredity looms as destiny, and with the force of a miracle people persist in being themselves: "But Duncan, who had changed her whole life and taken her past away from her, slept on as cool as ever, and on the crown of his head was the same little sprig of a cowlick he had had when he was four."

The family's conservatism and longevity defy time while embodying it; a nonagenarian father sits next to his elderly son on a couch, and "they might have been brothers. . . . In the end, the quarter-century that divided their generations amounted to nothing and was swept away. . . . Everything was leveled, there were no extremes of joy or sorrow any more but only habit, routine, ancient family names and rites and customs, slow careful old people moving cautiously around furniture that had sat in the same positions for fifty years."

Yet not all the Pecks hold fast to the household established by the first Justin in northern Baltimore after the Great Fire of 1904. Caleb, his second son, whose "tilted brown eyes must have snuck in from the Baum side of the family," literally gives his father apoplexy with his love of music—the old man's left side is paralyzed by the young man's defiance, and his mother tells Caleb, in one of the book's many astounding sentences, "You have killed your half of your father." Caleb repentantly works for a decade in the family shipping business, then vanishes, leaving the fortune and the dynasty to his brother, Daniel. There are other runaways. Daniel's wife, Margaret Rose, bears him six children, one a year, and in the seventh year leaves him and flees to her parents in Washington. The six children do what is expected of them, as the family business becomes law instead of trade, but of *their* children (and there are oddly few)

Duncan, the oldest's son, runs away at the age of eighteen, and a little later Justine, the youngest's daughter, defies her parents and marries him, joining him in a life of job-to-job vagabondage in the small towns of Maryland and Virginia. Their daughter, Meg, defies them in turn and also marries to escape. And even old Daniel, the patriarch of Peckishness, allows himself in retirement to drift away in search of Caleb, and takes up residence with the shabby, fortune-telling, forty-year-old Justine, the one other member of the family willing to spend time "chasing rainbows on the Greyhound bus line."

Searching for Caleb is, among other things, a detective novel, with an eccentric detective, Eli Everjohn (he looks like Abraham Lincoln, "even to the narrow border of beard along his jawline"), and an ingenious unraveling; readers should be permitted unhampered enjoyment of the plot's well-spaced turns. Suffice it to say that, with the quest for Caleb as her searchlight, Miss Tyler warmly illumines the American past in its domestic aspect. Old Justine's turn-of-the-century illness evokes this: "Therefore he undertook his own cure. He had all the panes in his windows replaced with amethyst glass, which was believed to promote healing. He drank his water from a quassia cup and ordered Laura to send away for nostrums advertised in the newspaper—celery tonic, pectoral soup, a revitalizing electric battery worn on a chain around the neck. His only meat was squirrel, easiest on the digestive tract."

Miss Tyler, who was twenty-three when her first novel was published and is now only in her mid-thirties, seems omniscient about the details of old Baltimore. When Laura finally dies, Daniel reflects that she was the only person who with him could remember "the rough warm Belgian blocks that used to pave the streets downtown." We are told that the 1908 Ford had "a left-hand steering wheel and splashless flower vases," and that in the 1900s women wore Pompeiian Bloom rouge, and little Caleb leaned out a window to hear an Irish tenor sing "Just a Lock of Hair for Mother." Such tender erudition never feels forced. Contemplation of the vanished induces in Miss Tyler a totally non-academic ecstasy: "Whenever you hear distant music somewhere in the town, maybe so faint you thought you imagined it, so thin you blamed the whistling of the streetcar wires, then you would track the sound down and find Caleb straddling his little velocipede, speechless with joy, his appleseed eyes dancing."

The whistling of the streetcar wires is another motif that recurs, and the search for Caleb feels to become a search for the lyrical, mystical, irrational underside of American practicality. Duncan spouts facts but he rarely applies them, and Justine is, matter-of-factly, a fortune-teller. Her fortune-telling, along with Caleb's invisible presence, keeps this scrupulously exact novel of furniture and manners spooky and suspenseful. The career of fortune-telling—the methods and habitats of its practitioners—occasions another fine display of curious information, and of Miss Tyler's subtle psychologizing. Madame Olita, offspring of a gypsy and a high-school civics teacher, instructs Justine: "You must think of these cards as tags. . . . Tags with strings attached, like those surprise boxes at parties. The strings lead into your mind. These cards will pull out what you already know, but have failed to admit or recognize."

So, too, Miss Tyler's details pull from our minds recognition of our lives. These Pecks, polite and snide and tame and maddening and resonant, are *our* aunts and uncles; Justine and Duncan's honeymoon, when they are "isolated, motionless, barely breathing, cut loose from everyone else," is everybody's escape from a suffocating plurality of kin into a primitive two-ness; the America they truck their fraying marriage through is our land, observed with a tolerance and precision unexcelled among contemporary writers. Paragraph after paragraph, details kindle together, making heat and light. For, along with the power to see and guess and know, Anne Tyler has the rare gift of coherence—of tipping observations in a direction, and of keeping track of what she has set down. Reading letters from Baltimore as a newlywed, Justine notes that "each envelope let out a little gust of Ivory soap, the smell of home." A generation later, when her daughter, Meg—who in rebellion against her mother's rebellion has become a super-Peck, prim and conventional—leaves home, Justine in the girl's abandoned room takes "a deep breath of Meg's clean smell: Ivory soap and fresh-ironed fabric." Dozens of such strands of continuity glint amid the cross-woven threads of this rich novel of nostalgia and divination, genes and keepsakes, recurrences and reunions.

Miss Tyler does not always avoid the pawky. Her ease of invention sometimes leads her to overdo. The secret of Caleb's departure, she would have us believe, was harbored for sixty years by a family servant whom no one ever thought to ask, and who therefore, with the heroic stubbornness of a Faulkner character, declined to tell. Such moonbeams of Southern Gothic, without a sustained sense of regional delirium, shine a bit stagily. In a note following the text, the author's biography sounds cosmopolitan (born in Minneapolis, married to an Iranian psychiatrist, herself once a graduate student of Russian), but she says she "considers herself a Southerner"; and she does apparently accept the belief, extinct save in the South, that families are absolutely, intrinsically interesting. Are they? Her Pecks contain not only their milieu's history but every emotion from a mother's need "to be the feeder" to an old man's perception that "once you're alive, there's no way out but dying." Does Miss Tyler share Daniel Peck's preference when he says, "I would prefer to find that heaven was a small town with a bandstand in the park and a great many trees, and I would know everybody in it and none of them would ever die or move away or age or alter"? No other kind of goodness is suggested in this book, except Justine's hopeful forward motion. Miss Tyler gives us a border South, busy commercializing its own legends, a New South where the traditional slave-boy iron hitching post has had its face (but not its hands) painted white and where faith healers live in hideously slick decors of sculptured carpets and glass knicknacks. The America she sees is today's, but, like the artist-hero of her previous novel, *Celestial Navigation*, she seems to see much of it through windows. There is an elusive sense of removal, an uncontaminated, clinical benevolence not present in the comparable talent of, say, the young Eudora Welty, whose provincial characters were captured with a certain malicious pounce. Powerhouse and Old Mr. Marblehead and the narrator of "Why I Live at the P.O." have an outrageous oddity they would disown if they could decipher the fiction, whereas we can picture Anne Tyler's characters reading through her novels comfortably, like Aunt Lucy in "her wing chair in which she could sit encircled, almost, with the wings working like mule's blinders. . . . The upholstery was embroidered in satin-stitch, which she loved to stroke absently as she read." Sit up, Aunt Lucy. This writer is not merely good, she is *wickedly* good.

11 / Loosened Roots

Anne Tyler in her seventh novel continues to demonstrate a remarkable talent and, for a writer of her acuity, an unusual temperament. She is soft, if not bullish, on America: its fluorescent-lit banks and gas stations, its high schools and low life, its motels and billboards and boring backwaters and stifling homes and staggering churches and scant, innocent depravities and deprivations are all to her the stuff of a tender magic, a moonlit scenery where poetry and adventure form as easily as dew. Small towns and pinched minds hold room enough for her; she is at peace in the semi-countrified, semi-plasticized, northern-Southern America where she and her characters live. Out of this peace flow her unmistakable strengths—her serene, firm tone; her smoothly spun plots; her apparently inexhaustible access to the personalities of her imagining; her infectious delight in "the smell of beautiful, everyday life"; her lack of any trace of intellectual or political condescension—and her one possible weakness: a tendency to leave the reader just where she found him. Acceptance, in her fiction, is the sum of the marvelous—or, as *Earthly Possessions* would have it, the end of traveling is to return. This is not untrue. Nothing Anne Tyler sets down is untrue. But the impending moral encloses the excitements of her story in a circle of safety that gives them the coziness of entertainment. It may be that in this Protestant land, with its reverence for sweat and constipation, we distrust artificers, peaceable cultivators of the imaginary. Miss Tyler tends her human flora for each book's season of bloom and then latches the garden gate with a smile. So, one could say, did Shakespeare; but in the tragedies, at least, the enclosure of final order is drawn around a group of chastened survivors, while Miss Tyler here gathers in to safety the very characters she has convincingly shown us to be sunk in "a rich, black, underground world . . . where everyone was in some deep and dramatic trouble." The depths that her lucid vision perceives through the weave of the mundane are banished, as it were, by a mere movement of the author's eyes. *Earthly Possessions* contains, for instance, a chilling portrait of a habitual criminal, Jake Simms, Jr., who blames every destructive and chaotic act of his own on someone else. He kidnaps our heroine, the surpassingly amiable Charlotte Emory, because while he was robbing a bank a bystander happened to produce a gun. "I could be clean free," he tells his victim, "and you safe home with your kids by now if it wasn't for him. Guy like that ought to be locked up." As the chase continues, and the kidnapping lengthens into a kind of marriage, he persuades himself, "It ain't *me* keeping you, it's them. If they would quit hounding me then we could go our separate ways. . . ." This is perfect loser psychology, the mental technology for digging a bottomless pit; but Anne Tyler would have us believe that Jake is saved from falling in by the doll-like apparition of a wee seventeen-year-old girl he has impregnated, Mindy Callender: "She really was a tiny girl. The biggest thing about her was that stomach, which Jake carefully wasn't looking at. . . . She raised a thin, knobby wrist, with a bracelet dangling heart-shaped charms in all different colors and sizes. The pink stone in her ring was heart-shaped too, and so was the print of her dress. 'Hearts are my *sign*,'

Mindy said. 'What's yours?'" With such a figure, the Shakespearean ambience of dark comedy turns Spenserian; we are traveling in an allegory, and Love (Mindy) on page 193 points to the Grail with one of those bursts of articulate insight that overtake even the dimwitted in Anne Tyler's animated world.

The excitements of *Earthly Possessions* include both headlong suspense and surprises of retrospective revelation. Charlotte, the narrator and heroine, tells in her wry, patient voice two stories: she describes, hour by hour, the few days of her southward flight with Jake Simms, and, synopsized in alternating chapters, the thirty-five years of her life. The two accounts flow parallel, to the same estuary of acceptance. As in the author's previous novels, a fundamental American tension is felt between stasis and movement, between home and escape. Home is what we are mired in; Miss Tyler in her darker mode celebrates domestic claustrophobia and private stagnation. Charlotte is the late and only fruit of a very fat first-grade teacher and a faded, fussy "travelling photographer named Murray Ames." Ames stops traveling, and sets up a studio in his wife's "dead father's house," where a child is born with grotesque inadvertence: the mother's obesity and innocence have hidden the pregnancy. "One night she woke up with abdominal spasms. . . . All around her the bed was hot and wet. She woke her husband, who stumbled into his trousers and drove her to the hospital. Half an hour later, she gave birth to a six-pound baby girl." The little girl grows up lonely. The common American escape from home into the "whole new world" of public school is feelingly evoked:

> I hadn't had any idea that people could be so light-hearted. I stood on the edge of the playground watching how the girls would gather in clumps, how they giggled over nothing at all and told colorful stories of family life: visits to circuses, fights with brothers. They didn't like me. They said I smelled. I knew they were right, because now when I walked into my house I could smell the smell too: stale, dark, ancient air, in which nothing had moved for a very long time. I began to see how strange my mother was. I noticed that her dresses were like enormous flowered undershirts. I wondered why she didn't go out more; then once, from a distance, I watched her slow progress toward the corner grocery store and I wished she wouldn't go out at all.

From embarrassing parents Charlotte moves to an embarrassing husband, Saul Emory, a boy who had lived next door, returns from the Army, courts her, weds her, and abruptly announces that he has been called to preach, in the local fundamentalist Holy Basis Church. Charlotte is a nonbeliever; while her husband preaches, she sits deafly in church scheming how to get him into bed. "He was against making love on a Sunday. I was in favor of it. Sometimes I won, sometimes he won. I wouldn't have missed Sunday for the world." They live in what has become *her* dead father's house; she diffidently runs the studio that she has inherited, and the house fills up with charity cases and Saul's brothers. Charlotte says, "I felt like something dragged on a string behind a forgetful child. . . . I gave up hope. Then in order not to mind too much I loosened my roots, floated a few feet off, and grew to look at things with a faint, pleasant humorousness that spiced my nose like the beginnings of a sneeze." Childhood fantasies of flight recur; she keeps giving away the furniture; she finally decides to leave, goes to the bank "to get cash for the trip," and is seized by Jake Simms. Her adventure begins.

Writing a self-description for the *Washington Post*, Anne Tyler said, "Mostly it's lies, writing novels. You set out to tell an untrue story and you try to make it believable, even to yourself. Which calls for details; any good lie does."[1] Her details are superb, tucked in with quick little loops of metaphor: "When she was angry, her face bunched in now as if gathered at the center by a drawstring." "When he lifted me up in his arms I felt I had left all my troubles on the floor beneath me like gigantic concrete shoes."

Without pushing it, she establishes her characters in authentic occupations. Murray Ames's photography and his daughter's continuation of it becomes very real, and a paradigm for art:

"Move that lamp off somewhat," he would tell me from his bed. "You don't want such a glare. Now get yourself more of an angle. I never did like a head-on photograph."

What he liked was a sideways look—eyes lowered, face slanted downward. The bay window displaying my father's portraits resembled a field full of flowers, all being blown by the same strong breeze.

The author's attention to American incidentals is so unblinking that we are rather relieved when she seems to nod, as when Charlotte observed the "snuff adds" ("ads," surely) in Georgia, or a "pair of giant fur dominoes" (dice, more likely) hung from a rearview mirror. Every bit of junk food the fugitives nibble as they drive their stolen car south is affectionately noted, and the subtle changes in scenery and climate are continental in their cumulative effect. When, having at last arrived in Florida, Charlotte says, "It was one of those lukewarm, breezy evenings that makes you feel you're expecting something," we have arrived, too, and feel exactly what she means.

What else do we feel, after our two hundred pages with Charlotte Emory? She belongs to what is becoming a familiar class of Anne Tyler heroines: women admirably active in the details of living yet alarmingly passive in the large curve of their lives—riders on male-generated events, who nevertheless give those events a certain blessing, a certain feasibility. Jake comes to need his victim: "Charlotte, it ain't so bad if you're *with* us, you see. You act like you take it all in stride, like this is the way life really does tend to turn out. You mostly wear this little smile." Amos, a brother of Emory's who turns amorous, exclaims in admiration, "Now I see everyone grabbing for pieces of you, and still you're never diminished. . . . You sail through this house like a moon, you're strong enough for all of them." These intelligent, bustling, maternal, helpless moon-women trouble us with the something complacent in their little smiles, their "faint, pleasant humorousness." Their detachment has been achieved through a delicate inner abdication, a multiplication and devaluation of realities. Anne Tyler stated in the *Post*, "I write because I want more than one life."[2] Charlotte Emory as a photographer poses her subjects in odd bits of costume, "absent-mindedly" holding feathers and toys, antique swords and pistols; she has come to believe that such elaborations "may tell more truth than they hide." In the crisis of her mother's dying, Charlotte says, "My life grew to be all dreams; there was no reality whatsoever." Her life, from lonely childhood to lonely marriage, spent in an old house between two gas stations, photographing workaday people with dream baubles, has a terror and a sorrow of which the outlines are acknowledged but not the mass, the terrible heft. She seems less a character than a creator, who among the many lives that her fantasizing, emphathizing mind arrays before her almost casually chooses to live her own.

12 / Beauty and the Transformed Beast

Fairy Tales and Myths in *Morgan's Passing*

I
n her discussion of literary influences on Anne Tyler, Alice Hall Petry points out the relationship between some of Tyler's fictional qualities to Hawthorne's, noting Tyler's concerns, like Hawthorne's, "with the past, be it personal, familial, or (less commonly) historical."[1] Although people's problems are intertwined with history and their society, folklore deals with themes which the human race faces collectively.[2] Recognizing the influence of themes and stereotypes in fairy tales, psychiatrist Erich Berne has explored the use of fairy tales to show patients the roles on which they base their life scripts.[3] Even in the "liberated" 20th century, according to Karen E. Rowe, "many women internalize romantic patterns from ancient tales."[4] References to fairy tales appear in a number of Tyler's nov-

els—a narrative strategy that reflects her recognition of their cultural influence. In *Celestial Navigation* (which preceded the musical comedy that deconstructs fairy tales, *Into the Woods*), however, Tyler's use of fairy tales is more pointed than her allusions to them in earlier novels. Here, disenchanted Mary Tell, who has moved from an unsuccessful marriage to an affair to a common-law marriage which she deserts with her six children, comments: "Rapunzel. The Princess and the Pea. Rumpelstiltskin. . . . My mind runs ahead of the words. I play silent games with the tired old plots, I like to ponder the endings beyond the endings. How about Rapunzel, are we sure she was reallly happy ever after? Maybe the prince stopped loving her now that her hair was short. Maybe the Genuine Princess was a disappointment to her husband, being so quick to find the faults and so forthright about pointing them out. And after Rumpelstiltskin was defeated the miller's daughter lived in sorrow forever, for the king kept nagging her to spin more gold and she could never, never manage it again."

This cynical subversion seems to be a seed for, or to foreshadow, Tyler's treatment of fairy tales throughout *Morgan's Passing*. Puppets and fairy tales create a significant text in the work, for, just as fairy tales impel the puppeteers in manipulating the puppets' movements, behavior, and speech, so do cultural myths and stereotypes embedded in these tales appear to foster expectations and goals for the principal characters in *Morgan's Passing*, Morgan and Emily.

Ironically, although *Morgan's Passing* was Tyler's first novel to be honored with awards,[5] Alice Petry notes, "even Tyler's most ardent supporters were taken aback by these novels [*Morgan's Passing* and *Earthly Possessions*]."[6] Frank Shelton describes *Morgan's Passing* as "another runaway housewife novel" and Joseph Voelker disregards the novel, making only passing comments about *Morgan's Passing* while devoting chapters, or half-chapters, to Tyler's other novels.[7] Recognizing the rich intertextuality that goes beyond realism, Robert Towers addresses the figurative in his review of the novel, noting that "hints of myth, of fairy tale, abound in the novel. . . . Morgan is a protean figure . . . Emily an unawakened princess . . . Leon a glowering beast [hence his name], a truculent prince."[8] Towers adds that despite the "hints of myth," Tyler never loses sight of the realism in this novel. Through these "hints of myth" Tyler explores the ways in which a character's definition of self and the "other"[9] are affected by fairy tales.

Mythic discourse is introduced in the opening chapter of *Morgan's Passing* with the performance of a puppet show which is part of an Easter Fair sponsored by the Presbyterian church every year. As the Cinderella puppet (Emily Meredith) and the Prince (Leon Meredith) dance, "they held each other so fondly, it was hard to remember they were two hands clasping each other." Cinderella speaks in an unlikely manner: "The floors are like mirrors.... I wonder who scrubs them." The reader immediately becomes aware of (1) the comedic tone of the novel and (2) the function of the puppets as a reflection of the psyches of the puppeteers. The show reveals the puppeteers' closeness as Prince Charming embraces Cinderella, and we also perceive Cinderella's awareness that romance can be overshadowed by domesticity. According to Marcia R. Lieberman, Cinderella and various other tales perpetuate stereotypes and myths: the myth about courtship is "magnified as the most important and exciting part of a girl's life," after which the couple lives happily ever after.[10] Not only does the couple live happily ever after, but also, as Rowe suggests, fairy tales transfer fantasies that exalt "acquiescence to male power and make marriage not simply one ideal, but the only estate toward which women should aspire."[11] Throughout the novel, the commedia dell'arte performances of fairy tales by the puppeteers reveal their unconscious, or at times conscious, preoccupations, especially Emily's as she attempts to reconcile myths about love and romance with her reality.

The puppet show which opens the novel ends abruptly with a traumatic event when "Cinderella flops on her face" and the principals of the novel are brought together as Leon emerges from behind the stage, calling for a doctor. Morgan Gower, a "lank, tall bearded man" about forty-five, steps forth, clad in "a shaggy, brown suit that might have been cut from blankets"; his outfit is topped off with a red ski cap. Impersonating a doctor, Morgan attempts to get Emily, who is about to give birth, to the hospital. Since the baby begins to make its entrance, Morgan must stop his car and deliver the baby. Morgan delights in the Merediths' telling him that their baby will be sleeping in a cardboard box and fantasizes about their life as puppeteers, for he is a man who searches for meaning and romance in the lives of others. Tyler reinforces the fairy-tale motif at the end of the first chapter by describing Emily's impression of Morgan: "His hat . . . had made her think of a gnome. He really could have been someone from a fairy tale, she said: the baby elf, the troll, the goblin who finds children under cabbage leaves and lays them in their mothers' arms and disappears." Emily's early impression of Morgan becomes part of the web of fairy-tale stereotypes and imagery woven through the novel.

Morgan's Passing is written in the third person; however, the two voices we hear are those of Morgan Gower and Emily Meredith, both of whom seem to be somewhat powerless or puppetlike. For example, Morgan—who admittedly married his wife Bonny for money, which he says doesn't mean he didn't love her—lives in a large house, provided by her family, with their seven daughters. When his daughters are young, they enjoy their eccentric father, but as they become aware of his differences from other fathers, they are embarrassed by him and turn away from his companionship. Morgan supposedly manages the oldest of the chain of hardware stores owned by Bonny's family, although Butkin his helper actually does most of the work. His life seems to be orchestrated by other people while he preoccupies himself with outfits that are costumes and poses as multiple "others." In fairy tales, conjuring and spell-laying bring about transformations into creatures or into altered states. Ruth B. Bottigheimer indicates that in the Grimm tradition "wishing does not constitute conjuring, though wishes accompanied by unintended results appear often in Grimm's tales."[12] Morgan, in addition to being the hero (or anti-hero), also acts as a conjurer, initially by transforming himself through clothing and later by assuming Leon's identity and by transforming himself into Emily's prince.

Although Emily incorporates or reacts to fairy tales to create a life script, Morgan's views and behavior harken to eighteenth- and nineteenth-century romantic literary tradition. Not only should readers keep copies of Emerson, Thoreau, and Hawthorne on hand when reading Tyler, but they should also recall their Whitman, especially "Song of Myself." For, like the "I" in the poem, Morgan romantically seeks identity or heroism through becoming one with the "other" as he tests various roles, often masquerading as people in other professions. Also, not unlike Whitman, whose catalogs exalt

New York, people, and scenes, Morgan is absorbed by the urban Baltimore milieu he catalogs, riding on the bus:

> They passed more stores and office buildings. They whizzed through a corner of Morgan's old neighborhood, with most of the windows boarded up and trees growing out of caved-in roofs. (It had not done well without him.) Here were the Arbeiter Mattress Factory and Madam Sheba, All Questions Answered and Love Problems Cheerfully Solved. Rowhouses slid by, each more decayed than the one before. Morgan hunkered in his seat, clutching the metal bar in front of him, gazing at the Ace of Spades Sandwich Shop and Fat Boy's Shoeshine. Now he was farther downtown than he had ever lived. He relaxed his grip on the metal bar. He sank into the lives of the scattered people sitting on their stoops: the woman in her nightgown and vinyl jacket nursing a Rolling Rock beer and breathing frost; the two men nudging each other and laughing; the small boy in a grownup's sneakers hugging a soiled white cat. A soothing kind of emptiness began to spread through him. He felt stripped and free, like the vacant windows, frameless, glassless, on the upper floors of Syrenia's Hot Pig Bar-B-Q.

The Morgan-Whitman correspondence can be further extended, for Morgan, too, pursues the American Adam's belief in endless possibilities as he constantly seeks an eidolon woven from the fabric of otherness. Never losing sight of realism in her fiction, Tyler provides a clue to Morgan's constant search for identity as a possible search for a father figure, a clue which Joseph C. Voelker describes as the "thinnest mention of the mystery of his father's suicide" and Morgan's never having learned the reason for the action.[13]

Like Morgan, the female voice in the novel, Emily Meredith, appears to be disempowered as she defers to her husband Leon, reacting passively to his patriarchal choices about their future, his views about her puppets, and his anger throughout the novel. In examining female acculturation through fairy tales, Marcia R. Lieberman notes that good temper and meekness are "regularly associated with beauty," and she also indicates that frequently the girls in fairy tales are not only victims but martyrs as well.[14] Emily appears to follow these patterns, beginning with her meeting with "prince" Leon during her freshman year in college. Since there had been no major in acting, he had majored in English and appeared in every play on campus, appearances that influenced Emily's view of Leon and his otherness:

> For the first time Emily understood why they called actors "stars." There really was something dazzling about him whenever he walked onstage. Seen close up, he was a stringy, long-faced, gloomy boy with eyes that drooped at the outer corners and a mouth already beginning to be parenthesized by two crescent-shaped lines. He had a bitter look that made people uneasy. But onstage, all this came across as a sort of power and intensity. . . . He hung on to words lovingly and rolled them out after the briefest pause, as if teasing the audience. It appeared that his lines were invented, not memorized.

Leon's transformation into a prince occurs when he appears on the stage, a transformation that enables Emily to mythologize him and to see him as totally different from her own family which "had been so ordinary and pale."

Leon's "flunking out" and his parents' efforts to divert him from his obsession with acting result in his leaving college and going to New York to attempt an acting career. Atypically, Emily acts as the aggressor and asks him to take her with him. After they marry, Leon's abortive attempt at an acting career eventually leads the Merediths to Baltimore, where Leon and a troupe of actors perform in clubs. Leon fails in his efforts to be selected for roles in plays, in part because of his truculence. The Merediths subsist by performing puppet shows—Emily's idea—and by Emily's selling her puppets. The puppets become increasingly important as the "Other" for Emily; that is, as an expression of her unconscious. Emily's identification with the puppets and her husband's reaction to her "art" foment a rift between them; specifically, he refuses to use both the shadow puppets and the marionettes Emily creates, responding to her desire to use marionettes with "You just can't switch the universe around, any time you're tired of it." Like a mythic prince, Leon renders Emily powerless and silent, a condition she eventually finds unacceptable.

Not only did Emily initiate the performance of puppet shows, she also builds the stages and creates and repairs the puppets. Tyler's description of Emily's assembling and reconstructing her puppets takes on a metaphoric quality and a parodic tone when compared with Tyler's description of Morgan.

> She repaired the puppets and sewed more costumes for them. A few she replaced completely, which led to the usual question of what to do with the old ones. They were like dead bodies; you couldn't just dump them in the trashcan. "Use them for spare parts," Leon always said. "Save the eyes. Save that good nose. Put Red Riding Hood's grandmother's pockmarked cork-ball nose on any other puppet." It wouldn't work. It wouldn't be right. Anyway, how could she tear that face apart? She laid the grandmother in a carton alongside a worn-out Beauty from "Beauty and the Beast"—the very first puppet she'd ever made.

The parallel between the description of the puppets and of Morgan, whose self-identity is always linked to others—as is true for puppets—becomes obvious in the following passage: "You could say he was a man who had gone to pieces or maybe he'd arrived unassembled. Various parts of him seemed poorly joined together. His lean hairy limbs were connected by exaggerated knobs of bone; his black-bearded jaw as clumsily hinged as a nutcracker. Parts of his life, too, lay separate from other parts." Like the puppets, Morgan seems to be constructed and manipulated by outside forces. Tyler's characters live in a naturalistic world entrapped by romantic myths and controlled by genetic and familial influences, yet they hope and believe in freedom.

The puppet metaphor also appears later in the novel, when Emily, who is about twenty-nine towards the end of the book, falls in love with Morgan, who is fifty-one; despite her affection, she is struck by his separateness—his otherness—and realizes that "she would never really understand the smallest part of him." When they are eventually living together, she muses, "At night in bed, she never lost her surprise at finding herself alongside this bearded man, this completely other person. She felt drawn to him by something far outside herself—by strings that pulled her, by ropes. Waking in the dark, she rolled toward him with a kind of stunned sensation. She was conscious of their two surfaces meeting noticeably: oil and water." The "strings" and "ropes" reinforce the puppet trope: a trope John Updike perceives as the dominant metaphor in the novel.[15]

Fairy tales, which are projected through the puppets, serve as refractors of Emily's self-image. She has chosen "Beauty and the Beast" for their first show because it is her favorite fairy tale. However, "Leon didn't seem to care. . . . He hardly noticed when Emily came prancing up to him with her hand transformed into Beauty." Emily's attachment to the puppets and her attempt to garner some attention or praise from Leon reveal her desire to be identified with Beauty. When the show is performed, both Leon's and Emily's lines become expressions of the "Other," or their alter ego or unconscious, as they reconstruct fairy tales. Leon appears as the Beast, but instead of roaring he asks plaintively, "Who's gobbled up all my food?" . . . "Who's been sleeping in my bed?" . . . "My lovely bed, with the satin sheets to keep my hairdo smooth!"—dialogue that reveals his egocentricity and his fracturing of fairy tales. The audience responds with laughter. Then the Beast queries the audience, "Who?" When the children point to the father puppet, the Beast begins to act beastly and the father puppet shrinks back. This behavior is significant in view of Leon's refusal to communicate with his parents after his father disowned him for not pursuing his college education and attempting to become an actor.

As their first show ends, Mrs. Tibbitt, who has commissioned the puppet show for her daughter's birthday party, says, "Just one thing puzzles me."

> "What's that?" [said Leon.]
> "Well, the Beast. He never changed to a prince."
> Leon glanced over at Emily.
> "Prince?" Emily said.
> "You had her living happily ever after with the Beast. But *that's* not how it is; he changes; she says she loves him and he changes to a prince."
> "Oh," Emily said. It all came back to her now. She couldn't think how she'd forgotten.

The puppetry has become, like other arts and crafts in Tyler's novels, an extension of her characters' unexpressed and unacknowledged desires, frustrations, and fears—that is, a technique for revealing character. For Emily, Leon is no longer the prince she desired when she ran off to New York with him. Viewed in light of Bruno Bettelheim's analysis of "Beauty and the Beast," the misplaying of the scene becomes symbolic of Emily's modified view of Leon.

Bettelheim describes the beginning of Beauty and the Beast as the expression of a view of the dual existence of man, as both animal and mind (symbolized by Beauty), but, he says, when the Beast's true nature of being kind and loving is revealed, there is a happy ending.[16] Tyler reverses the fairy tale with Leon's conversion from loving prince to unloving beast in marriage, for he is described by Emily as becoming subject to rage during the course of their marriage.

Not only is Leon subject to fits of anger, but he also seems uncaring, a trait that especially reveals itself when other men are attentive to Emily. Emily's view of her relationship with men as the "other" is revealed in several ways. When Victor, a fellow actor younger than Emily, professes his love for her, the announcement doesn't evoke Leon's anger or any other emotion, but elicits a dispassionate "Do you want to go away with Victor?"—which makes Emily feel "flattened," but she assures Victor that she is fine and will stay. Emily recalls that other men have affixed themselves to her in the past, "but not to her personally. . . . What they liked was the idea of her." She feels that she must have reminded Victor of someone else; she has a minimal sense of self-identity and seems to be a character in search of a role: one she appears to be seeking as she fractures fairy tales.

All of these events in the Merediths' lives had occurred before they met Morgan Gower. However, after Morgan delivered Emily's baby, the Merediths could not find a Dr. Gower Morgan listed anywhere, so they could not thank him for the delivery of their daughter, Gina, nor compensate him. However, Morgan has not disappeared from their lives; in fact, he becomes obsessed with the Merediths, peering at their apartment and imagining their lives, and even following Leon and Emily. Morgan becomes part of the Merediths' lives from the day of his daughter's wedding, when he goes to their apartment in the guise of a puppet buyer. He "admires the marriage very much," attends the Merediths' performances, and seeks out Emily as she walks to school with Gina.

Over the next five years, Leon and Emily's relationship worsens; for instance, when they are interviewed about their puppet shows, Emily resents Leon's indicating in the newspaper article that the shows are improvised, adapted moment by moment, and that Emily's puppets are made "according to a fixed pattern. They're not improvised." Emily wishes she had defended herself during the interview, for she sees Leon's comment as downplaying her originality and the part of her that is revealed in her puppets. For, like other artists or artisans, her identification with these puppets, these "other," is a means of creating an identity, of empowerment.

A turning point in the novel occurs when Morgan, on an impulse, invites Leon and Emily to Bethany Beach, where the family is vacationing. Morgan becomes dismayed by Emily's appearing in her "unbecoming pale blue swimsuit that exposed her thin, limp legs, . . . for he wants her to be always wearing her liquid black skirt and ballet slippers," and when she does, he feels she is her "old, graceful fairy-dancer self," a revelation of Morgan's mythic view of Emily. Emily, for whom the Bethany stay is her first real vacation, bares her feelings about Leon to Morgan, indicating that Leon either wants to give shows or stay at home, telling her that they can't spare the time for vacations. During this conversation, her conscious identification with fairy tales is revealed as she tells Morgan, "I sit in my room with that sewing machine. . . . I feel like the miller's daughter, left to spin gold out of straw." The significance of the spinning becomes greater than that of its just being a menial task when examined in the light of Greek mythology. Ann Bergren has analyzed the role of weaving and spinning in Greek tales, arguing that "the semiotic activity peculiar to women throughout Greek tradition is not linguistic. Greek women do not speak, they weave. Semiotic woman is a weaver. Penelope is, of course, the paradigm."[17] Additionally, this preference for silent retiring women is represented in the German tradition by Wilhelm Grimm's fairy tales.[18]

After Emily's catharsis, she finds her voice as she begins to express other dissatisfactions with Leon, and she begins to weep. Morgan clumsily holds her and is startled "by a sudden ache that made him tighten his arms and pull her hard against him." On his return trip to Baltimore, Morgan realizes he is in love with Emily. After everyone returns to Baltimore, Morgan playfully begins to proposition Emily, often in Leon's presence. His visits become more frequent and he also finds opportunities to encounter Emily when she is outside the home.

As in several other Tyler novels, the death of an aunt evokes introspection by a protagonist. When Emily's great-aunt dies, Emily drives four hours to attend the funeral. This visit to the house with its familiar possessions and to the town of Emily's childhood evokes layers of remembrances. Emily's remaining aunt urges her to take

furniture or jewelry; however, Emily only asks about a marionette that had belonged to the deceased aunt. She examines the
marionette:

> Her tangled strings were tied to a single-cross control bar, just
> like the one that Emily had invented. Or maybe (it began to seem)
> she had not invented it after all, but had remembered it from
> childhood. Though she couldn't recall ever being shown this little
> creature. Maybe it was something that was passed in the dark—
> the very thought of giving puppet shows, even. And here she
> imagined she had come so far, lived such a different existence.
> She saw her Red Riding Hood scene in a whole new light now, as
> something crippled.

This "passing in the dark" has cultural as well as genetic overtones,
since the myths underlying Red Riding Hood and other tales have
become part of Emily's psyche. The revelation that her marionettes
might be something less than her own creation, and that her talent
for puppet shows is not an indication of her breaking away from
a colorless past, seems to mark a turning point in Emily's self-
perception as well as in her relationships with Morgan and Leon.
Emily's view of Morgan undergoes a transformation, for Morgan the
conjurer has cast his spell on her. He is no longer a frog; she notes
"how odd he had seemed when they first knew him—his hats and
costumes, his pedantic, elderly style of speech. Now he seemed . . .
not ordinary exactly, but understandable." Conversely, her relationship with Leon continues to worsen, especially in their disputes
about the puppet shows. One major confrontation occurs when Leon
questions the choice of Rapunzel for the puppet show (Rapunzel is
a character who escapes imprisonment), insisting that they had
agreed on Sleeping Beauty (a figure who, like Emily, is trapped by
her passivity). He also suggests that Gina, their daughter, cut school
to help them with their show. Emily turns on Leon about his trying
to set the puppet agenda and his suggestion about Gina's missing
school. Their fight impels her towards Morgan's hardware store,
where she confides in Morgan, telling him that Leon has become
rigid and narrow and that he insists that she is the narrow one. The
meeting initiates Emily and Morgan's affair, an affair which eventually results in Emily's becoming pregnant. Morgan's discovery of
the pregnancy and his wife's throwing him out when she learns of it

lead to his making the decision to take care of Emily and the baby. This decision leaves him "drunk with his own decisiveness." Heretofore, he had operated on whims and, puppetlike, had allowed others to shape his life. When Morgan approaches Leon about his relationship with Emily, Leon reacts unemotionally and even offers their apartment to Morgan. Emily and he accept, and Morgan becomes eager "to start his new life": the practitioner of impersonation is eager for a major transformation. Morgan's final transformation to another identity occurs when Reverend Linthicum visits the Meredith apartment and—assuming that Morgan is Leon—reiterates a request he had made by mail that they become part of "Holy Word Entertainment Troupe" in Tindall, Maryland. Taking Leon's name, Morgan completes his transformation into the prince that Emily had sought in Leon. However, the spell is not complete until Bonny, his wife, who has become something of a witch, publishes Morgan's obituary in the Tindall newspaper. A witch emerges as an important mythic component for this story; this mythic turn is foreshadowed in Tyler's description of Emily, who "stayed up late and repaired the witch, the all-purpose stepmother-witch that was used in so many different plays."

In this contemporary fairy tale, the "living happily ever after" becomes life in a small trailer with puppetry as a livelihood, a conclusion that appears to invert the conclusions of "Cinderella" or "Beauty and the Beast." Traditionally, as Maria M. Tatar has indicated, the fundamental law of a fairy tale is that with the "reversal of all conditions prevailing in its introductory paragraphs, the fairy tale ends by enthroning the humble and enriching the impoverished."[19] Despite the seeming lack of enthronement and enrichment, one of the last scenes in the novel describes a performance of Cinderella, a performance which is at once comedic and magical:

> "I'm certain I can fit into it," the second stepsister said. "It's only that I've been shopping all day and my feet are a little swollen."
>
> "Madam. Please," the Prince said in his exhausted voice.
>
> "Well, maybe I could cut off my toes."
>
> "What about you young lady?" asked the Prince. He was looking at Cinderella, who peered out from the rear of the stage. Dressed in burlap, shy and fragile, she inched forward and ap-

proached the Prince. He knelt at her feet with the little glass slipper, or it may have been a shimmer of cellophane. All at once her burlap dress was mysteriously cloaked in a billow of icy blue satin. "Sweetheart!" the Prince cried, and the children drew their breaths in. . . . Their expressions were dazzled and blissful, and even after the house lights came on they continued sitting in their chairs and gazing at the stage, open mouthed.

Like the children who delight in myth and illusion, Morgan and Emily bask in their romance. After the performance, when Morgan walks to the mailbox, he is mistaken for a mail carrier and given additional mail to be taken to the post office. Unable to resist prying into other lives, he must take a peek at the mail; the attraction of the mystery of the "other" has not left Morgan, but when he sees Emily and his son, he suddenly feels lighthearted and begins walking faster. "By the time he reached Emily, he was humming. Everything he looked at seemed luminous and beautiful, and rich with possibilities." Although he still yearns for the mystery of the other, he is able to create his own life script by incorporating and modifying myth, "living happily ever after," and romantic "endless possibilities." Morgan and Emily have discovered "rich possibilities" that enable them to seemingly transcend the limitations of their personal foibles and their economic status. Tyler has demonstrated the need for romance and myth in people's lives, yet, like the puppets, these characters are caught by roles in fairy tales that hold sway over their behavior; as Erich Berne's therapy indicates, like these characters, people can follow these roles or subvert them or convert them to map out their life scripts.

13 / Everybody Speaks

Anne Tyler's fictional landscapes may hover around the vicinity of Baltimore, Maryland, but the fields of play in her novels are located in the realm of the family romance. Beneath the even surface of her works, the troubled world of familial relationships works out its contorted designs. Indeed, Tyler's signature effects as a writer of fiction come largely from the muted dissonance between her surface prose (which often beguiles the unwary reader) and the painful inner work of human creatures seeking meaning and self-authority in a suffocating social world. Tyler's novels typically offer the reader a beguiling surface because the omniscient narrative voice invariably suggests a calm reasonableness, seemingly immune to outrage, large or small. Precisely because Tyler's language does not create oppositional heroes and villains, paper tigers of any stripe, because she democratically parcels out reason and unreason so evenly, individual voices in her novels seem to have an equal claim on the reader, who, through the distribution of point of view in the novels, is invited to participate in the act of creating meaning. Tyler's work is a veritable Quaker meetinghouse in which every voice may be heard as possessing equal opportunity for authority.

When Tyler tells a *New York Times Book Review* interviewer that her interest is in character and day-to-day endurance, she identifies this kind of focus as the result of having "no world view,"[1] which means, I think, that she is not conscious of having an overriding stance which might be identified as ideological. Yet she says in another interview, in regard to Saul, a character in *Earthly Possessions*, that she has nothing against ministers except a concern "with how much right anyone has to change someone, and ministers are people who feel they have that right."[2] This statement suggests a clear point of view with definite ideological implications, even though it denies by its nature the kind of advocacy often associated with ideology. Within Tyler's work the rule of laissez faire governs her fictional practice, and indeed seems to suggest a coherent and consistent view for social democracy—a practice which ideally includes the reader. In the Michaels interview, Tyler speaks of the ideal relationship with the reader, and it is precisely the one we would expect. She indicates that when she receives letters from her readers, she feels that "they in their solitude, and I in mind [*sic*], have somehow managed to touch without either of us feeling intruded upon. We've spent some time on neutral territory, sharing a life that belongs to neither of us."[3] One hopes that among world views, there is room for a view which values with such equanimity respect for all voices, that resists domination, appropriation, and final authority.

Even though "Something You Should Know," the title of the first chapter of *Dinner at the Homesick Restaurant*, suggests a voice of authority speaking of an absolute, the title refers to a number of issues; it is never a single or simple imperative. It is, among other possibilities, an invitation to the reader to understand Pearl Tull, who, in the hands of a different novelist, might have been the character most likely to be nominated Domineering Mother of the Year (among many such stereotypes in contemporary fiction one has only to think of the mother figure in William Styron's *Lie Down in Darkness*, for example). Yet Tyler wants us to *know* Pearl, to know her own frightening and unhappy journey through life, and for this reason she gives Pearl a voice sympathetically (and traditionally) mediated by her imminent death. The reader enters the world that has created Pearl's isolation, her abandonment, her anxiety over the only role which has given her definition and continuing authority: she is a mother. But she can, in her own voice, with the fictional clarity and awareness of last moments, identify herself, in an act of self-knowledge, as an "angry sort of mother"—"continually on edge," "too burdened," "too much alone." It was not a single mother but rather a wife that she had set out to be, for that role was the only one culturally imaginable for a young woman in her time. Her husband Beck's decision to leave her and the children changed her into the anxious, confining, suspicious mother she became; it also made her a household handyman, a clerk at the local grocery store, and an unrealistic liar whose pride made her conceal over a long period of years the permanence of Beck's absence from everyone, including her children.

While "Something You Should Know" speaks to the reader about Pearl's story, which itself will mediate her children's accusations and problems, it also refers to Pearl's desire on her deathbed to advise her youngest son, Ezra, that the children should have had an extra mother, since, although her children are grown (two of them have children of their own), her anxious desire to control cannot permit her, even now, to envision them in the world without the guidance of the protecting figure of a mother. Pearl's fierce definition of family is the nuclear family, a culturally constructed definition she holds to rigidly even in the face of the absence of the father and all of Ezra's desperate attempts to loosen the family's bonds and widen the family's boundaries. The reader is not meant to forget Pearl's failures but to understand them through hearing her voice. And when she settles her head for her final sleep upon the pillow embroidered "*Sleep o faithful warrior upon thy carven pillow*," the reader understands both the irony and the tribute the motto contains.

"Something You Should Know" may also be an announcement to the reader that Pearl is and will continue to be a speaking subject, a voice so intimately bound up in the family romance that it will continue to resonate beyond the moment of her physical death. It seems to me clear, although critics like Mary Elkins disagree,[4] that Pearl's death is indeed an accomplished fact at the end of the first chapter. The long final paragraph, which begins, "It was such a relief to drift, finally. Why had she spent so long learning how," ends with the kind of formal symbolic nexus established by Emily Dickinson's poem, "Because I could not stop for death." Pearl remembers an antique brass bed, complete with linens, that she had seen at an auction years ago, when it was wheeled onto the platform by two men. It is this bed into which now, "behind her eyelids" she climbs and reclines: "Pearl Tull . . . laid her head on the pillow and was borne away to the beach, where three small children ran toward her, laughing, across the sunlit sand." The investment in this symbol is prepared for by Pearl's earlier thought that her end would come with a flash of knowledge and by her subsequent awareness that such a notion is only wishful thinking: "She'd supposed that on her deathbed . . . deathbed! Why, that was this everyday, ordinary Posturepedic, not the ornate brass affair that she'd always envisioned." And in the penultimate chapter of the book, before the announcement of Pearl's death at the beginning of the final chapter, Jenny, the daughter, who has become a physician, tells Ezra that their mother had called to ask if it were true that a person would develop pneumonia from lying on her back for a long time. As the reader learns in the first chapter, Pearl's illness is diagnosed by the family physician as probably pneumonia, although it is not until late in the book that we learn the significance of her pneumonia as a time marker for the novel's structure as well as an instance of Pearl's heroic final attempt at control.

The construction of *Dinner at the Homesick Restaurant*, then, I would argue, chronologically sets the first chapter and the last in a contiguous time frame, with the large center of the novel existing as a kind of space in which the voices, both public and private, of all the characters can be heard in turn and in chorus, making it possible for the reader to enter into the meaning that is completed in the final chapter with all its possible insights, all its ironies. For, at the end of the book, the family at last sits down to dinner, an action that cannot be accomplished while Pearl is alive. The infinitely deferred occasion, the restaurant dinner that could never successfully be enacted, is completed as a family funeral feast, a ritual in which Pearl's absence is marked by presence, as the whole family comes together and breaks bread.

The voice that authorizes this novel and, almost without exception, Tyler's other works, is that of the omniscient narrator using what is most clearly described as indirect discourse. Yet Tyler's third-person narrative practice is so open to the concerns in time of her characters that the voice of authority, that is, the voice of the narrator who knows what is going on inside and outside the characters she creates, operates with almost complete openness and nonjudgmental representation in language. The result of Tyler's narrative treatment gives the reader the sense that her characters are as subjectively whole and completely represented as if they were themselves speaking in the first person at all times, as in the case, for example, of Virginia Woolf's six characters, who are embodied in self-defining soliloquies in *The Waves*. Finally, "Something You Should Know," then, if you are one of Tyler's readers, is that her novels require a readerly attention that is defined by the absence of a traditional narrative omniscience, which, by choice of linguistic markers, irony, etc., privileges the omniscient narrator and creates a hierarchy of reliability and awareness among characters, thereby smoothing the road of reading. Tyler's novels demand a careful and equal attention to voice at all times, whether the voice is that of the narrator or the direct speech or interior thought of individual characters.

In spite of what we think of as a modernist tendency towards the distribution of subjectivity and its effects in Tyler's fiction, her novels have the look of belonging to the kind of work generally identified as classic realism or, in terms of modern and postmodern experimental texts, what might be called "old fashioned" narrative, which is defined by Christopher Nash as a kind of narrative that has a subject "in two important senses of the word: first, as a 'subject matter' that demands to be 'told,' to be 'borne witness to it'"—a narrative that, in short, is *about* something which is "stable, clear, and readily identifiable." For the definition Nash is working with, the second important sense of *subject* involves the presence in narrative of a "'subjectivity'—a person, a 'subject' who experiences this truth to which he or she must bear witness; a being, a mind that is in some vital respect stable, clear, and readily identifiable. 'Old fashioned narrative' wants to be information-full and meaning-full, coming from a solid someone whose intention simply awaits discovery."[5] Although this definition is much too facile and general to be of much use in dealing with the specific novels of, say, Dickens, Austen, or the Brontës, it at least reflects our nostalgic imaginary sense of what narrative was like in a simpler and less self-conscious world of fiction.

The effect that Tyler's work gives of being "old fashioned" grows in part out of her scrupulous attention to the details of her chosen social scene and its domestic rituals, but even a cursory survey of her novels makes it clear that there is not in Tyler's usual fictional practice a single character in a dominant subject-position. Instead, there is, as in Virginia Woolf's best novels, a collection of competing voices, of competing positions, each with its own truth which requires equal witness. One cannot, for example, say that any single character or combination of characters in *Dinner at the Homesick Restaurant* has the story right, even with the revisions that they are forced in the end to make. There is also not, in most of Tyler's novels, an intention that "awaits discovery" from "a solid someone," since Tyler's narrator almost invariably is not given to taking sides, to pushing an ideological or moral claim, or even to finding satisfaction in a "right" or "neat" ending. "Solid someone" is not a phrase that describes any of Tyler's characters either, except perhaps in an often temporarily perjorative way, since for Tyler *solid* usually means rigidly bound and socially overly determined—a condition that the plot of the novel usually works towards changing, as in *The Accidental Tourist* or *Saint Maybe*, in which there are clear reversals of expectation. Tyler's treatment of "solid" characters makes the reader understand their solidity as growing out of a lack of self-realization, which inevitably impinges on their own freedom as well as on that of others, and at the same time also understand the socially constructed nature of such characters, whom Tyler tends to see as victims. The term *solid citizen*, would, I think, have no appeal to Tyler, for the novels suggest that it marks certain characters as *frozen*, solid as ice, incapable of change or of openness to the unexpected, for change seems to present positive possibilities and value in Tyler's novels. Although Tyler tends to conceive the family as an essential and inescapable social force, she is not essentialist in her treatment of characters or their conditions. Whatever is understood as socially constructed can be reconfigured in a moment; the solid can become fluid once again.

If the family romance is the severest and most natural testing ground for the formation of subjectivity, self-awareness, and social relationships with others, we should not be surprised to discover Tyler's consistency in making it the ground of her novels. Even the professional traveler Macon Leary is thrust back into the house of his childhood and forced to set out again on an unexpected journey towards difference, which has nothing to do with his physical presence in London or Paris or Madrid. And *Dinner at the Homesick Restaurant*, which describes a family for whom Pearl has made the house a fortress against the outside world, is full of the obligatory journeys we find in Tyler's novels, which inevitably seem part of an attempt to "find" something or to create a separation, a physical distance from home which may make maturation possible. Yet the characters, for all their journeying, with the possible exception of Beck, must come home to experience some sense of self-awareness.

Tyler's treatment of characters as self-conscious subjects, with power to define and understand themselves as far as possible at any given moment in time, makes it clear that movement through time and experience enables a rereading and new understanding within the potentially ongoing formation of self. The meaning, the triumph of *Dinner at the Homesick Restaurant* resides, I think, in the family members' ability to learn to reread the texts of self and family relationships that have been previously constructed under immense pressure (amid the agony of loss and the terror of adolescence in a dysfunctional family). Even Pearl, blind in her last year of life, searches for a way to read the self that has been lost under the pressure of the role that life has constructed for her. Beck's absence has created a space that she must try to fill: both mother *and* father, she is forced into a compensatory gender role for which nothing has prepared her. During Pearl's last days, Ezra, the "extra" child who is most closely tied to the mother, patiently reads to Pearl from the diary she kept as a girl and as a young woman, until he comes across the entry she has been searching for:

> *I went out behind the house to weed. Was kneeling in the dirt by the stable with my pinafore a mess and the perspiration rolling down my*

back . . . reached for the trowel, and all at once thought, Why I be-
lieve that at just this moment I am absolutely happy. . . . The Bedloe
girl's piano scales were floating out her window, . . . and a bottle fly
was buzzing in the grass, and I saw that I was kneeling on such a
beautiful green little planet. I don't care what else might come about,
I have had this moment. It belongs to me.

After Ezra's retrieval of this moment of potential, after his voice
retextualizes it as a part of the person that is Pearl, she tells him there
is no need to read further, that she has found the confirmation that
she was looking for. What has come after her youthful moment of
epiphany has not often been happy, and it is clear that the promise,
the potential of the disheveled girl, is lost to the demanding, defen-
sive, locked-in person Pearl of necessity becomes.

Shortly before Beck's abandonment, Pearl is shot by an arrow
misfired because of Ezra and Cody's adolescent acting-out of a sib-
ling rivalry. The wound is a visible symbol of the love-hate relationship which both makes separation an imperative and binds the
family together. It is a communal wound from which Ezra never
recovers, because he has never been blamed and so can never be
forgiven, and for Cody, upon whom the blame falls for the shooting
of the mother, the incident is an unimpeachable example of Ezra's
position as the privileged son, since the real guilt belongs to Ezra.
Wounded themselves in many ways, each of the children, like Pearl,
has an experience of rereading the past in order to complete their
understanding of the people they have (and may yet) become. Cody
is the last to come to a revisionary reading of the past, and hence of
the present in which he formulates the self, and it is his father's
articulation of the text of Pearl's life which makes this new vision
possible: "Haven't you all turned out fine—leading good lives, the
three of you. She did it; Pearl did it. I knew she would manage."
Cody for the first time can admit the good times into his memory of
his mother and his family; he can even return to the hateful "archery
trip" and see his mother's "upright form along the grasses, her hair
lit gold, her small hands smoothing her bouquet while the arrow
journeyed on."

One of Pearl's last acts is to make Ezra promise to invite everyone
in her address book to her funeral. The entries are few to begin with,
and the only address not yet canceled by death is Beck's; the perpetu-

ally traveling father is called upon to materialize, to share the funeral feast with his burgeoning family. Pearl's surrogate summoning of Beck to attend the occasion created by her death can be read in several ways, but surely, given the results, the reader is once again asked to remember that in Tyler's fictional practice, character is an open matter, that characters are not set pieces to be moved about on the chessboard of plot, that part of the reader's job is to honor the possibility that a complex subjectivity cannot ever be fully or completely *read*. Pearl's last act is for me an unselfish, healing act that acknowledges the potential of her diary's epiphany. Even though she is not a living participant in the dinner at the Homesick Restaurant, she is, through her action, still a speaking subject. Understanding this is part of "something we should know."

14 / Exploration of a Not-So-Accidental Novel

Anne Tyler's *The Accidental Tourist*, certainly one of her most popular novels, is built on a series of paradoxes and contradictions that somehow lead the reader to a positive conclusion. From the word "Accidental" in the title to the last "Oof" uttered by the protagonist at the end of the book, Tyler walks a thin line balanced between control and chaos, a balance that Macon Leary and the other colorful characters that wander through this novel are constantly losing and regaining. Let us be honest: accidents do not really happen in well-crafted novels, yet a series of accidents in the plot and the characters' attempts to avoid or compensate for these accidents create a pattern of accident/non-accident, control/chaos, and finally order. There is nothing accidental in *The Accidental Tourist*.

Notwithstanding the last statement, the tension and action in this novel are based on an accident that happened before the novel began. Ethan Leary, the twelve-year-old son of Macon and Sarah Leary, "a tall blond sprout of a boy," was murdered by a holdup man in a hamburger joint. Ethan was not supposed to be there; the man had no reason to shoot him. This accident is the catalyst for the other events in the story. Yet if Ethan had been a rule-player, like his father, he would not have "snuck away from the camp" where he was spending the summer. If there is someone to blame—Ethan, a careless camp counselor, the parents for allowing him to go to camp, or the murderer—if there is a mistake made, then is the event an accident? An accident is not just an event that is unintended, but one that is unexpected. Tyler allows Ethan and the other characters to control, yet mismanage, their fates in such a way that we take refuge in the pragmatic proverb, "Accidents do happen."

An inability to accept this truth and a determination to avoid accidents at all costs drive the Leary family close to the edge of comedic eccentricity. The members of the Leary family, Porter, Charles, Rose, Macon, and Sarah (through marriage), consider themselves the epitome of normalcy and conventionality. These traits are pursued with almost religious fervor, as they attempt to lead orderly, reasonable, logical lives. This determined control over events leads to a series of accidents that somehow seems almost logical and planned. This family is not dysfunctional, as modern psychology labels us all, but almost ultra-functional. They have figured out how life can and should work; unfortunately for outsiders, it is a closed system.

Tyler provides, in flashbacks, some reason for the family's behavior. In Chapter 9, we learn about Grandfather Leary, the founder of the bottle-cap business where Charles and Porter still work. Lost in senility, he invented much—nonexistent islands off the coast of Bolivia, a motorcycle that would run a plow, a floating telephone, and even flowers especially grown for funerals that close up in the presence of tears, all while sitting quietly on the porch or in his red leather armchair. Only his daughter Rose (the responsible one) cared for him, maintaining order around the chaos of his mind. Later, after Grandfather Leary's death, and after Macon's wife Sarah has left him, Macon dreams that Grandfather Leary appears and speaks to him: "You've lost the center of your life, Macon." Macon immediately thinks of Ethan, whose death has left such a gaping hole in his and Sarah's life that they no longer have a marriage. (One of the first actions in the book is her telling him she wants a divorce.) Grandfather Leary, however, says that Sarah is "the best of all of us." Like Yeats and other twentieth-century poets, Macon fears "the center cannot hold." He tries to "hold steady" in a world he feels is more and more out of control.

With the exception of Alicia, Macon's mother, all the other Learys lead eccentric conventional lives, another of Tyler's contradictions. Alicia, "a giddy young war widow," disturbed the three serious-minded children with her enthusiasm and spontaneity. Her unexpected treats, such as messy, sticky cotton candy at the circus, an experimental learning community where no one wore clothes, and wild forages in costume on Halloween, were fraught with accidents; "she believed in change as if it were a religion." Leaving the children in the safe environs of Baltimore, the city that for most of Macon's life would be the measure against which he held every other place on earth, she would visit infrequently and comment on how stodgy they had grown. Thus Macon, Charles, Porter, and Rose experienced "accidental" people early in their lives, an experience that for the most part was, if not frightening, at least unpleasant.

Frightened by the chaos they saw in their mother, Macon, his brothers, Porter and Charles, and his sister Rose attempt to prevent other such accidents from occurring in life and to avoid change whenever possible. Both Porter and Charles still work at the factory founded by their grandfather, and they still live in their grandparents' house. Porter whistles; Charles doesn't. Charles, a dreamy, "soft, sweet-faced man, who never seemed to move," deals with the production end of the bottle-cap factory. Porter, the most practical Leary and the only one who understands money, was married once and had three children, but after his divorce he came back home to ·run the family business. Rose, the caretaker of first the bedridden grandmother and then the senile grandfather, takes care of the house and her two brothers. When Macon returns home with a broken leg, he is simply someone else for Rose to care for. Her life is full of polishing silver, planning menus, ironing all the clothes, including the socks, and keeping the food in the pantry in alphabetical order.

Accidents do not occur in Rose's life; she is the antidote for accidents. Until the return of Macon, the three of them had maintained a lifestyle that seemed not to have changed at all, in a sanctuary where no one visited and no one answered the phone. Their evenings were often spent playing a complicated card game invented when they were children. The rules are so convoluted and idiosyncratic that no one outside the family unit, not even Macon's wife Sarah, can figure them out. The game, appropriately called "Vaccination," symbolically keeps them from the contagion of the outside world, making them safe from accidents, which only happen to other people. Because all the Learys have a poor sense of direction, getting lost and wandering around looking for one's destination is not considered an accident, but normal and expected behavior. Control, convention, and planning reach the state of the art in the Leary household.

After Sarah leaves, Macon's own attempts to organize his life so that it requires as little effort as possible, to simplify laundry, meals, and even animal feedings, result in the dreaded accident. As Macon steps on Ethan's skateboard, which he has adapted to roll the laundry basket from the clothesline to the laundry chute, he sets in motion a series of carefully orchestrated "accidents" that create both chaos and change in his well-ordered life. A significant participant in the accident, Ethan's dog Edward, is, paradoxically, Macon's connection with his past life, but leads him into the future and to the Meow-Bow Animal Hospital. There Macon meets Muriel Pritchett, the woman who eventually pulls him out of his safe, cocoon-like life into a world where accidents, both pleasant and painful, are possible.

Muriel Pritchett's life is a series of unplanned events and accidents, the antithesis of the controlled lives of the Leary family. But it is Muriel who rescues Macon from the chaos caused by Edward's sudden aggressive and uncontrollable behavior. She may not be in control of her own life, but she can control animals. Macon notes that even her voice "wandered too far in all directions. It screeched upward; then it dropped to a raspy growl," and that she talks too much. Her out-of-control hair is symbolic of her out-of-control life. Her marriage (ironically, to a man named Norman, who, in spite of his name, suggesting "normal," cannot create an ordinary safe life for Muriel) was the result of an accidental pregnancy, which produced her now seven-year-old son, Alexander, an allergic, scrawny, awkward child. But Muriel is not a whiner or complainer; she and

Alex are survivors. She has "about fifty jobs, if you count them all up. You could say I'm lucky; I'm good at spotting a chance." She has adapted to the chaotic world that Macon fears. When Macon looks at the childhood snapshot which she gave him, he sees "her fierceness—her spiky, pugnacious fierceness as she fought her way toward the camera with her chin set awry and her eyes bright slits of determination." Muriel's accidental entrance into Macon's life when, although unaware, he is in a state of crisis, is the accident that saves his life.

Macon's accident, however, has repercussions beyond the changes in his own life. Although he finds that, in the Leary family at least, one can go home again (which he does quite easily), he cannot quite shut out the disorderly elements of the outside world. One of these is his publisher, Julian Edge, whose last name suggests what he may present to Macon and his family. Julian, long fascinated by the behavior of the Leary family, and attracted to Rose, who has always been too busy caring for someone to ever consider marriage, worms his way into their lives, like a snake into the Garden of Eden. The conventionality of their lives, with its order and stability, seems a little like paradise when compared to his own messy divorce and his life in a singles apartment building. By Thanksgiving Julian has become a part of the family, to some extent, sharing Thanksgiving dinner with them, even eating Rose's suspect, dry turkey, which the others avoid for fear of food poisoning, based on their experience with other cooking disasters. Julian, the voice from the edge, stands between the real world and the world created by the Learys; he does not destroy this paradise that he has discovered. Instead he falls in love with Rose and marries her, with Macon's apprehensive blessing. Although Rose protests that "Love is what it's all about," the pull of the old way of life proves too strong. Shortly after the honeymoon in Hawaii, she is back at home taking care of Charles and Porter. She suffers from the Leary family's inability to find places, and each time she leaves Julian's apartment, she cannot find her way back. Julian, however, has a secret strength, foreign to the Learys: he is flexible. He not only hires the efficient Rose to organize and run his office, but also moves into the house with her and her brothers. Julian is the man in the middle, the one with a foot in both worlds, able to appreciate and function in both. Unlike Charles and Porter, he is not caught in a rut so narrow and so comfortable that there is no need for change, nor is he as volatile and unpredictable as Muriel, who thrives on change and the unexpected but needs the steadiness of Macon for a center.

If Julian is the middle of the continuum between total control and chaos, and his marriage to Rose is presented as a working model, what are we to think about the un-accidents or the non-accidents that made up the marriage of Macon and Sarah? Macon was aware of the need to control the relationship from the outset. Although they met accidentally at a party, the "accident" was the result of Sarah's misinterpreting Macon's shyness as his being stuck-up. Macon decided he needed to control his eagerness by maintaining an emotional distance. The more distant he was, the more attracted she was by his unavailabilty. They were engaged for three years, a conventional, safe time period, and by the time they were married, Macon "was locked inside the stand-offish self he'd assumed when he and she first met." Sarah would always see him as cool-headed, unemotional, and safe. There was nothing accidental in Ethan's birth, which occurred seven years after they were married; he was, of course, an only child. It is only after Ethan's death, after Sarah has filed for divorce, after Macon's fall (both literally and symbolically), that Macon, in a desperate attempt to regain stability and control, agrees to meet Sarah at his favorite restaurant, The Old Bay. As Sarah talks about a legal separation, Macon asks, "Have you ever considered we might have another baby?" The loss in their lives, the loss that doomed the marriage, is not so much the accidental death of their son as it is their inability to share and deal with the suffering. Macon, in his attempt to "hold steady" and to adjust to the loss of their only son in a world that he had always believed was dangerous and evil, has shut out Sarah. She sees him as "ossified," "encased," "like something in a capsule." The Old Bay restaurant symbolizes to both of them the Old Way of life. Even the names of restaurants are not accidental in this novel.

In spite of her complaints, it is Sarah who makes the last effort to save the marriage. She has lived in the real world, the one that Macon feared, and has decided to return to the safety and security of marriage. Macon returns after a flight to Canada to their old house where Sarah has been living alone, and the two attempt to re-create the safe and conventional marriage they had shared before Ethan's death. Both have been cowed by the uncontrollable chaos of the real world. They pursue "normal" married activities; they buy fertilizer, read the newspaper, buy a needed couch. Sarah has decided that "there are worse things than boring," and Macon agrees that "after a certain age, it seems to me you can only choose what to lose." Although both seem to have accepted marriage as a sanctuary, a place where accidents would not happen anymore, Macon's dreams tell him that something is missing. Unlike Sarah, who has tried the world of accidents and mishaps and found it unpleasant, Macon misses the accidental, uncontrollable world to which Muriel introduced him.

There is pattern and order in this book of accidental happenings. Even though Macon's final decision, to choose possibility rather than certainty, non-conformity over convention, and chance over regulation and control, is heroic and difficult, it does not guarantee success, happiness, or less pain for himself, Muriel, or Sarah. Unlike Julian, who was able to compromise and bring both worlds together, Macon must choose between the certain and the unsure; compromise is not an option. Although many of the events that trigger responses in this novel are the result of or the reaction to accidents, the two events that bring the novel to a close are deliberate and planned. Muriel deliberately goes to Paris to be with Macon, but also for the joy of traveling. Sarah goes to Paris to help Macon and to finish his work for him. Change wins out over stasis. Macon and Sarah change places on the continuum between control and chaos. She settles for safety and control; he balances in the middle, finally being able to admit that accidents do happen and not all of them are bad. He leaves the comfortable winged armchair in which he has traveled most of his life; he forsakes his identity as an "accidental tourist" and becomes a participant in life.

Anne Tyler's *The Accidental Tourist* is a tightly crafted, balanced novel. If one believes that in the eye of God there are no accidents, then it is easy to see the connection and meaning behind the "accidents" in this novel. Unlike a moralistic fable, *The Accidental Tourist* admits the frailties of human beings and the possibility of choices which are not simply between good and evil. The characters make choices throughout the novel, change their minds, and attempt to undo what they have done. Somehow, however, even at the end of the novel, the joke is on us, for it is one of Macon's accidents—in giving directions to the taxi driver, something we know he is no good at—that facilitates the fortuitous meeting with the woman he has chosen. "Arrêtez!" he cries, but Macon's life does not stop here; it begins again, and accidents are waiting to happen.

15 / *The Accidental Tourist* and *The Odyssey*

his is very much an accidental paper. I took the first step towards writing it four years ago, when my department still required all freshman composition students to read *The Odyssey*. I had then read *The Accidental Tourist* only once and not liked it much (perhaps because Macon dumps an old wife *with my name* to find happiness with a younger woman), but I thought idly that the plot might make it a good companion piece to *The Odyssey*. And it did. My students ended up loving the book—and writing about it well— and I ended up loving the book, and being convinced that the re- semblances between it and *The Odyssey* were more than accidental.

Of course, the situations of the protagonists are similar. Odysseus has to choose between returning to his wife or deserting her for one of a number of alluring consorts—Nausikaa, Kirke, the Sirens, and, most importantly, Kalypso—just as Macon must choose between Sarah and Muriel. But the resemblances between the protagonists do not end there.

Odysseus and Macon are both famous travelers and accidental tourists. Odysseus is literally a legend in his own time: in Book VII, he hears his own exploits sung twice by the Phaiakian bard. Macon's guidebooks make him a famous traveler too, as we are reminded when he meets his fan Lucas Loomis, who tells him, "You're my hero! You've improved my trips a hundred percent. You're the one who told me about those springy items that turn into clotheslines." Macon is also, of course, the quintessential accidental tourist: he never looked for a job involving travel any more than he chose the loss of his son, the departure of his wife, his broken leg, or the nervous breakdown of his dog, that all together precipitate him into a new life. It may seem odder to think of Odysseus as an accidental tourist—yet he is, at least, an extremely reluctant one. He feigned madness to try to avoid the Trojan War, and his single most important goal, during the war and thereafter, is to get home. He knows nothing of the natives anywhere he goes, and his wanderings, at least from the time he is told to go to Hades, are entirely involuntary. The subtitle for Macon's first article—"*I Feel So Break-Up, I Want to Go Home*"—could as easily apply to Odysseus, who is increasingly prone to crying as his journey continues. Just as Odysseus expects exotic creatures like the Kyklops to observe Greek customs of hospitality, Macon seeks out places abroad that remind him of home: the "Yankee Delight," the "New America," the "U.S. Open," "My American Cousin." Both Odysseus and Macon are wary of foreign food—unlike his crew, Odysseus seldom gets in trouble by eating—and Macon refuses alcohol on planes as resolutely as if it were the fruit of the lotus. Odysseus ends his travels at the lavish banquet of the Phaiakians, where even feasting and merrymaking have become wearisome to him. Homer says:

> Only Odysseus
> time and again turned craning toward the sun,
> impatient for day's end, for the open sea.
> Just as a farmer's hunger grows, behind
> the bolted plow and share, all day afield,

drawn by his team of winedark oxen: sundown
is benison for him, sending him homeward
stiff in the knees from weariness, to dine;
just so, the light on the sea rim gladdened Odysseus.[1]

Macon, of course, reacts to travel in the same way: "It was one of
Macon's bad habits to start itching to go home too early." He ends
his trip to England "subsisting on imperishable groceries and lukewarm soft drinks because he couldn't face another restaurant,"
hating the long afternoon of the plane flight—"It was afternoon for
hours and hours, through drinks and lunch and drinks again—all
of which he waved away," dreaming irrationally that his wife would
greet him at home.

The resemblances between Penelope and Sarah are more tenuous,
partly, of course, because the plot of *The Accidental Tourist* ironically
inverts that of *The Odyssey*. In *The Accidental Tourist*, it is the wife
who leaves home and the husband who stays, first in the house of his
marriage and then in the one of his childhood. But Sarah has something of Penelope's timeless beauty, with her "halo of curls, the way
her coat fell around her in soft folds, her firm, springy walk in trim
pumps with wineglass heels," and something of the vanity that
Penelope shows when she displays herself before the suitors; Sarah
seems concerned with maintaining her tan. Like Penelope, Sarah
remains chaste even during her separation from Macon, and of
all the major characters in *The Accidental Tourist*, she seems least
changed by her experiences. In Paris she tries to help Macon's back
heal by giving him "deadly" pills to induce a sleep that is not "normal" but "a kind of burial"; Odysseus also is deeply, unnaturally
asleep in the boat that finally returns him to Ithaka. After his twenty-
year absence, Odysseus returns to a wife who seems changed not at
all; during her brief reunion with Macon, Sarah also seems un-
changed, and their marriage seems exactly the same. As Macon complains to her, "By God, if that doesn't sum up every single thing that's
wrong with being married. 'The trouble with you is, Macon—' and,
'I know you better than you know yourself, Macon—.'" The sameness of marriage that is reassuring in *The Odyssey* comes to seem a
trap in *The Accidental Tourist*.

The funniest and most intriguing resemblances between characters in the two books, though, are between Muriel Pritchett and the

various enchantresses who try to lure Odysseus, to make him stay with them. Muriel is pushy (so much so that my students, all women, typically do not like her when they first meet her) and as persistent as any Siren, from her very first meeting with Macon—"I'm a divorsy myself. I know what you're going through"—to the end of the book: "She sent him an anonymous letter pasted together from magazine print: *Don't FoRget tO BUY plANe Ticket for MuRiel.*" Muriel certainly dresses like a seductress, wearing "a V-necked black dress splashed with big pink flowers, its shoulders padded and its skirt too skimpy; and preposterously high-heeled sandals" to meet Macon at the Meow-Bow. At other times she wears ankle straps—Macon "never could figure out why ankle straps were so seductive"—and "silvery dust . . . on her eye lids." Her lipstick is dark red, like her outrageously long fingernails. And the scene with Muriel's parents suggests, seriously enough, that "Muriel was just on the lookout for anybody in trousers." As definitely as Kirke and Kalypso seduce Odysseus, Muriel seduces Macon.

Especially striking are the parallels between Muriel and Kalypso. When we first see Kalypso in *The Odyssey*, she is weaving; so does Macon think that Muriel has "webbed his mind with her stories, wound him in slender steely threads from her life." Kalypso lives in a cave shrouded by vines; Muriel draws Macon into her house as if it were a cave ("She took one of his wrists very gently and she drew him into the house, still not fully opening the door, so that he had a sense of slipping through something, of narrowly evading something"). Kalypso takes Odysseus in when he is absolutely desperate, washed naked and alone onto her shores; so Muriel takes Edward in at the Meow-Bow, telling Macon that the dog can stay "if you're desperate." When forced to relinquish Odysseus, Kalypso complains to Hermes:

But it was I who saved him. . . .
I fed him, loved him, sang that he should not die
nor grow old, ever, in all the days to come.[2]

She sounds remarkably like Muriel telling Macon about an earlier relationship:

His divorce was awful. . . . He said he didn't think he could ever trust a woman again. It was months before he would spend the night, even; he didn't like going to sleep when a woman was in the same room. But bit by bit I changed all that. He relaxed. He got to be a whole different man. . . . We started talking about getting married. Then he met an airline stewardess and eloped with her within the week. . . . It was like I had, you know, cured him, just so he could elope with another woman. . . . Would you leave me and go home to your wife?

I think that just for a moment in *The Odyssey* Homer lets Kalypso's claim to Odysseus seem valid, just as Muriel's claim to Macon seems to be. *Both* women are therapeutic for the heroes, and both heroes *need* therapy sometimes.[3]

Thus both Odysseus and Macon, battered by the world, find themselves compelled to hurt one woman or the other. And this idea leads to their deepest resemblance: their scars. Odysseus, of course, has a scar on his leg, acquired during a boar hunt in his youth, the scar that enables Eurykleia to identify him. Macon's leg is likewise scarred from his accident in the basement. When the cast comes off, "Macon's leg emerged dead-white and wrinkled and ugly. When he stood up, his ankle wobbled. He still had a limp. Also, he'd forgotten to bring different trousers and he was forced to parade back through the other patients in his one-legged summer khakis, exposing his repulsive looking shin. He wondered if he'd ever return to his old, unbroken self."

Odysseus's scar is more than just a mark on his leg: his very name, in ancient Greek, means "Trouble," and may imply both that he suffers trouble and that he inflicts it on others.[4] Odysseus's scar is an emblem of who he is. Macon's scar also becomes a metaphor for his identity, an outward and visible sign of his depression over Ethan's death and Sarah's departure. In a climactic passage in the novel, after Macon has first slept with Muriel, Tyler describes him: "He turned over and found Muriel. She sighed in her sleep and lifted his hand and placed it upon her stomach. The robe had fallen open, he felt smooth skin, and then a corrugated ridge of flesh jutting across her abdomen. The Caesarean, he thought. And it seemed to him, as he sank back into his dreams, that she had as good as spoken aloud. *About your son*, she seemed to be saying: *Just put your hand here. I'm scarred, too. We're all scarred. You are not the only one.*" Macon seems to accept his psychic scars as part of his identity when he tells Charles, "I'm kind of, you could say, damaged merchandise."

Other resemblances between *The Odyssey* and *The Accidental Tourist* are smaller and more teasing—*Is* it an accident that Macon's cat is named Helen?—but fun to play with anyhow. One of the strangest things about *The Odyssey* to modern readers is that Ithaka seems hardly to have changed during Odysseus's twenty-year absence: when the hero returns, his wife still loves him, the old servants are still faithful, his dog still remembers him. Macon's grandfather's house is just like Ithaka: Macon comments when he returns that Charles "made it sound as if Macon had been gone just a few weeks or so—as if his entire marriage had been just a brief trip elsewhere." And Macon's family does not take well to the outside suitors Julian and Muriel. Dreams and omens play a prominent role in *The Odyssey*, invariably foreshadowing the hero's successful return home. So are Macon's dreams important in *The Accidental Tourist*: they do not foretell the future, but they reveal truths about his feelings at the time, his regret over Ethan and Sarah as well as his desire for Muriel.

This difference between the functions of dreams may point to one of the most important differences between the two works as a whole. From Book I in *The Odyssey*, when Athena speaks to Zeus, Odysseus's return seems a foregone conclusion: willed by the gods, predicted by omens, naturally and inevitably right. The universe of *The Accidental Tourist* does not work that way; we sense that Macon could have made the other choice. Both times when I taught the novel, there was a vocal minority of students who finished the book still thinking that Macon should stay with Sarah.[5] And it is interesting to speculate that that was the ending Tyler originally intended. In a 1989 interview with Alice Hall Petry, Tyler said, "I wrote an entire final chapter in which Macon stayed with Sarah and then realized I couldn't do it—not only because it spoiled the dramatic line of the plot but also because it meant abandoning Alexander."[6] Alexander (Muriel's son from a previous marriage) is, of course, another essential difference between the two works. In *The Odyssey*, the only character who definitely changes through time is Odysseus's son Telemakhos. But for Macon and Sarah, the changing, growing person who could have held their marriage together is Ethan, their son, and he is dead. It is Alexander who can tie Macon to life, its trouble as well as its joy: "Macon tightened his grip [on Alexander's hand] and felt a pleasant kind of sorrow sweeping through him. Oh, his life had regained all its old perils. He was forced to worry once again about nuclear war and the future of the planet. He often had the same secret, guilty thought that had come to him after Ethan was born: *From this time on I can never be completely happy*."

I prefer the ending of the novel as we have it. Muriel is a seductress, all right, but she offers Macon not death—as the Sirens offer Odysseus—but life; not eternal, monotonous sameness and isolation—as Kalypso offers Odysseus—but "the real adventure . . . the flow of time . . . as much adventure as anyone could wish." It is Muriel, not Sarah, who offers Macon the fuller identity, as a husband, a substitute father, an in-law, a neighbor. But Tyler's ending is merely happy, not inevitable.

16 / *Breathing Lessons*

A Domestic Success Story

Although Anne Tyler's 1988 novel, *Breathing Lessons*, won the Pulitzer Prize for Fiction, it was criticized by a number of readers—even those who usually praise her fiction.[1] Perhaps part of this dissatisfaction with the work stemmed from the position Tyler had reached by the end of the 1980s. Seen as a chronicler of the macabre contemporary Southern life she treated with such poignance and understanding, she had a good reputation as a comparatively "undiscovered" writer. Critics liked to think they had found a new voice in fiction. Unfortunately, they often saw her as a latter-day Flannery O'Connor. Tyler's world was less grotesque than O'Connor's had been, with more of the real South about it, but it was definitely a local-color construct. Characters were defined through their idiosyncrasies, and place played a large share in the fiction's success.

With *Breathing Lessons*, Tyler left the Southern milieu and wrote a more universal story. Maggie, the spunky but hardly radical wife, could have lived anywhere; her problems were those of women anywhere in the United States—perhaps anywhere in the world. They were problems of autonomy, of dependence, of confusion about roles. (Was the mother-and-grandmother role more important than the wife role, and where did the mother-in-law role fit in?) Maggie was plagued with Everywoman's role confusion, not just that of a Southern woman.

Breathing Lessons also shared what critic Ann Romines has recently labeled "the home plot," a narrative about the value, the ritual, of domestic life that runs the risk of shutting readers out, particularly those who do not cope with housekeeping and family on a daily basis.[2] When attention to housekeeping becomes the dominant narrative line, readers trained to look for more visibly dramatic plots are confused. Few other Tyler novels had been "domestic" in this way, with the protagonist more concerned about fixing lunch or celebrating a holiday in a ritualized way than about "big" life-enhancing, or life-threatening, decisions. That there are very few "big" decisions in *Breathing Lessons* may be one of Tyler's themes: that most life decisions are not announced by spectacular fireworks.

When Maggie runs away from her loving, long-suffering but inarticulate husband Ira in a fit towards freedom, her longing for Fig Newtons in Nell's Grocery is hardly the stuff of Greek tragedy. Yet her act signals her recognition of her own perilous balance: her quest to discover who Maggie is. The answer seems to be that Maggie is the woman married to Ira. She must then ask who Ira is. She must also bring herself to ask the haunting question, unexpressed until the novel's end, what their life, filled as it is now with frustration about their children, has finally meant. Accidental as Ira's courtship of Maggie seems, in those moving flashbacks that are a trademark of Tyler's fiction, his love is unquestioning; at this time in her life, however, Maggie needs reassurance. Her self-image ("She was only forty-eight and her health was perfect, and in spite of what some people might think, she was capable of anything she set her mind to") is at variance with other people's views of her: "Ira thought she was a klutz. Everybody did. She had developed a sort of clownish, pratfalling reputation, somehow. . . . She had assumed when she married Ira that he would always look at her the way he'd looked at her that first night, when she stood in front of him in her trousseau negligee. . . . He had looked directly into her eyes, and it seemed he wasn't even breathing. She had assumed that would go on forever."

The importance of this seemingly unadventurous novel is that it charts so accurately the unadventurous life of a middle-aged American couple. The Morans maintain their individual personalities, and their individually complicated relationship, through the twenty-eight years of their marriage. It is here that the novel opens, with a narrative strategy so clearly chosen to alienate the reader that one begins to appreciate the story-telling skills Tyler has honed to perfection. Tyler does not ask a reader to accompany her and her characters out of sympathy for the personae she creates; rather, she forces the reader to read her story with admiration for her artistic daring throughout the book.

The brilliance of Tyler's casting the novel as a journey to the funeral of a man their age, defined only as the husband of Maggie's friend Serena, becomes clear as the novel draws to its purposely unsatisfying end. As primal rituals of life, weddings and funerals merge and become one; Serena underscores this trope when she asks her friends to sing the same songs at Max's funeral that they had sung at his wedding. As if re-creating the marriage scene were not enough, at Max's wake Serena shows silent movies of the wedding—forcing her friends back into not only the aural enactment of the past but the visual as well. When Book I ends with Ira and Maggie having sex in Serena's bedroom chair and Serena angrily banishing them from the wake, Tyler returns the reader to the sexually charged atmosphere of the courtship and wedding era. Twenty-eight years earlier, when Maggie and Ira, and Serena and Max, married, the rituals legitimized their sexual relationships.

For all the novel's uneventfulness, desire chronicles the characters' emotions in *Breathing Lessons*. The closing scene of Book I enables the reader to better understand Ira's break with his dependent family, his asserting himself and marrying Maggie despite his other financial responsibilities. And understanding Ira gives the reader momentum to untangle the rest of the Moran family story, as Tyler focuses on the failed marriage of young Jesse Moran—Maggie and Ira's son—to his even younger wife Fiona. Although Maggie yearns to care for Leroy, her lone granddaughter, her plotting to reconcile Jesse and Fiona is not only futile; as Tyler presents the situation, it is unsympathetic. By the time of what might have been Jesse and Fiona's reconciliation, Ira has lost patience with both his son and his wife. Instead of urging Fiona to return, Ira tells her that Jesse is no good, and that Maggie has been misleading her:

> "She had no business telling you that," Ira said to Fiona. "It's Maggie's weakness: She believes it's all right to alter people's lives. She thinks the people she loves are better than they really are, and so then she starts changing things around to suit her view of them."
>
> "That's not one bit true," Maggie said.
>
> "But the fact is," Ira told Fiona calmly, "Jesse is not capable of following through with *anything*, not even a simple cradle. He's got some lack; I know he's my son, but he's got some lack, and you might as well face up to it. He's not a persevering kind of person. He lost that job of his a month ago. . . . He's seeing another girl too."

Ira's brusque honesty about his son returns the reader to the key early scene of his confrontation with his manipulative father, in which Tyler shows Ira doing whatever is necessary to marry Maggie—even if it means leaving his kin. In contrast to Ira's healthy willfulness, Jesse finishes nothing, not even the clumsy cradle for his coming child.

Ira's relentless truthfulness counters Maggie's pervasive confusion. In her need to make everyone happy, she has lost sight of what she needs to be happy herself, but the resolution of *Breathing Lessons* shows the middle-aged woman coming to some sense of what will be necessary. Watching their young, childless, romantic neighbors, Maggie turns away from the window and towards Ira with the omnipresent question of her life, "Oh, Ira . . . what are we two going to live for, all the rest of our lives?" She has come to the point of being able to voice the major problem of her middle age; Tyler's structure suggests that she is on her way to being able to answer that query as well as ask it.

As a woman once trapped in social convention and finally able to act to bring change to her life, Maggie hardly qualifies as the "meddlesome" character critic Sandra Gilbert finds her. Neither Gilbert's comparison of the novel with a soap opera, nor her criticism of what she reads as Tyler's "condescension" towards the "dreary and dull" Morans, is accurate.[3] *Breathing Lessons* is an integral part of Tyler's oeuvre, particularly when it is read as a continuation of her 1977 novel, *Earthly Possessions*—and a possible foreshadowing of the 1991 *Saint Maybe*. Although both these novels have a more sensational cast of characters, including some of Tyler's most grotesque Southerners, they are linked with *Breathing Lessons* through their attention to the way characters come to beneficence. Tyler's focus during these fifteen years moved from a sharp interrogation of peculiar characters to a creation of often ordinary characters that are somehow blessed. By the time of *Saint Maybe*, she had switched genders, using a man rather than a woman as the long-suffering head of a loving family. Or perhaps the character of Ira Moran was more central to *Breathing Lessons* than readers had recognized.

In retrospect, *Earthly Possessions* seems to be a first step in Tyler's changing narrative aim. That novel centers on the identity, and the difficult self-determination, of Charlotte Ames. Webbed in by the demands of many helpless family members and parishioners from her husband's church, Charlotte (suggestive of the title *Charlotte's Web*) has decided to leave her husband. Marriage seems the reason for her draining life, even though Tyler is careful to leave Charlotte's relationship with Saul shadowy; the novel suggests that Saul is not intentionally at fault. Ironically, at the moment of her decision to leave him, as she stands in line to draw money out of the bank, Charlotte is taken hostage by Jake, a bank robber. Working, as she often does, to equate narrative line with metaphor, Tyler here makes Charlotte a hostage of both the gunman and her own life. She may as well go with the armed young robber; she has no personal volition anyway.

Tyler's opening description is more dramatic than her writing in *Breathing Lessons*: Charlotte recounts, "The marriage wasn't going well and I decided to leave my husband." Her terse idiom is at odds with the kind of good woman she appears to be (even her affair with her brother-in-law seems aimed at helping him); Charlotte is about to take action. Younger than Maggie, she has finally learned that no one is going to save her, fairy tales about princes to the contrary. But Charlotte's victimization has begun in infancy, with her confused sense of her own parentage, and therefore she has trouble sloughing off the socially approved role of good woman. Married to a preacher, programmed to help everyone in need, Charlotte lives at the center of the fragile web of human life.

One of her personal dilemmas is her need to separate herself from her dying mother, a woman as parasitic in death as she has been in life. Incapacitated by her obesity, Charlotte's mother has taught her passivity. But she has also bound her daughter to her because of her physical helplessness. In a memorable death scene, which is also Charlotte's coming-to-life episode, Tyler writes, "Then I had my mother to myself. For I couldn't let loose of her yet. She was like some unsolvable math problem you keep straining at, worrying the edges of, chafing and cursing. She had used me up, worn me out, and now was dying without answering any really important questions or telling me a single truth that mattered. A mound on the bed, opaque, intact. I was furious." After her death, and after having identified the child in the salvaged photo as her mother, not herself, Charlotte comes to her own truth: "I saw that all of us lived in a sort of web, criss-crossed by strings of love and need and worry."

Another of her psychological problems has been to fill the gap left by her father's absence. When she takes over his photography studio, professing to be unskilled at his art but taking successful pictures anyway, she never commits herself to the profession. She dodges the responsibility of naming her role. Her dreamlike reveries in the studio, photographing people who come to her at all hours of day and night, distance her from the work that might define her. Tyler's portrayal suggests that neither action nor time has any reality for Charlotte—has it been seventeen years since she took over the studio? Has it been all these days that she has been held hostage by the young, needy bank robber? Although intellectually she "knows" certain things, Charlotte's socialized role keeps her from acting.

In fact, despite new levels of understanding, it is not until the end of *Earthly Possessions* that Charlotte acts for herself. When she does walk away from Jake, who threatens to shoot her even though he really wants her not as a hostage but as a grandmother for his baby, she relies for the first time on her sense of what she wants to happen. She takes a risk. "I continued up the street, already feeling the hole that would open in my back. I passed an elderly couple in evening clothes. Still no shot rang out. I saw now that it never would. I released my breath, marveling at my slipperiness: I had glided through so many dangers and emerged unscathed. As smooth as silk I swerved around a child, passed a glass-boxed woman in front of a theater. . . ." Breathing on her own, achieving the autonomy of self-regulation, the dreamy Charlotte resumes her life at home with Saul and his misfits—but with the great difference that she is now living the way she wants to live.

The impatience the reader feels for Charlotte accrues partly from Tyler's making *Earthly Possessions* a kind of character study: there is little to follow, narratively, except the character's development. That irritation is softened somewhat in Tyler's characterization of Maggie in *Breathing Lessons*, a novel which embroiders the theme of women's being used and worn, left without ambition for themselves as they dutifully help others. Maggie is caught in the same web of dependency that traps Charlotte. People depend on her, and she initiates their dependence because she is comfortable in that role. Whether a hostage in fact, or a willing hostage to marriage and motherhood, Tyler's Charlotte and Maggie lead similar lives.

Tyler's wry irony makes itself known as she draws Charlotte and Maggie as different from Serena, a woman who could, and did, look out for herself. As she said when Maggie asked how she knew Max was the right man to marry, "It's just time to marry, that's all. . . . I'm so tired of dating! I'm so tired of keeping up a good front! I want to sit on the couch with a regular, normal husband and watch TV for a thousand years. It's going to be like getting out of a girdle; that's exactly how I picture it." Forthright in the direction she intends to go, Serena dyes her wedding dress so that she can wear it again, orders her friends to take part in Max's funeral, and throws Ira and Maggie out of her house for their misbehavior at the funeral. She makes rules that benefit her, and stands by them. *Breathing Lessons* is enriched by Serena's presence, because she differs from both Maggie and the victimized women of *Earthly Possessions*.

The sympathy with which Tyler presents Maggie's devastated dream of romance so that the reader shares that sympathy marks *Breathing Lessons* as both realistic and suggestive. Like beings from other atmospheres who must learn to breathe the earth's air, human beings too need survival skills. For women who are forced to be givers, one of those survival skills is finding oxygen to breathe for themselves. Tyler's fictions are filled with women hyperventilating, choking, struggling with the most basic of life processes, self-assertion. Usually, women who have difficulty breathing also have difficulty being.

In Maggie's case, her understanding of social paradigms is faulty. She has led her life on the premise that "love" leads to weddings, and after weddings come children, children who then lead lives that culminate in other weddings and other children. When the pattern is broken, life provides few alternative scripts—it asks characters to write their own. Ira had long since been writing his own life, but Maggie was new at understanding such responsibility.

In *Saint Maybe*, Tyler plays with the definition of "saint" by creating yet another self-effacing protagonist. In this 1991 novel, however, the giving, womanly figure is a man. Ian Bedloe is the adolescent who knows that he has driven his beloved older brother to his death; because of his guilt, he cares for the three children that remain from Danny's marriage to Lucy (only one of whom may be his brother's, perhaps not even that one). His self-abnegation as an otherwise normal young man is both commendable and strange, and Tyler's wry title suggests the possible ambivalence in his situation.

In this novel, the theme of building—and finishing—a baby's cradle becomes a key metaphor. Once Ian has finally married, after more than twenty years of caring for his inherited family, and his wife is pregnant, he spends loving hours building a cherry cradle for his unborn child. Unlike Jesse, who had the whimsical notion of making a cradle from a kit for his child, but never did the work, Ian becomes a master craftsman. In his serious concern for the cradle's exact balance, the careful dovetail fit of the wood, he rises above the common. He becomes the hero of Tyler's modest narrative.

The goodness of Ian's sacrifice of twenty years of his adult life, caring for the sometimes unappreciative children, only one of whom was his blood kin, is reified in the closing scene of *Saint Maybe*. Here Ian lifts his infant son from the safety of his cradle and carries him joyfully into the downstairs living room, where his relatives and friends await him. As he starts down the stairs, Tyler writes, "He felt a kind of echo effect—a memory just beyond his reach." The scene he visualizes is Danny's presenting Daphne, but "then the moment slid sideways like a phonograph needle skipping a groove" and it was Lucy, his wife-to-be, he was presenting. The separation between characters, and between events, is one of the "facts" Tyler calls into question in her novel about lives lived out of necessity rather than will. As Ian had concluded in another of the novel's final scenes, "In the end you had to accept that the day would never arrive when you finally understood what they [other people] were all about."

By featuring the same kind of character in her latest novel, Tyler suggests that it is the trait of lovingness in which she is interested, not so much women's roles and their problems of definition. For Ian Bedloe risked none of his masculinity—as Rita's memory of his waiting for her to come to bed on their wedding night suggests—spending his years waiting on his children, the children that were not in any way his. And one of the closing narratives of *Saint Maybe* is the children's retelling an episode when they all had the flu and Ian rose from his sickbed to dress and go to the store for the hearts of palm that they wanted. His act, then, of thanking them for remembering that taste, and making him go for the food, caps the characterization of the man as saint, serving others in the fullness of his love, and working past the conflicts between self-abnegation and self-recovery in the penance for his own earlier misunderstanding.

His early injustice to Danny's young wife, the impoverished and frantic Lucy, drives Ian's great love for her children—and, years later, his great love for his wife Rita and their son. Tyler has again left grotesques behind as she inscribes a narrative not just of domesticity, but also of family love and sacrifice. Jay Parini, in his review of what he calls Tyler's "most sophisticated" novel, praises its ability to "celebrate family life without erasing the pain and boredom that families almost necessarily inflict."[4] Parini marvels, too, at the way Tyler manages to make Ian so appealingly heroic.

Religion and community, and Ian's active part in both, also mark a difference between *Saint Maybe* and the earlier *Earthly Possessions* and *Breathing Lessons*. Charlotte tried to find family meaning and tradition in the objects of her existence, whereas Maggie's search was inner-directed, and often focused on her physical stability (her breathing itself). Each woman lived separate from a larger community. In Charlotte's case, such isolation was ironic, because she could easily have been involved in her husband's ministry; her isolation, however, was self-imposed, and could not diminish until her sense of self was repaired. In Maggie's case, although she wanted to create a community, it was to be the community of her own nuclear family. The young Ian, who left college to care for his brother's family, had little rationale for his behavior. Becoming an active church-goer, a part of the brotherhood and sisterhood that linked people by their names ("Brother Ian," "Sister Harriet"), led him to enough self-confidence that he could make good decisions about his children—and, accordingly, his own marriage and family.

Ian lived within the church, and its structure supported his life. In contrast, the suicide of his sister-in-law Lucy stemmed from her complete isolation: standing alone, uneducated and untrained, bewildered by the bad luck she has had with both her marriages as well as with married men who pretend to be unmarried, she is isolated also from the seemingly kind Bedloe family, who snobbishly refrain from giving her and her three young children any real help. Part of Lucy's difference lies in her not knowing how to keep house, how to assess and accomplish the domestic rituals the Bedloes perform efficiently. Her strange menus, complete with candles, separate her from her in-laws, just as her attire when she goes for an unsuccessful job interview shows her to be naive. Bell Bedloe comments to the children that their mother is "overdressed"—but she does not offer Lucy any practical help.

Yet, in contrast to their behavior towards Lucy, Bell and Doug Bedloe are integral to Ian's community. An active, normal father, Doug is a source of strength; he helps raise the orphaned children, and, as a part-time carpenter, he works with his hands for comfort. There are several scenes in his basement workshop when he sustains Ian as they work. Fathering has come into its own in a very positive sense in Tyler's work. What Edward Hoagland in the *New York Times* referred to as "a sort of golden mean" in *Breathing Lessons*,[5] responding to the place Ira had in that fiction, here blossoms into Ian's coming of age.

Again, Tyler's narrative brilliance lies in working from the unexpected. Early in *Saint Maybe*, Ian is the interfering, jealous younger brother who tells tales that turn out to be false and cause the deaths of both his brother and his unfortunate young wife. Rather than labeling him a murderer, however, Tyler uses Ian's persona to show that human nature can change. Whereas in Jake, the bank robber in *Earthly Possessions*, she had drawn that same crude rightness, and in Ira in *Breathing Lessons* she had made the wise older man a source of unspoken good sense, both portraits are combined in Ian. But she asks her reader to take the leap of faith and believe that such a crass adolescent, angry because his sexual tryst has been interrupted, can become a loving and wise paterfamilias. It is in this transformation of the young Ian that Tyler makes a further-reaching statement than she has in either of the other novels discussed here.

What Tyler suggests in *Saint Maybe* is the perfectibility of human nature. In 1991, with the world reeling from the liberalization of social codes set in conflict with a punitive religious paternalism, to attempt the greatest of humane plots—the sanctification of a human soul—is no small task.

Part of Tyler's immense skill, in telling the stories of *Saint Maybe* and *Breathing Lessons* as quietly and sustaining the languid rhythm as long as she does, is that she writes as if the story did not matter. There is no artificial buildup of action, no resolution that seems imminent. It is hard for today's reader, so accustomed to violence and visible denouement, to find excitement in those shopping-for-supper scenes in the supermarket. But in these novels, Tyler's prose rhythm is that of tranquility. She uses a mixture of sentences that combine compound clauses with prepositional additions, elongating pace in an unexpected but natural way. Her paragraphs, too, share this elongation. They tend to be longer than most paragraphs in modern prose, comprising six to seven relatively long, and often balanced, sentences.

Stylistics seem germane when one notices that her narrative "events" share in this elongation. Most of Tyler's novels contain very few happenings or separate scenes. No longer are Tyler's books plum pudding–rich with idiosyncratic characters and events, as were *Dinner at the Homesick Restaurant* and *The Accidental Tourist*. Her recent novels have fewer characters, and the protagonists are much less idiosyncratic than some of her earlier characters. In fact, many of Tyler's people might live next door.

Throughout fiction, making such ordinary people interesting has been the prerequisite of narrative tour de force. Faulkner used the term to describe what he thought he had accomplished in *As I Lay Dying*—the motive being to see whether the writer could take a mundane, and in this case unremittingly unpleasant, situation and make compelling fiction from it. Tyler plays the same game, her choice of subject and event forcing her to write like a demon to draw the reader into the narrative with anything like interest, much less suspense. In fact, she deliberately tries to distance the reader by focusing the initial forty pages of *Breathing Lessons* on a wife's troubles in walking to a garage, driving a car home, and having an accident on the way. Through the near lack of action, Tyler makes the reader pay attention to the rhythms and tone of the text.

Reading *Breathing Lessons* is, in a way, an indoctrination into good reading. When there is seemingly little to pay attention to, given the blandness of the plot, Tyler makes the reader attend to the way she makes the uninteresting narrative fascinating. Once the reader understands that Maggie is going to drive the car from the garage to meet Ira, and that is all the suspense ahead, the weave of the text becomes more interesting than the text itself. Peter Prescott comments on Tyler's "awesome ability to make an exceedingly complex structure look effortless, even casual";[6] Tyler deserves similar praise for making the narrative itself look casual. It looks like Maggie's life, unrolling with no causation or consequence; but it comes near the edge of both self-disillusionment and the breakdown of a marriage.

Tyler's reliance on the flashback is another integral part of her belief that a human life is, in some ways, timeless. As the reader figures out why the flashback operates—what is being recalled, and from the vantage point of what moment in more immediate time— the distinction between "present" and "past," like that between "fiction" and "truth," or "male" and "female," comes into question. One of the problems with writing about Tyler's fiction is that, in some ways, it is intentionally amorphous: it defies easy categorization. Minimalist and feminist as it may seem at times, in other texts Tyler is decorative and anti-feminist. The real sin of pride, in a Tyler lexicon, is that of thinking one has all the answers.

What such a position might mean with regard to *Breathing Lessons* is that a reader's tendency to conclude the text on the basis of what happens in the ending goes awry. Everything that happens in the novel does not in any way end with its final scene—yet, in some ways, the tapestry of tone that Tyler has been building does come to a calculated end. *Breathing Lessons* ends with the Morans together. Maggie tries to cuddle up to Ira, who continues playing solitaire. True, he does put an arm around her, and she does appear to gain solace from his three-word reassurance. But she has just asked him the central question of her life, of their life as a married couple— what the value will be of their having lived that life, "what are we two going to live for, all the rest of our lives?" He does not answer, and his acceptance of her troubled self seems only cordial. Some readers and critics have felt concern: what does Tyler's ending "mean" for the Moran marriage?

Perhaps here the tone and pace of the writing are intended to provide reassurance. The comfort we know Maggie finds in Ira's response, though it is largely non-verbal, comes through the prose as carefully as it does through the couple's interaction. As Tyler herself said in 1975, "[In] anything I've ever written I've wanted to know how much dependency is allowed between people, how much right people have to want to change other people. All that business. And I resent the fact that blurbs on my books always say I'm concerned with lack of communication because I don't think communication is really all that hot between people. I don't think it's necessary or desirable in lots of cases."[7] Maggie sits at rest at the end of *Breathing Lessons*. She has learned some skills, and she has others yet to learn. And Ira meanders towards her, as full of love and confidence as he has been during their twenty-eight years together. The Morans' is not a swift journey, or even a completed one, but it is the same kind of passage Tyler has created before in her fiction, and it is a passage most readers take their own kind of comfort in experiencing.

As she describes Ira's finesse in finishing the card game before him and Maggie watching with real appreciation for his skill, Tyler gives the reader the explicit "ending" that is appropriate for this late novel: "He had arrived at the interesting part of the game by now, she saw. He had passed that early, superficial stage when any number of moves seemed possible, and now his choices were narrower and he had to show real skill and judgment." But Tyler knows her readers too well to add, life in middle age is exactly like Ira's card game.

17 / Tyler's Literary Reputation

What is Anne Tyler's literary reputation today? This is not the same question as "How good are Anne Tyler's novels?" Although I am going to take my best shot at answering the first question, I will not attempt to answer the second. It cannot, in fact, be answered without asking several other questions, e.g., "Good for whom?" and "Good for what?" I can give my own personal judgment of Tyler (and I probably won't be able to keep the reader from guessing what it is, even if I want to); I can give John Updike's evaluation (and I certainly will); and I can give the judgments of other individuals or groups, such as those who write for the *National Review* (and I'll do that too). However, in our postmodern universe, in which, as we now understand, values are socially chosen and are shared only within communities bound together by such things as ideology, life experience, and location in social space, it is no longer fashionable (or, in my opinion, accurate) to talk about universal or objective value.

As we know, there is not and has never been complete agreement in judgments about literary quality. The way that divergent evaluations were dealt with in the past was to ascribe to the "true critic" a special ability, based on training and on innate sensitivity, to make judgments about quality. Judgments diverging from the norm of institutionally sanctioned evaluations were pathologized—presented as the work of the inept, the untrained, the auslander.[1] Objective theories of value work in tandem with the "test of time," a notion somewhat at odds, it must be acknowledged, with the notion of the "true critic," for if the true critic has the ability to judge quality, what need is there for the "test of time"?[2] As we analyze the judgments that have been made of Anne Tyler's novels, we will see that individual evaluations vary widely. My ongoing study of literary evaluation and reputation, much of which has been based on the analysis of book reviews, has led me to proclaim the following "law of literary evaluation": For every evaluation, there is an equal and opposite evaluation. The viewpoint of those who write for the *National Review*, for example, is quite different from the community that John Updike represents.

But let us leave the subject of evaluation for the moment and turn to the related but separate matter of literary reputation. Individual readers make evaluative judgments, whereas institutions mediate reputations. Only institutional readers have the authority to confer reputation, which represents a public and collective assessment of value. Reputation is a contingent phenomenon, which can be understood only within a sociocultural and institutional context. While the common reader may play an important role in bringing a work to the attention of cultural authorities,[3] ultimately it is only through the dedicated and persevering attention of these authorities that a work gains reputation. As Grace Paley has noted, "to remain in print in the United States means to be read in classrooms."[4]

In this essay, I will follow Tyler's reputation through the stages of evaluation by book reviewers and then by academics. My narrative will explore the role of the literary press in the creation of Tyler's reputation and will highlight the part played by influential individuals associated with that institution. I will show how Tyler's reputation has been affected by matters of ideological and literary "fit" in relation to late-twentieth-century literary and academic culture. Finally, I will suggest what Tyler's standing is today by "summing up" her place in the rankings of the literary set.

Tyler's reputation has been enormously influenced by one institution in particular—the literary press. There is no doubt that Tyler has profited from being widely reviewed in a number of influential publications. Of enormous benefit has also been the fact that many reviewers have been persons of significant stature. Among these—in the category of creative writers—John Updike leads the list, and he is followed by Gail Godwin, Larry McMurtry, Francine du Plessix Gray, Wallace Stegner, Lynn Sharon Schwartz, Brad Leithauser, Diane Johnson (with the last-named critical of Tyler), and others. Other reviewers are important cultural spokespersons because of their influential standing in the literary press. These include Benjamin DeMott, Jonathan Yardley, Vivian Gornick, and, in the British press, Hermione Lee, Michael Wood, and Paul Binding. Tyler's reputation has also been given a boost by Reynolds Price, her teacher at Duke, whose generous praise is often quoted.

Among these influential individuals, John Updike has played an especially important role. His influence on her success can not easily be overestimated. His pronouncement that Tyler is "wickedly good,"[5] made in his review (reprinted in this volume) of *Searching for Caleb* in the *New Yorker* and widely quoted thereafter in reviews and articles, made claims on her behalf that brought her national attention. And Updike helped even more by reviewing five Tyler novels in succession. Such attention to Tyler hinted that Updike was following her career with an eye to ascertaining whether she could be counted among America's foremost novelists, and indeed Updike suggested that he was interested in her in just such a way. Not all Updike's reviews were highly positive, though they were always respectful. The striking phrase "wickedly good" is the one most often quoted, even though Updike reviewed Tyler's subsequent novels, and in those reviews, with the important exception of *Dinner at the Homesick Restaurant*, he was less enthusiastic, and sometimes offered muted but serious reservations. It seems safe to say that with one well-made phrase, Updike provided the nudge that raised Tyler to the rank of "important writers." That he was able to do so is, of course, a testament to his vast cultural influence. Obviously, Updike did not singlehandedly "create" Tyler's reputation, and I choose my language carefully to give what I think is the proper emphasis to his influence.

Tyler's reputation has also been helped by the fact that she herself is a prolific reviewer: she has written hundreds of reviews.[6] Tyler has been reviewed by some of the same people whose books she has reviewed, e.g., Stegner, Leithauser, Godwin. This is, of course, not surprising, given the fact that she writes so many reviews. In any case, Tyler's work as a reviewer has probably been good for her own fiction, having promoted its visibility in various ways. For one thing, editors who know her and have worked with her as a reviewer are more likely to make certain that her books are reviewed. She has reviewed numerous books for the *National Observer*, the *New York Times Book Review*, the *Washington Post Book World*, and the *New Republic*, and her books have also been regularly reviewed by these publications.[7] Of course, her stature now is such that she can expect her books to get top billing in a number of journals, and her recent novels have often received page-one reviews in such publications as the *New York Times Book Review*, the *Washington Post*, and the *Chicago Tribune*. Apart from her activity as a reviewer, Tyler, a very private person who gives few interviews and those only in writing, has clearly done little to promote her career (and to be sure, she surely must do the voluminous review-writing because she enjoys it). Tyler is known as a generous reviewer, and she has said that she prefers to review books she thinks she will like.

Tyler has also been awarded prestigious literary prizes, including the Janet Heidinger Kafka Prize for Fiction by an American woman for *Morgan's Passing*, which was also nominated for the National Book Critics Circle Fiction Award and for an American Book Award. *Dinner at the Homesick Restaurant* was nominated for a Pulitzer Prize and was given the P.E.N./Faulkner Award. *Breathing Lessons* received the Pulitzer Prize. These prizes were an acknowledgment of her increasing visibility and recognition, but they in turn made her better known.

According to Richard Ohmann's important article, "The Shaping of a Canon: U.S. Fiction, 1960–71," reputation formation takes place in three general stages.[8] In the first stage, a writer is brought to the attention of the literary set through sales in hardback and then in paperback. The second stage involves a favorable response from reviewers (or the literary press), and the last stage consists of attention by scholars and professors, who promote literary reputation in important ways by including a writer in course syllabi and writing about him or her in scholarly books and journals.

But the making of a literary reputation is not simply a matter of being promoted by certain influential individuals (however important that is). Of crucial importance is the matter of ideological and sociocultural "fit." Literary reputation is a product of the intersection of readers and writers within a particular sociocultural context, and to understand the place of a writer in any culture, we must analyze the fit that obtains.

Like most or all American writers who gain reputations in the United States, Tyler is also read in Great Britain, and her British reception provides interesting contrasts with her American reception and helps to make clear how cultural traditions, literary and otherwise, have an effect on a writer's reception. Restrictions on the length of this essay permit only a brief overview of the British reviews. In general, British responses are more subdued than American reactions. There is a certain drama—with nationalistic overtones—played out in the American reviews, revolving around the question, "Is Anne Tyler worthy to be ranked with the foremost American writers?" To the British, Tyler is an interesting writer, one who can offer enjoyment and insight into human life and American society, but in evaluating her work British reviewers do not have to become exercised about such matters as the rise or decline of their own national literary tradition. Somehow ranking the artistic productions of one's own countrymen and -women and evaluating their visions of one's own culture is fraught with more emotion than making evaluations of writers that represent another national literary tradition. Perhaps this helps to explain why the British reviews are generally uniformly positive, lacking in the outspoken negative criticism that is a minor refrain in the American reviews. The British have a respected tradition—the comedy of manners— in which to place Tyler, and this may be another reason for her favorable reception. Thus it appears that British reviewers do not have to worry as much as some American critics do about Tyler's lack of attention to the dark side of reality.[9]

As one reads through the reviews, one is made aware of the criteria, pertaining to the culture, that are the basis for judging a novel. These criteria probably would not surprise any undergraduate English major who has been put through several English courses. Reviewers who write for America's leading journals and magazines expect the following things from a good novel: (1) characters who have psychological credibility but who are, at the same time, arresting in some way, that is, characters who strike the reader as universal but are, nonetheless, the highly individual creations of a particular artist; (2) a plot that interests and pleases and has no extraneous or awkward elements; and (3) something that can be called philosophical verity or "wisdom." It is often noted that Tyler writes realistic fiction, and the particular criteria applied to her have been devised for this type of fiction. Whether Tyler would be granted higher praise or more recognition if she wrote metafiction, à la Barth, Pynchon, and the like, is a good question. (I comment on this matter at the end of the essay.)

Those who have followed the reviews of Tyler's novels or have read some of the academic essays on her work will be aware that a major issue for Tyler's reputation is her "rosy" vision of human life. Tyler has been charged with a tendency to present a false or sentimentalized view of reality and an inability to sound the depths of human experience. A related matter is the status of Tyler's novels as comedy. Comedy has never had much respect, and certainly in our time genial comedy such as Tyler's is often suspect. (Black comedy, which dwells on the horrors of modern existence, is, of course, a different matter.)

Anne Tyler published her first novel, *If Morning Ever Comes*, in 1964; it was followed by *The Tin Can Tree* (1965), *A Slipping-Down Life* (1970), and *The Clock Winder* (1972). Tyler reportedly dislikes her first two books.[10] Her early novels were reviewed, but often without much enthusiasm, and for the most part not in major reviewing organs. Tyler came to wider public attention when Gail Godwin reviewed *Celestial Navigation* for the *New York Times Book Review*.[11] This review, while not a "rave review," is generally very positive. The fact that it is mentioned by nearly everyone who has commented on her reputation or her rise to prominence suggests that Godwin's "clout" was of significant assistance to Tyler. While the novel was not widely reviewed, certainly not in comparison to the novels that followed, *Celestial Navigation* (1974) has been named as a favorite novel by several influential readers, and, at one time at least, it was Tyler's favorite.[12] In addition to Godwin's endorsement, a highly positive review, praising the novel as "altogether stunning," appeared in the *National Observer*.[13]

But it was John Updike who put Tyler firmly on the cultural agenda with his review of her next novel, *Searching for Caleb*. For Updike, *Searching for Caleb* is a "lovely novel, funny and lyric and true-seeming, exquisite in its details and ambitious in its design."[14] Updike has praise for the plot's "well-spaced turns," for the realism of its "scrupulously exact" depiction of furniture and manners, and for "the subtle psychologizing" of its characters. For Updike, Tyler has done more than entertain: she has shown us something about America. In this novel about the family as the "vessel of Time," the Peck relatives "are our aunts and uncles," and the land is "our land," with Tyler showing us, in the search for Caleb, the "lyrical, mystical, irrational underside of American practicality." "This writer is not merely good; she is wickedly good," says Updike, in the oft-quoted summation of the review.

Updike's praise for the characters, for the realism of the surface of the novel, and for the Tyler's "craft" are themes that recur in the reviews. They are certainly the focus of Katha Pollitt's review in the *New York Times Book Review*.[15] While noting that Tyler is not concerned with the contemporary moment and is uninfluenced by feminist novels, Pollitt praises Tyler for the success of her craft: "the unfolding of character through brilliantly imagined and absolutely accurate detail." Stella Nesanovich, writing for the *Southern Review*, is equally prone to superlatives: with this novel, Tyler demonstrates "greater depth and keener insight into human nature" and has produced a novel that "literally bristles with vitality."[16]

Tyler's next novel, *Earthly Possessions*, was seen by many as a slight backward step.[17] Nicholas Delbanco, in a review in the *New Republic*, says straightforwardly, "I do not feel this novel represents advance." Delbanco is bothered by a schematic repetitiveness of motif and fuzziness of theme. Similarly, Katherine Bouton, though she pronounces Tyler one of the "best young writers around," is disappointed by the novel; she feels that the novel's message is all too clear: many characters feel "trapped by events." Walter Sullivan, writing for the *Sewanee Review*, likewise agrees that Tyler has little to say in the novel: "The characters and action are interesting enough, but what you see is what you get. Everything that is to be gleaned here is on the surface." Angela Wigan, the reviewer for *Time*, agrees that *Earthly Possessions* is "not her best book," but adds that Tyler's own standard is so high that even her "secondary works are compelling." Even Updike's favorable review (also reprinted here) echoes these same criticisms. Updike continues to like Tyler's evocation of America: "She is soft, if not bullish, on America; its fluorescent-lit banks and gas stations, its high schools, its motels and billboards and boring backwaters . . ." But he echoes the other reviewers of this novel in his remarks on "her one possible weakness: a tendency to leave the reader just where she found him."

Morgan's Passing provoked a divided response.[18] Although it had some loyal fans, Tyler received some of her harshest criticism for this novel. Tyler herself worried about the response to the novel, thinking that some readers might not like Morgan, and this has sometimes proved to be the case. David Evanier of the *National Review*, who has little praise for the novel, feels that "the problem may be the novel's determined celebration of Morgan's eccentricity." Similarly, A. G. Mojtabai, writing for the *New York Times Book Review*, announces that "Morgan is a problem, not only to friends and relatives, but to author and reader as well." Mojtabai speculates that Tyler's relation to Morgan may be the problem: she may be "too casually fond of Morgan to subject him to a truly loving, yet deeply probing scrutiny." James Wolcott, writing in the *New York Review of Books*, agrees that Morgan is the problem: "What finally undoes *Morgan's Passing* is the characterization of Morgan himself." Tyler is uncritical about Morgan, he believes: "Tyler seems to adore Morgan, polishing his buttony eyes, as if he were a toy panda."

But Morgan also has admirers.[19] Francine du Plessix Gray (*Commonweal*) finds him "one of those interesting maternal men (increasingly prevalent in our best fiction)." Gray gives high praise to Tyler's "engrossing and superbly crafted book." Paul Gray, in *Time*, considers Morgan a worthy addition to Tyler's gallery of eccentrics. Stella Nesanovich, who has never offered negative criticism of Tyler, is outspoken in her praise of this novel, calling it "a marvel of a book deserving full critical recognition." Nesanovich's evaluations of Tyler have appeared in the *Southern Review*, but she also wrote a dissertation on Tyler. Most enthusiastic of all is the review by Thomas M. Disch in the *Washington Post Book Review*. Disch approves of Tyler's practice of creating, not "sexist gargoyles," but "entirely ordinary men of limited competence and probity." He takes to Morgan, whom he sees as "at once so implausibly flawed and so improbably lovable." His admiration for the novel is related to his enjoyment of Tyler's comedy: "The flavor in the book is alternately lyrical and rambunctiously comic—as though Chekhov were to rewrite one of Kaufmann and Hart's comedies of confusion; as though Flannery O'Connor were to forget all about religion and write a whole novel as droll as her tales; as if Dickens were alive and well and living in Baltimore."

While continuing his support of Tyler as a promising and impressive writer, Updike seems to take a step backward from his earlier outspoken praise in his review of *Morgan's Passing* in the *New Yorker*. From his first review, Updike placed Tyler in the company of Eudora Welty, Flannery O'Connor, and Carson McCullers. He has, in effect, been posing a question (which to my knowledge he has not yet answered), which could be phrased as follows: "Is Tyler as good as the three older Southern writers?" or, rather, "Is Tyler getting closer in her race with the three accomplished artists who started the course ahead of her?" My reading of the review of *Morgan's Passing* is that Updike is not as sure of her ultimate success after reading her latest novel as he was earlier. Tyler is accomplished as a realist, and her characters live emotionally, but her books may lack substance: "Still, her books, their dazzlements subsided, leave an unsettling impression of having been writ in water, or with a cool laser of moonlight." "There is a certain melancholy in 'Morgan's Passing'—the puppetmaster's ennui," Updike writes, and he speculates that Tyler may herself be suffering from fatigue "in a work so forcedly buoyant, so scattered and manic in its episodes, so enigmatic and—dare we say?—fey in its central character." Tyler has a gift, to be sure, but Updike concludes that "something of that gift is still being withheld."

With *Dinner at the Homesick Restaurant*, Anne Tyler's reputation reached new heights. The novel "made her famous."[20] Those critics and reviewers who had been asking themselves, "How good is Anne Tyler?" finally felt able to answer the question with confidence. *Dinner* has been called Tyler's "breakout book," a term used in publishing to designate a book that wins an author a larger audience and a new level of recognition.[21] Tyler's novel received the significant accolade of a highly favorable page-one review in the *New York Times Book Review*. The review was important for the stature of both the publication and the reviewer, Benjamin DeMott. DeMott, professor of Humanities at Amherst, has written both scholarly books and numerous reviews in the *Times Book Review* and other publications, has had his hand (or pen) in many literary judgments, and (we can assume) has had influence on several literary reputations. The comments of DeMott, Updike, and others suggest that those who have the most authority to influence reputations are also those most interested in speculating about the ultimate reputation a given author is capable of achieving. It's probably a matter of a subjective feeling of entitlement. The propensity to make literary judgments is proportional to the degree of cultural authority one has. I am reminded here of Pierre Bourdieu's comments on political opinions: one has political opinions if one is authorized by the social structure to do so.[22] DeMott reveals that he has been speculating on what Tyler's final achievement might be for some time. With *Dinner* he feels authorized to stop "brooding" about "her direction and destination, her probable ultimate achievement."[23] Considering the novel a "border crossing," he finds it a great success in every way: a plot that avoids the static and the predictable, unforgettable scenes, interesting characters (he praises particularly Tyler's young women). But one senses that it is the seriousness of her themes and the technical complexity he finds in *Dinner* that DeMott feels justifies a new level of praise. Her novel, DeMott informs us, is about the uses of adversity, but it merely hints at the mysterious way the lessons—hardly known to the consciousness of the learners—are learned. DeMott speaks of Tyler's wisdom, particularly on the subject of "the complications of our nature and of our nurturing arrangements."

The novel was praised by other American reviewers in *Time*, *Saturday Review*, and other publications,[24] but the praise of John Updike deserves special attention. Like DeMott, Updike is pleased that Tyler has taken a leap towards greater complexity and greater seriousness—towards a "darker" vision.[25] As Updike states explicitly: "Her art has needed only the darkening that would give her beautifully sketched shapes solidity." In her novels, Tyler has consistently shown us an authentic and convincing America, but this novel is more "complex and somber." We see the family "as a theatre for intimate cruelties," and time brings "a blackness of loss," but also brings epiphanies to its characters, who in this novel have "real psychologies."

As a result of the success of *Dinner at the Homesick Restaurant*, the appearance of Tyler's next novel, *The Accidental Tourist*, was accompanied with a certain amount of hype: paperback and book club deals netted $1.3 million before the novel was released.[26] When the novel appeared, it enhanced Tyler's reputation. Once again the novel was accorded the honor of a page-one review in the *New York Times Book Review*, again by a distinguished reviewer—novelist Larry McMurtry. He awards high praise indeed: from the "fusty" soil of the South, Tyler is "steadily raising a body of fiction of major dimensions."[27] *Accidental Tourist* is "one of her best books," in which she makes new accomplishments in the realm of metaphor. McMurtry thinks the metaphor of the "accidental tourist" captures not only the dilemma of the central character but also some larger point about men that Tyler has been making in all her novels: "they are frequently accidental tourists in their own lives."

Jonathan Yardley, influential reviewer for the *Washington Post Book World*, is even more impressed with what he refers to as a "beautiful, incandescent, heartbreaking, exhilarating book."[28] To Yardley, it is becoming "ever more clear that the fiction of Anne Tyler is something both unique and extraordinary in contemporary American literature." Yardley is drawn to the "abiding sympathetic nature of [Tyler's] characters" and the lessons about endurance that he finds in the book: that "life leaves no one unscarred, that to live is to accept one's scars and make the best of them—and to accept as well the scars that other people bear." Yardley concludes the review with one more generous, even extravagant, compliment: "Words fail me; one cannot reasonably expect fiction to be better than this."

Richard Eder, also a well-known reviewer, in this case for the *Los Angeles Times Book Review*, is equally complimentary. His evaluation of Tyler could hardly be more positive. He writes, "I don't know if there is a better American writer going. When a writer is good enough, he or she, by definition, is impossible to compare; the vision is too individual. But I can't think of another major novelist who so plainly is still gaining on herself."[29] Eder, too, praises Tyler's characters, who "do not in the first instance stand for anything but themselves, yet they manage to stand for a good deal more." The novel is about "moral choice," a theme of high seriousness even though it is articulated in the midst of a "carnival of comic events."

The novel received praise from other reviewers also, including unqualified kudos from two feminist journals: *Ms.* magazine and the *Women's Review of Books*.[30] Brigitte Weeks, in *Ms.*, agrees with the male reviewers quoted above that Tyler "has steadily progressed toward excellence." Praising Tyler's characters, who have "the elements of Everyman," and the complex mosaic-like structure of the book, Weeks concludes that "*The Accidental Tourist* is, quite simply, her best novel yet." In the *Women's Review of Books*, Barbara Rich praises Tyler's evocation of Baltimore—claiming a special authority for her opinion as a long-time resident of the city—and her characters, especially Muriel, "one of the most captivating characters Tyler has ever produced for her readers." She concludes that the novel is so good that "it's difficult to see how Anne Tyler can top it, but there's little doubt that she will."

Less impressed with the novel is an important reviewer, novelist Diane Johnson. In a review in the prestigious *New York Review of Books*, Johnson reviews *The Accidental Tourist* along with Bobbie Ann Mason's *In Country*, characterizing both novels as Norman Rockwell–like creations, characterized by "fashionable settings in rural or small-town America among lower-middle class people."[31] According to Johnson, the strategy of the novel is to "urge a whole agenda of comforting, consoling ideas." These ideas are "powerfully attractive. It's just that they are not true." Johnson concludes that Tyler's "Reaganesque dream novel" may suit the national mood.

In his review in the *New Yorker*, Updike's kind remarks about the novel did not equal the almost extravagant praise of some of the other reviewers. His praise is of this order: "Miss Tyler never fails to produce a fluid, shapely story sparkling with bright, sharp images drawn from the so-called ordinary world."[32] Updike has kind words for several aspects of the novel, including the delineation of "the moral evolution of male character," but there may be a key to his more muted praise in this comment: "'The Accidental Tourist' is lighter than its wholly admirable and relatively saturnine predecessor, 'Dinner at the Homesick Restaurant.'" Seemingly chiding himself for his lack of enthusiasm, Updike comments, "If Anne Tyler strikes us as too benign, too swift to tack together shelter for her dolls, it may be that we have lost familiarity with the comedic spirit, the primal faith in natural resilience and the forces of renewal."

With two highly acclaimed novels to Tyler's credit, the reviewers of her eleventh and Pulitzer Prize–winning novel, *Breathing Lessons*, had two choices: proclaim the novel to be the culmination of her talent, or declare that it was a falling-off. The former view is expressed most succinctly by Peter Prescott in *Newsweek*: "Anne Tyler moves from strength to strength. Each of her novels is more impressive than the one before and her new one, her 11th, reveals an awesome ability to make an exceedingly complex structure look effortless, even casual."[33] Prescott is one of a number of people who have reviewed several of Tyler's novels, and perhaps a reviewer is motivated to continue to praise a novelist he or she has previously described as a great talent. Those, like Prescott, who like the novel, find in the work a recognition of common humanity and a story of human endurance. These reviewers praise the comedy in the character Maggie and like her for her heart and her innocence. Other reviewers think the novel is a less substantial work than Tyler's previous efforts. These reviewers tend to dislike Maggie, and they also often criticize Tyler's vision in this novel (and sometimes, by implication, in all her work) as too rosy, not hardheaded enough. Updike did not review this novel, nor has he reviewed Tyler's latest novel, *Saint Maybe*.[34]

To take the novel's admirers first,[35] the *Washington Post Book World*'s Wallace Stegner offers unqualified praise. The last two novels should have been hard acts to follow, he suggests; "*Breathing Lessons* shows us a writer who should have had trouble matching herself, surpassing herself." One can't like the novel without liking Maggie, it seems, a generalization that is borne out by Stegner's review. Though he characterizes her as "a scheming flibbertigibbet" and an incorrigible meddler, his affection for Maggie is apparent. Her actions are motivated by affection, he believes, as well as an essential innocence. Stegner enjoys all aspects of Tyler's comedy, from her powers of comic observation to the broad comedy of the automobile trip and the funeral observances.

Others who are similarly enthusiastic are Lee Lescaze in the *Wall Street Journal*, Barbara Rich in the *Women's Review of Books*, Richard Eder in the *Los Angeles Times Book Review*, R. Z. Sheppard in *Newsweek*, and Hilma Wolitzer in the *Chicago Tribune Book World*. Lescaze, who refers to Tyler's "extraordinary talents," identifies the theme as an exploration of "the resilient spirit that rescues us from moments of despair." Barbara Rich, who calls Tyler a "splendid writer," makes an explicit defense of Tyler against the charge of superficiality, and expresses particular admiration for Maggie. Richard Eder also gives high praise to Maggie, and to Ira as well: they are "not heroes, but they are, in a sense, heroic." R. Z. Sheppard, who also reviewed the previous novel, praises Tyler's characters and the truthful depiction of reality. Hilma Wolitzer calls the book Anne Tyler's "gentlest and most charming novel and a paean to what is fast becoming a phenomenon—lasting marriage."

The novel got less than enthusiastic reviews in the *New York Times Book Review* (Edward Hoagland) and the *New York Review of Books* (Robert Towers).[36] While Hoagland has praise for Tyler's accomplishments, he is lukewarm about this novel. He admires Tyler's "kindly, wise, and versatile" eye and applauds "the utter absence from her work of a fashionable contempt for life." For Hoagland, *Breathing Lessons* is, however, a "slightly thinner mixture," and Hoagland thinks that the "unfunny slapstick" of the final pages seems like "an effort to corral extra readers." Towers believes that Maggie is "too awkward, too silly, to carry the burden that has been assigned to her." The novel also got unfavorable reviews in the *Nation* and the *National Review*. These reviews are discussed below, with other reviews that are of especial usefulness in helping to place Tyler ideologically.

Reviewers of Tyler's most recent novel, *Saint Maybe*, note that Tyler ventures into new territory in her treatment of religion.[37] Two reviews that comment on Tyler's handling of religious experience mirror the division that characterizes the general response to her novels—on the one hand, there is the complaint that her vision is too superficial, and, on the other hand, the assertion that she presents everyday experience authentically and insightfully. Reviewer Bruce Bawer of the *Washington Post* says that Tyler's novels "lack something central to Christianity," namely an awareness of evil. She "holds up unreflectiveness as a virtue," and "we never get inside of Ian's faith, or longing for forgiveness, or whatever it is that binds him to his church." In contrast, Ann-Janine Morey of the *Christian Century* believes that Ian's religious commitment does inform the novel, and concludes that "Tyler displays an acuity about everyday holiness that is all the more effective for being understated." Joyce Sister of the *Chicago Tribune* also finds in the novel a successful portrayal of "making the leap of faith, taking the crazy chance, and then taking the consequences."

Several reviewers have little patience with Ian Bedloe, the young man who gives up college and normal life to raise his brother's children in an attempt to assuage the guilt he feels for the brother's death. "He may be a saint," says Crystal Gromer of *Commonweal*, "but he's awfully boring." Paul Gray of *Time* and Richard Eder of the *Los Angeles Times Book Review* agree, the latter remarking that Tyler's work is "high risk stuff . . . writing at the borderline of dullness." Eder still counts himself an admirer of Tyler's, but thinks her last novel "stands some ways behind" previous efforts, largely because of the character Ian, whose "muted spirits, justifiable as they are, mute the book."

Marilyn Gardner of the *Christian Science Monitor* and Michiko Kakutani of the *New York Times* like the novel, and their positive response seems to have to do with the fact that they see the novel as about a family rather than one individual. Gardner writes, "Few families appeal with more heartbreaking charm than the Bedloes, the 'ideal, apple-pie household' at the center of 'Saint Maybe.'" Kakutani finds that "each character in 'Saint Maybe' has been fully rendered . . . and each has been fit, like a hand-sawed jigsaw-puzzle piece, into the matrix of family life."

The best news for Tyler's reputation in the response to her most recent novel is the fact that she got very glowing reviews in the two publications that count the most: the *New York Review of Books* and the *New York Times Book Review*. In a lengthy and substantive review in the *New York Review of Books*, Brad Leithauser has nothing but high praise for Tyler's oeuvre and her latest novel. Not only does she offer interesting characters and plots that "brim with surprises," she also possesses the writerly virtue of wisdom. Her craft is so strong that she is able to offer the reader a pleasure "that distinguishes first-rate realistic fiction": the conversion of skepticism about certain plot devices into a sense of inevitability. Leithauser's defense of Tyler from the charge that she stints on sex and violence is predicated on an understanding of her work as an example of the comedy of manners. He writes, "Among gifted contemporary American writers, she is unusual in treating the comic not as a branching of her art but as its taproot." Tyler writes the "amiable social comedy" largely set aside by most American writers, who have "arguably conceded it to Hollywood." Tyler is "bold in a number of quiet ways"—in her creation of male characters "of immediate authenticity," for example.

Jay Parini is equally complimentary in a page-one review in the *New York Times Book Review*. For Parini, the novel is "vintage Tyler, delicately stamped, like a watermark, with her intimate and unmistakable voice." He praises her rendering of children ("Anne Tyler is one of the few contemporary novelists who can really 'do' children"), her comic gift as displayed in the amusing but affectionate description of the Church of the Second Chance, and her portrayal of family life. In summary, he says he "adored" *Saint Maybe*: "In many ways it is Anne Tyler's most sophisticated work, a realistic chronicle that celebrates family life without erasing the pain and boredom that families almost necessarily inflict upon their members."

A full discussion of Tyler's contemporary reputation must include further discussion of what are seen as her strengths and weaknesses and an attempt to suggest an ideological fit (or lack of fit, in some cases) between Tyler and her readers. Let us examine first the serious criticisms that have been made of Tyler. These criticisms echo charges often leveled against popular literature: its sole aim is to console, and in so doing it deludes, falsifying reality, and simplifying to the point of untruth. Tyler is accused of being unable to treat the full range of human experience and of deliberately trying to please and to charm by painting a rosy picture of reality and ignoring the darker side of human experience and the deep flaws in American society. This point of view is epitomized by John Blades in a 1986 article in the *Chicago Tribune*. Blades says he finds something "annoyingly synthetic"[38] about Tyler's work: it is "seriously diluted by the promiscuous use of artificial sweeteners, a practice that has made Tyler our foremost NutraSweet novelist." Blades's association of Tyler's art with popular forms is indicated by his invocation of Neil Simon, the sitcom, and Lake Wobegone. Blades wonders "how a writer can affirm life without ever seriously facing it."

Several critiques that can be identified as coming from the right and the left help to establish the politics, in the narrow sense of the term, of Tyler's reception. One of Tyler's sternest critics is Vivian Gornick, known for her association with left and feminist causes, who wrote a piece on Tyler for the *Village Voice* that is in part a review of *Dinner at the Homesick Restaurant*.[39] Gornick thinks that Tyler's is a case of "arrested development": "In Tyler's world there is neither terror nor rapture because there is no sex. Instead there is an endless child-parent interchange prolonged into listless adulthood." It is adulthood that Tyler is unable to depict satisfactorily: "(To be precise, the fearful years between 25 and 50, when one is required to act. These are the years that, in a Tyler novel, must pass in fantasy-ridden sedation; after that, everyone can calm down and start moving toward senility.)" The novel succeeds only in being "strikingly direct in communicating the depression behind the adopted whimsy of her middle books." Such chronicles of arrested development can have no depth, says Gornick, because they represent a form of escapism. Gornick suggests that Tyler's readers share her propensity for escapism: "Ironically she is beloved precisely because her writing skill invests the ordinary infantilism of American family life with a tender glamour. She allows the middle-brow middle class to love itself for all its poignant insufficiency. A pity: A good writer being rewarded for making virtue out of the fear of experience."

After Tyler won recognition with *Dinner at the Homesick Restaurant* and *The Accidental Tourist*, her work drew attention from journals identified with distinct political philosophies: the *Nation* (recognized as a left publication) and the *National Review* (a voice for conservatism). These magazines, which review few novels, illustrate that ideological issues are always a factor in literary evaluation, even though, much of the time, matters of ideological "fit" may be unnoticed or invisible. Both journals made criticisms of *Breathing Lessons*, though those made by the *National Review* are the more serious. The *Nation*'s reviewer, Robert McPhillips, who calls Tyler "the most benign of our novelists," sees Tyler moving, in *Breathing Lessons*, from romance to realism.[40] But, alas, she fails in her attempt to broaden her fictional universe and venture into the realm of social realism, where, in the reviewer's mind, a critique of society is required. Unable to see Maggie as the symbol of endurance that some other reviewers find her, McPhillips says of Maggie that "her skirmishes with reality outside the claustrophobic confines of her family life make her resilience seem forced and finally insignificant." As Tyler moves beyond the romance of her previous novels, she attempts too little, and fails in "her attempt to invest Maggie with a genuine social conscience." McPhillips may be charged with liberalism of the bleeding-heart variety for criticisms of two particular episodes in the novel, one dealing with an encounter with a elderly black man and the other with Maggie's appearance at an abortion clinic.

David Klinghofer, who reviewed Tyler's novel for the *National Review*, takes on the role of champion for the middle class, whom, says Klinghofer, Tyler, like others in America's artist class, "never quite learned to like."[41] Such a failing is the cause for the failure of her novel, whose characters are boring (Ira) and pathetic (Maggie).

Tyler got a more thorough dressing-down in an issue of the *National Review* that appeared a year later, in 1989, after she had won the Pulitzer Prize. Carol Iannone, who became known to academics as the nominee to the National Endowment for the Humanities who was opposed by the Modern Language Association and other professional groups, suggests that Tyler is an unworthy prize winner. Iannone's conservative leanings are apparent in the review, in which she criticizes not only Tyler but her audience as well—on the grounds that an audience that overpraises an author deserves criticism, too. What Tyler's audience wants is assurance that they can continue on their course of quietism and blind hopefulness. This Tyler gives them with her "all-encompassing, non-judgmental, low-grade-soap-opera formats."[42] Iannone's criticisms are similar to those perennially made about works judged to be artifacts of low culture: they flatter the audience and relieve them of thinking. Iannone places Tyler's work firmly in the category of low culture and makes connections between emotionally soft romance creations and the female pen (the sort of thing that has been said about many women writers). The ideological position from which Iannone makes her critique is especially clear in the article's conclusion, where she laments Tyler's lack of attention to evil in the universe: "If she were any better than she is at what she does, she could not exert her peculiar charms. If the elements in her fiction were more vividly realized, some things might turn out to be at risk and the stakes would rise alarmingly. The disruptive heart of darkness in some behavior might actually peep through, the irreconcilable discontinuity between certain choices might become more tragically apparent."

But such harsh criticisms are the minority report. Most of the people who have written about Tyler in reviews, articles, and books have praised her ability to show us the ordinary in a new way, to teach us something about ourselves, and to strengthen or even inspire us. As Wallace Stegner says of Tyler's characters in his review of *Breathing Lessons*: "First they surprise us, then we recognize them, then we acknowledge how much they tell us about ourselves."[43] Tyler's Quaker background is often cited by those who are attracted to her benign outlook.

Many who have praised Tyler have predicated their positive evaluations on the assumption that Tyler is writing comedy—a genial comedy or a comedy of manners. Readers who situate her within a comic tradition do not expect her to dwell on the dark side of life and do not see her tendency to be hopeful as a flaw. Reviewers praise her for a range of comic gifts. Several reviewers cite her ability to create eccentrics, à la Charles Dickens; others appreciate the elements of broad, even slapstick, comedy (such as that associated with Maggie in *Breathing Lessons*); many have commented on such things as "witty invention,"[44] comic scenes "that explode with joy,"[45] the exuberance and the vitality of her novels, and the combination of "joie de vivre and endurance."[46] That the utilization of a comic mode does not equal superficiality of treatment is suggested by many reviewers who comment on such things as an "alternation of laughter and tears"[47] or Tyler's ability to "personify moral choice both gravely and winningly amid a carnival of comical events."[48] She might, however, be rated even higher by academics if her comic art resembled more closely the ironic and verbally complex comedy of Thomas Pynchon, for example.

Thus, Tyler is getting praise from those who are attuned to comic art for reasons that have to do with personal makeup and literary taste. But what is the "political" profile of the Tyler fancier? Tyler's readers may not think of themselves as highly "political" beings. They are part of a broad section in the middle of the spectrum of American political opinion that excludes the ideologies of the left and the right. If not "bullish" on America, they at least accept the basic premises of American culture and relate to the themes of family life, or "the mysteries of kinship and blood,"[49] and day-today middle-class existence. Tyler is sometimes called an apolitical novelist, but it would be more accurate to say that she shares the politics of the American majority. It is part of the understanding of the concept of ideology that one does not recognize one's own ideological position as an ideological position.

But we cannot talk about Tyler's reputation without dealing with her reception among scholars and academics.[50] We can assert, first of all, that she is assuming an important place among writers adopted by the academy. Tyler has been the subject of a number of books and articles as well as dissertations. Tyler's work has received thorough analysis and high praise from Alice Hall Petry in *Understanding Anne Tyler* and Joseph C. Voelker in *Art and the Accidental in Anne Tyler*. She has been placed in good company in Margaret Morganroth Gullette's *Safe at Last in the Middle Years: The Invention of the Midlife Progress Novel: Saul Bellow, Margaret Drabble, Anne Tyler and John Updike*. She has been included in the following collections: *Contemporary American Women Writers: Narrative Strategies*, edited by Catherine Rainwater and William J. Scheick; *The Writer on Her Work*, edited by Janet Sternberg; and *Women Writers of the Contemporary South*, edited by Peggy Prenshaw. A recent volume, *The Fiction of Anne Tyler*, edited by C. Ralph Stephens, contains essays presented at the Anne Tyler Symposium in Baltimore in 1989; and a number of additional essays have appeared in journals, particularly those dealing with Southern literature.

The construction of reputation by scholars and teachers involves establishing the literary value of a work by claiming for it literary qualities which are held in high esteem. Establishing the quality of a writer's work has several facets, including placing the writer in recognized literary traditions (a process begun by reviewers) and validating his or her work by applying current methodologies. Several books and articles make much of Tyler as the heir of Welty, McCullers, and, for some, O'Connor.[51] Tyler has gone on record about her admiration for Welty, but has otherwise de-emphasized her connection with a Southern school.[52] It can be interpreted as a compliment to Tyler, however, that she has also been considered in relation to the author regarded as the grandmaster of the Southern tradition, William Faulkner.[53] And Petry places Tyler in illustrious company by tracing her connections to the giants of the American and Russian traditions, e.g., Hawthorne and Chekhov. Among her contemporaries, Tyler is linked with America's most respected writers. Voelker pays Tyler an indirect compliment by setting up a dichotomy between Quaker Tyler and Puritan Updike. Tyler is also associated with John Cheever and John Irving.

Those who have chosen to interpret and analyze her work make a high estimation of her novels. Novelist Doris Betts, who has written a number of essays on Tyler, remarks in her essay in the Prenshaw collection that Tyler, like Welty, has made character bear "her heaviest load of meaning."[54] Tyler is praised for the depth of her insight into character, with praise divided between her men, her women, and her children. Let me cite in particular the praise of her male characters. Paul Binding says unequivocally of Tyler's men: "I know of no woman writer who writes more sympathetically about men than Anne Tyler; she can describe them with affection as well as with stronger emotions and sees them not as objects of desire or embodiments of impersonal forces but simply as individual human beings."[55] This high praise is echoed by others, and it may be that Tyler's benign attitude to men has been a factor in her reputation.

Tyler is seen as having important things to say about the nature of art in *Celestial Navigation, Dinner at the Homesick Restaurant,* and *Morgan's Passing* in essays by Barbara Harrell Carson and Sue Lile Inman.[56] The reputation of this last novel, which was not exactly favorably reviewed, is repaired in several scholarly essays, especially the one by Gordon O. Taylor, who makes a highly sophisticated analysis of Tyler's treatment of identity in the novel.[57] Taylor makes a virtue of Tyler's resistance to classification—her ability to elude literary trends—as does Betts in her article in the Stephens collection. Originality and a distinctive vision are of course necessary characteristics for a reputation as a great writer, and praise for going beyond the formulas of one's time is a compliment of a high order.

Tyler's art is praised for its subtlety, its philosophical and metaphysical qualities, and its formal complexity. In her essay on Tyler's use of narrative pattern, Mary F. Robertson applies a highly sophisticated theoretical approach to Tyler's art, one which could be read as a refutation of the assertions that Tyler's work belongs in the category of low culture.[58] Mary Ellen Gibson comments on an "almost metaphysical intelligence" often "overlooked" by her reviewers,[59] and Margaret Morganroth Gullette cites Tyler's ability to answer "philosophical questions" in "plain concrete language."[60]

Other writers employ current methods of analysis, especially psychoanalytic criticism.[61] These writers include Joseph B. Wagner, who deals with the oedipal struggle in Tyler's novels, and Anne Ricketson Zahlan, who invokes Lacan in a discussion of Tyler's treatment of the unconscious. An anthropological approach to kinship is utilized by Virginia Schaeffer Carroll.

The many men and women scholars who have associated their own academic careers with Anne Tyler have sometimes expressed regret that Tyler is not getting more scholarly attention, and have suggested that other contemporary writers no more deserving of recognition have been preferred to her by the academic establishment. Some of these scholars have alluded to John Updike's remark in his review of *Dinner at the Homesick Restaurant* that Tyler's "humane and populous novels have attracted . . . less approval in the literary ether than the sparer offerings of Ann Beattie and Joan Didion."[62] The opinion that Tyler is underrated is, of course, the personal and qualitative assessment of her admirers. Those who make this assessment sometimes say that she is denied the highest academic accolades because she has not pioneered in techniques of experimental fiction. That "failing," along with her rosy vision, which makes her vulnerable to the criticism that she ignores the darker elements in American life, probably does mean that some people will place her in a lower rank. I want to point out, however, that in terms of the number of scholarly studies, Tyler is doing as well as Beattie and Didion. There are more entries on Tyler in the MLA bibliography than on Beattie. Entries on Didion exceed those on Tyler, but a number of the Didion entries relate to articles in journals of composition and communication, not publications concerned with literary analyses. I concur that Tyler's reputation is less than it could be because of her realistic forms, her preference for a comic mode, and her hopeful—bittersweet, but more sweet than bitter—outlook. Nevertheless, my estimate is that Tyler is doing very well. In reputation, she stands with a select group of America's most respected writers, and if there are arguments about the precise rankings among this group, that is the name of the game in the study of literary reputation.

Notes on the Contributors

Frances H. Bachelder, concert pianist and teacher for over forty years, studied at the University of Massachusetts and Purdue University. She now resides in San Diego, California, and while continuing her career as pianist also writes poetry and nonfiction. She is the author of an essay on Barbara Pym and of the study *Mary Roberts Rinehart: Mistress of Mystery*.

Sarah English teaches English at Meredith College in Raleigh, North Carolina.

Elizabeth Evans taught in the Department of English at the Georgia Institute of Technology from 1964 until her retirement in 1990. A former head of the department, Evans is the author of *Ring Lardner*, *Eudora Welty*, *Thomas Wolfe, May Sarton, Revisited*, and *Anne Tyler*. She now lives in the mountains of western North Carolina.

Donna Gerstenberger is professor of English at the University of Washington, Seattle. She works in the fields of modern American, English, and Irish literatures and narrative theory.

Lin T. Humphrey is professor of English at Citrus College where she teaches composition and folklore. She has received three National Endowment for the Humanities Summer Seminar Grants, at Indiana University, the University of Wisconsin, and the University of Virginia where she pursued her interests in American folklore, women's social history, and the study of traditional foodways. Her publications include articles in various folklore journals, and she is also coauthor of a collection of essays about food and community entitled *"We Gather Together": Food and Festival in American Life*.

Karen L. Levenback, who has served as president of the Virginia Woolf Society (1990–93) and as secretary-treasurer (1986–89), has published widely and is currently writing a book on Virginia Woolf and the Great War. She has taught in Europe and, since 1984, at George Washington University.

Stella Nesanovich is associate professor of English at McNeese State University. Besides being the author of the first doctoral dissertation on the fiction of Anne Tyler (Louisiana State University, 1979), she is also a fiction writer and a poet. Her work has appeared in various periodicals, including the *Southern Review*, *Xavier Review*, *Christianity and Literature*, *America*, and *Poet Lore*. She is the author of "The Pearl," a short story which appeared in *Something in Common: Contemporary Louisiana Stories*, and the compiler of "An Anne Tyler Checklist, 1959–1980," published in the *Bulletin of Bibliography*.

Alice Hall Petry, professor of English and chair of the Department of English at the Rhode Island School of Design, Providence, is a former Fulbright Scholar in Brazil (1985), USIA lecturer in Japan (1991), postdoctoral fellow of the American Council of Learned Societies (1987–88), and visiting professor of American literature at the University of Colorado, Boulder (1987). She has published widely on Southern fiction and American women writers, including *A Genius in His Way: The Art of Cable's "Old Creole Days," Fitzgerald's Craft of Short Fiction, Understanding Anne Tyler, Critical Essays on Anne Tyler*, and the forthcoming *Critical Essays on Kate Chopin*.

Rose Quiello, assistant professor of English at Western Connecticut State University, has been involved in women's and children's issues, in literature, and in life by her active work as a teacher and a practicing registered nurse. In addition to having published several articles in professional journals, she is the editor of *Breakdowns and Breakthroughs: The Figure of the Hysteric in Contemporary Novels by Women*.

Dale Salwak is professor of English at Citrus College. He was educated at Purdue University and then the University of Southern California under a National Defense Education Act competitive fellowship program. His publications include studies of Kingsley Amis, John Braine, Philip Larkin, Barbara Pym, Carl Sandburg, and John Wain. In 1985 he was awarded a National Endowment for the Humanities grant. In 1987 Purdue University awarded him its Distinguished Alumnus Award. His forthcoming books include *The Wonders of Solitude* and a collection of essays, *The Literary Biography: Problems and Solutions*.

Ruth O. Saxton is associate professor of English at Mills College. She edits the *Doris Lessing Newsletter* and has written on undergraduate archival research as well as on Lessing and Virginia Woolf. Her current work focuses on female dress, the body, and mothers and daughters. She is also coeditor (with Jean Tobin) of a collection of essays on Woolf and Lessing.

Aileen Chris Shafer, associate professor of English at West Virginia University, has published articles on T. S. Eliot, Mark Twain, Anne Tyler, and Walt Whitman.

Charlotte Templin, professor of English and chair of the Department of English at the University of Indianapolis, is the author of *Feminism and the Politics of Literary Reputation: The Example of Erica Jong* and (with Carole Taylor) *Literary Reputation and the Woman Writer*. She has held summer fellowships from the Lilly Foundation and the National Endowment for the Humanities. In the fall of 1992 she was a research associate at the Five College Women's Studies Research Center at Mount Holyoke College.

John Updike was born in Shillington, Pennsylvania, and attended Harvard College and the Ruskin School of Drawing and Fine Arts in Oxford, England. From 1955 to 1957 he was a staff member of the *New Yorker*; since 1957 he has lived in Massachusetts. He is the father of four children and the author of some thirty-six books, including sixteen novels and four collections of criticism. His novels *Rabbit Is Rich* and *Rabbit at Rest* both won the Pulitzer Prize for Fiction and the National Book Critics Circle Award.

Joseph Voelker, chair of English at Franklin and Marshall College, is the author of *Art and the Accidental in Anne Tyler*.

Linda Wagner-Martin, Hanes Professor of English and Comparative Literature at the University of North Carolina, Chapel Hill, has authored books on Hemingway, Faulkner, William Carlos Williams, Ellen Glasgow, Frost, Dos Passos, and other modern American writers. Her recent study of American fiction, *The Modern American Novel*, will be joined soon by a book on the novel at mid-century, and her biography of Sylvia Plath has led to a family biography of the Stein family, now in progress.

Kathleen Woodward, professor of English and director of the Center for Twentieth Century Studies at the University of Wisconsin-Milwaukee, is the author of *Aging and Its Discontents: Freud and Other Fictions*; coeditor (with Murray Schwartz) of *Memory and Desire: Aging/Literature/Psychoanalysis*; and editor of *The Myths of Information: Technology and Post-industrial Culture*. She is at work on a book on representations of older women in twentieth-century fiction.

Notes to the Text

Unless given below, full publication details on the sources may be found in the Selected Bibliography that follows the Notes.

Preface

1 Carolyn Wilkerson Bell, "*Saint Maybe*," *Magill's Literary Annual 1992*, ed. Frank N. Magill (Pasadena: Salem Press, 1993), pp. 706, 703.
2 Anne Tyler, "From England to West Virginia," *New York Times Book Review*, 13 February 1983, p. 1.

1. Early Years and Influences

1 Anne Tyler, "Varieties of Inspiration," *New Republic*, 12 September 1983, p. 32.
2 Ibid.
3 *In Praise of What Persists*, ed. Stephen Berg (New York: Harper and Row, 1983), p. 206.
4 Ibid., pp. vii–viii.
5 Ibid., p. ix.
6 Ibid., p. vii.
7 Ibid., p. 187.
8 Ibid., p. 33.
9 Anne Tyler, "Varieties of Inspiration," p. 33.
10 *In Praise of What Persists*, p. 10.
11 Ibid., p. xi.
12 Marguerite Michaels, "Anne Tyler, Writer from 8:05 to 3:30," *New York Times Book Review*, 8 May 1977; reprinted in Alice Hall Petry, ed., *Critical Essays on Anne Tyler*, p. 43.
13 Lucinda Irwin Smith, *Women Who Write: From the Past and the Present to the Future*, pp. 141–42.
14 Ibid., p. 139.
15 Phyllis Tyler to Elizabeth Evans, November 1990. Subsequent undocumented quotations are from this letter.
16 Anne Tyler, "Still Just Writing," in *The Writer on Her Work*, ed. Janet Sternburg (New York: Norton, 1980), p. 13.
17 Ibid.

18 Anne Tyler, "Why I Still Treasure 'The Little House,'" *New York Times Book Review*, 9 November 1986, p. 56.

19 Anne Tyler, "Fairy Tales: More than Meets the Ear," *National Observer*, 8 May 1976, p. 21.

20 Anne Tyler, "On the Uses of Genius, Daydreams, and Idle Hours," *National Observer*, 10 July 1976, p. 17.

21 Ricki Morell, "Orchids *for* Mrs. Peacock," *Charlotte Observer*, 6 December 1991, p. A8.

22 Betty Hodges, [Interview with Anne Tyler], (Durham, N.C.) *Morning Herald*, 12 December 1982, p. D3, Anne Tyler Papers, Perkins Library, Duke University.

23 Ricki Morell, "Orchids *for* Mrs. Peacock," p. A9.

24 Ibid.

25 Ibid., p. A8.

26 Interview with Phyllis Peacock, Raleigh, N.C., 25 February 1993.

27 Interview with Alice Ehrlich, Raleigh, N.C., 25 February 1993. Subsequent undocumented quotations are from this interview.

28 Telephone interview with Reynolds Price, 7 March 1993. Subsequent undocumented quotations are from this interview.

29 Reynolds Price, *Clear Pictures, First Loves, First Guides* (New York: Atheneum, 1989), p. 12.

30 Barbara Ascher, "A Visit with Eudora Welty," *Yale Review* 74 (1984): 149.

31 These stories by Anne Tyler appeared in *Archive*: "Laura," 71 (1959): 36–37; "The Lights on the River," 72 (1959): 5–6; "The Bridge," 72 (1960): 10–15; "I Never Saw Morning," 73 (1961): 11–14; "The Saints in Caesar's Household," 73 (1961): 7–10.

32 Reynolds Price, *Clear Pictures, First Loves, First Guides*, p. 204.

33 Anne Tyler, "Still Just Writing," *The Writer on Her Work*, pp. 14–15.

34 Interview with Eudora Welty, Jackson, Mississippi, 5 March 1993. Subsequent undocumented quotations are from this interview.

35 Anne Tyler, "The Fine, Full World of Welty," *Washington Star*, 26 October 1980, pp. D7–8.

36 Anne Tyler, "A Visit with Eudora Welty," *New York Times Book Review*, 2 November 1980, pp. 33–34.

37 Eudora Welty also made this statement to Barbara Ascher, who includes it in "A Visit with Eudora Welty," *Yale Review*, pp. 147–53.

38 Nina Auerbach, *Romantic Imprisonment: Women and Other Glorified Outcasts* (New York: Columbia University Press, 1985), p. 6.

39 See Carol S. Manning, "Welty, Tyler, and Traveling Salesmen: The Wandering Hero Unhorsed," in *The Fiction of Anne Tyler*, pp. 110–18.

40 Alice Hall Petry, *Understanding Anne Tyler*, p. 6.

41 For example, Alice Hall Petry notes from her 1989 interview that Tyler claims no conscious link between *Dinner at the Homesick Restaurant* and Eudora Welty's *The Golden Apples*. Although several critics have drawn parallels between *Dinner at the Homesick Restaurant* and Faulkner's *As I Lay Dying*, Tyler indicated in the Petry interview that "to the best of my knowledge, I've never read *As I Lay Dying*" (Ibid., pp. 19–20n.).

Bruce Cook in "New Faces in Faulkner Country" (*Saturday Review*, 4 September 1976) includes Tyler's disavowal of any identification with Faulkner. When she read Faulkner's work, Tyler says, "I didn't feel any sort of identification with it at all. He is, after all, an extremely masculine writer. There couldn't be a woman Faulkner at all. Then, too, I guess I should make it clear that when I did get around to reading him, I had already started writing myself. And his whole approach to writing—obviously he was knitting off in all directions—was completely wrong for me. If it were possible to write like him, I wouldn't. I disagree with him. I want everyone to understand what I'm getting at" (p. 40; reprinted in *Critical Essays on Anne Tyler*, pp. 157–58).

42 In Alice Hall Petry's 1989 interview, Tyler said, "I love Tolstoy because of a single book, *Anna Karenina*, and that's for its fresh, subtle, surprisingly modern style" (*Understanding Anne Tyler*, p. 19n).

43 Millicent Bell, "Tobacco Road Updated," *New York Times Book Review*, 21 November 1965, p. 77.

44 Alice Hall Petry, *Understanding Anne Tyler*, p. 12.

45 Anne Tyler, "Kentucky Comes," *New Republic*, 1 November 1982, p. 36.

46 Flannery O'Connor, *Letters of Flannery O'Connor: The Habit of Being*, ed. Sally Fitzgerald (New York: Farrar, Straus, Giroux, 1979), p. 99.

47 *In Praise of What Persists*, pp. vii–viii.

48 Anne Tyler, "End of a Love Affair," *New Republic*, 5 December 1983, p. 27.

2. The Early Novels: A Reconsideration

In 1976, when I first thought of writing a doctoral dissertation on the novels of Anne Tyler, I approached Dr. Donald E. Stanford, then coeditor of the *Southern Review* and professor of English at Louisiana State University. I was aware that he had begun publishing the short stories of Anne Tyler as early as 1965. I recall vividly the eagerness with which he accepted the project and the praise he had for Tyler's work. Though I cannot now quote him exactly, I remember his commenting on what a fine prose stylist Tyler was and his predicting that she would someday be a prominent literary figure. The rest, as the saying goes, is history.

1 Anne Tyler to Stella Nesanovich, 25 July 1977. Tyler is herself unsure of when she helped edit the *Archive*. Although an April 1977 issue of the magazine containing a new story by Tyler mentions her editing the magazine, it does not supply any other information.

2 See *Archive* 71 (1959): 36–37 and *Archive* 72 (1959): 5–6.

3 Anne Tyler to Stella Nesanovich, 25 July 1977.

4 *Archive* 23 (1961): 11–14.

5 *Antioch Review* 24 (1964): 379–86.

6 References to characters and parts of the plot in this story, particularly the observation of Ben Joe and Shelley's return by Shelley's younger sister Phoebe, are made several times in *If Morning Ever Comes*.

7 Anne Tyler, "Nobody Answers the Door," *Antioch Review* 23 (1974): 385.

8 Ibid., p. 382.

9 Clifford A. Ridley, "Anne Tyler: A Sense of Reticence Balanced by 'Oh, Well, Why Not?,'" *National Observer*, 22 July 1972, p. 23.

10 Marguerite Michaels, "Anne Tyler, Writer 8:05–3:30," *New York Times Book Review*, p. 43.

11 Clifford A. Ridley, "Anne Tyler: A Sense of Reticence Balanced by 'Oh, Well, Why Not?,'" p. 23.

12 In its portrayal of teenage musical obsessions, *A Slipping-Down Life* is especially reminiscent of the 1960s.

13 Clifford A. Ridley, "Anne Tyler: A Sense of Reticence Balanced by 'Oh, Well, Why Not?,'" p. 23.

14 Ibid.

15 Anne Tyler to Stella Nesanovich, 25 July 1977.

3. Tyler and Feminism

1 Clifford A. Ridley, "Anne Tyler: A Sense of Reticence Balanced by 'Oh, Well, Why Not?,'" *National Observer*, 22 July 1972, p. 23; reprinted in Alice Hall Petry, ed., *Critical Essays on Anne Tyler*, pp. 24–27.

2 Anne Tyler to Alice Hall Petry, August 1989.

3 Unsigned review of *If Morning Ever Comes* in *Time*, 1 January 1965, p. 71.

4 Edward Hoagland feels that Tyler had introduced elements of "unfunny slapstick" in "an effort to corral extra readers. I don't believe Ms. Tyler should think she needs to tinker with her popularity." See "About Maggie, Who Tried Too Hard," *New York Times Book Review*, 11 September 1988, p. 44; reprinted in Alice Hall Petry, *Critical Essays on Anne Tyler*, p. 140–44.

5 Marita Golden, "New Wives' Tales," *Ms.* 17 (1988): 86.

6 "The only way I could explain my life to myself was to imagine that I was living in a very small commune. I had spent my childhood in a commune, or what would nowadays be called a commune, and I was used to the idea of division of labor. What we had here, I told myself, was a perfectly sensible arrangement: one member was the liaison with the outside world, bringing in money; another was the caretaker, reading the Little Bear books to the children and repairing the electrical switches. This second member might have less physical freedom, but she had much more freedom to arrange her own work schedule. I must have sat down a dozen times a week and very carefully, consciously thought it all through." See Anne Tyler, "Still Just Writing," in Janet Sternburg, ed., *The Writer on Her Work*, p. 8. Also valuable is Marguerite Michaels, "Anne Tyler, Writer 8:05 to 3:30," *New York Times Book Review*, 8 May 1977, pp. 13, 42–43; reprinted in Alice Hall Petry, *Critical Essays on Anne Tyler*, pp. 40–44.

4. Manacles of Fear: Emotional Affliction in Tyler's Works

1 Carl E. Seashore, *Psychology of Music* (New York: Dover, 1967), p. 334.

2 Duane P. Schultz, *Psychology in Use* (New York: Macmillan, 1979), pp. 49–50.

5. Breakdowns and Breakthroughs: The Hysterical Use of Language

I am indebted to Regina Barreca, friend and colleague, who carefully read many drafts of my essay and gave me thoughtful criticism. I gratefully dedicate this to you, Gina.

1 Luce Irigaray, *This Sex Which Is Not One*, transl. Catherine Porter with Carolyn Burke (Ithaca: Cornell University Press, 1985), p. 76.

2 Sandra Gilbert and Susan Gubar, *The Madwoman in the Attic: The Woman Writer and the Nineteenth-Century Literary Imagination* (New Haven: Yale University Press, 1979), p. 37.

3 Virginia Woolf, *The Essays of Virginia Woolf*, vol. 1, 1901–1912, ed. Andrew McNeille (London: Hogarth Press, 1986), p. 35.

4 Tyler's *A Slipping-Down Life* has special affinities with Maxine Hong Kingston's compelling autobiography *The Woman Warrior: Memoirs of a Girlhood Among Ghosts* (New York: Random House, 1977), which begins with the memory of her mother's literally cutting the voice out of her: "She pushed my tongue up and sliced the frenum. Or maybe she snipped it with a pair of *nail scissors*. I don't remember her doing it, only her telling me about it, but all during childhood I felt sorry for the baby whose mother waited with scissors or knife in hand for it to cry—and then, when its mouth was wide open like a baby bird's, cut" (p. 190, italics mine). Maxine Hong Kingston's scars, like Evie Decker's scars, no doubt serve as both a fertile reminder and a visible manifestation of the price women have had to pay for transgressing cultural and linguistic conventions. In her fantasy, Maxine Hong Kingston is a warrior, like Fa Mu Lan, whose parents carved their grievances on her back and sent her off to battle: "My mother washed my back as if I had left for only a day and were her baby yet. . . . My father first brushed the words in ink, and they fluttered down my back row after row. Then he began cutting; to make fine lines and points he used thin blades, for the stems, large blades" (p. 35). Evie Decker, like Fa Mu Lan, has been inscribed literally with the word of the father; yet, like her antecedent, Fa Mu Lan, Evie goes on to become a woman warrior, escaping confinement to a female script.

5 For the most part, critical appreciation of Tyler's work centers on the family. Frank W. Shelton, in his essay "The Necessary Balance: Distance and Sympathy in the Novels of Anne Tyler," explores the difficulty Tyler's characters experience in attempting to find the "necessary balance" that will permit them to retain the distance from others necessary for a sense of autonomy and, at the same time, "achieve enough closeness to others to share necessary human warmth and sympathy." In her essay, "Family as Fate: The Novels of Anne Tyler," Mary Ellis Gibson examines the ways in which Tyler's characters repeatedly come up against the possibility of change. Mary R. Robertson, in "Medusa Points and Contact Points" (*Contemporary American Women Writers*,

eds. Michelle Zimbalist Rosaldo and Louise Lamphere [Stanford: Stanford University Press, 1974]), argues that the "family," in Tyler's novels, is "shown or implied to be the principal determinant of adult identity and the primary social unit" (p. 121). Robertson goes on to discuss the family as a sign of "order and disorder in personality and society" (p. 122). In "Home at Last, and Homesick Again: The Ten Novels of Anne Tyler," Anne G. Jones explores the conflict that Tyler's characters and her families experience when torn between wandering away from home in the world, and "staying at home in the hope of some bliss."

6 Margaret Homans, *Bearing the Word: Language and Experience in Nineteenth-Century Women's Writing* (Chicago: University of Chicago Press, 1986), p. 5.

7 Phyllis Chesler, *Women and Madness* (Garden City: Doubleday, 1972; San Diego: Harcourt Brace Jovanovich, 1989), p. xxxv.

8 The disruption in "traditional" logic becomes a marker of feminine discourse. Muriel's discourse is unconventional according to the standard of logic that has been imposed by men upon women. Central to Andrea Nye's argument in *Words of Power: A Feminist Approach to the History of Logic* (New York: Routledge, 1990) is the fact that women have been culturally positioned outside this arena of logic and language and have, consequently, been a threat to the potential feminization of logical thought (p. 2). The masculine gatekeepers of logic and language are seen as emblematic of the linguistic barriers women have been forced to face.

9 Sandra Gilbert and Susan Gubar, *The Madwoman in the Attic: The Woman Writer and the Nineteenth-Century Literary Imagination*, p. 26.

10 Helene Cixous and Catherine Clément, *The Newly Born Woman*, transl. Betsy Wing (Minneapolis: University of Minnesota Press, 1975), p. 7.

11 Ibid.

12 Sherry Ortner, "Is Female to Male as Nature Is to Culture?" in *Woman, Culture and Society*, eds. Michelle Zimbalist Rosaldo and Louise Lamphere (Stanford: Stanford University Press, 1974), p. 85.

13 Sandra Gilbert and Susan Gubar, *The Madwoman in the Attic: The Woman Writer and the Nineteenth-Century Literary Imagination*, p. 27.

14 Ibid., p. 79.

15 Margaret Morganroth Gullette, "Anne Tyler: The Tears (and Joys) Are in the Things," p. 110.

16 Caroll Smith-Rosenberg, *Disorderly Conduct* (New York: Knopf, 1985), p. 200.

6. Crepe Soles, Boots, and Fringed Shawls: Female Dress as Signals of Femininity

1 Sherry B. Ortner, "Is Female to Male as Nature Is to Culture?" *Woman, Culture and Society*, eds. Michelle Zimbalist Rosaldo and Louise Lamphere (Stanford: Stanford University Press, 1974), p. 73.

2 While there are codes of male dress in society—business suits, polo shirts, overalls—male dress is primarily associated with profession or class, not with self-expression. With obvious exceptions, masculine dress does not exist in the cultural imagination as a reliable way of reading a character's sexual status. For example, Grandpa Peck's shoes do not provide a clue to his sexual identity.

3 After reading an early draft of this essay, Kirsten T. Saxton introduced me to Joan Riviere's "Womanliness as a Masquerade" (*International Journal of Psychoanalysis* 10 |1929|: 303–13), and helped articulate these ideas. Katherine Saxton read the draft for clarity.

7. Functions of (Picturing) Memory

Virginia Woolf, "A Sketch of the Past," in *Moments of Being*, ed. Jeanne Schulkind (New York: Harcourt Brace Jovanovich, 1978), p. 64.

1 Ibid., p. 72.

2 That Tyler is concerned with connections made by her characters is widely acknowledged. As she revealed in an epistolary interview with Alice Hall Petry (see *Understanding Anne Tyler*), she is also concerned with connecting with her readers. She doesn't read reviews of her work, she said, because "I don't want to know how often I've missed connecting" (p. 3).

3 Ibid., p. 16.

4 Margaret Ferry, "Recommended: Anne Tyler," pp. 93–94.

5 Virginia Woolf, *To the Lighthouse* (New York: Harcourt Brace Jovanovich [1927], 1955), p. 310.

8. Marcel Proust, Involuntary Memory, and Tyler's Novels

1 Marcel Proust, "Overture," *Swann's Way, Remembrance of Things Past*, transl. C. K. Scott Moncrieff and Terence Kilmartin (New York: Random House, 1981), p. 4. All subsequent quotations from *Remembrance of Things Past* are from this edition and cited below.

2 Ibid., *The Captive*, p. 413.

3 John Updike, "On Such A Beautiful Green Planet" [review of *Dinner at the Homesick Restaurant*], *New Yorker*, 5 April 1982, p. 193.

4 Anne Tyler, "Olives Out of a Bottle" [Symposium at Duke University], *Archive* 87 (1975): 73; reprinted in *Critical Essays on Anne Tyler*, pp. 28–39.

5 Anne Tyler, "Because I Want More Than One Life," *Washington Post*, 15 August 1976, p. G2; reprinted in *Critical Essays on Anne Tyler*, pp. 45–49.

6 Anne Tyler, "Olives Out of a Bottle," p. 80.

7 Anne Tyler, "Because I Want More Than One Life," pp. G1, G7.

8 Marcel Proust, *Time Regained*, pp. 913–14.

9 Anne Tyler, "Because I Want More Than One Life," p. G7.

10 Marcel Proust, *Time Regained*, pp. 912–13.

11 Anne Tyler, "Why I Still Treasure the Little House," *New York Times Book Review*, 9 November 1986, p. 56.

9. Forgetting and Remembering: In Praise of Tyler's Older Women

1 I am borrowing the term "the middle years" from Margaret Morganroth Gullette's *Safe at Last in the Middle Years: The Invention of the Midlife Progress Novel: Saul Bellow, Margaret Drabble, Anne Tyler, and John Updike* (Berkeley: University of California Press, 1988).

2 The ostensibly heartless Amanda, too, in *Celestial Navigation*, having lost her mother and now her suitcase (she has come home for the funeral), rehearses the objects she has lost. It is also a way for her of conjuring up the realization of definitive loss, that is to say, the feeling of loss: "that one night I must have been at the low point and I lay on my back in the dark, long after Laura [her sister] was asleep, going over all the objects I had ever lost while some hard bleak pain settled on my chest and weighed me down."

3 Sigmund Freud, *Studies in Hysteria*, in *The Standard Edition of the Complete Psychological Works of Sigmund Freud*, transl. and ed. James Strachey, vol. 2. (London: Hogarth and Institute of Psycho-Analysis, 1953–74), p. 163.

4 Ibid., p. 162.

5 Ibid., p. 163.

6 Roland Barthes, *Camera Lucida: Reflections on Photography*, transl. Richard Howard (New York: Hill & Wang, 1981), p. 9.

7 Ibid., p. 117.

8 Susan Sontag, *On Photography* (New York: Farrar, Straus and Giroux, 1979), p. 14.

11. Loosened Roots

1 Anne Tyler, "Because I Want More Than One Life," *Washington Post*, 15 August 1976, p. G1; reprinted in *Critical Essays on Anne Tyler*, pp. 45–49.

2 Ibid.

12. Beauty and the Transformed Beast: Fairy Tales and Myths in Morgan's Passing

1 Alice Hall Petry, *Understanding Anne Tyler*, p. 8.

2 Not only did Freud explore the commonality of the Oedipal myth but he also discussed the meaning of Rumplestiltzchen, Red Caps, and the Wolf and the Seven Goats; Rank, Fromm, and Jung have also analyzed the behaviors contained in myths and fairy tales (see Julius E. Heuscher, *A Psychiatric Study of Myths and Fairy Tales* [Springfield, Ill.: Charles A. Thomas, 1974]). See also, Karen E. Rowe, "Feminism and Fairy Tales," *Women's Studies* 6 (1979): 237–57. She challenges "writers like Bruno Bettleheim who see fairy tales as gender-free stories that help children of both sexes to solve their problems and define themselves as human beings" (239).

3 Julius E. Heuscher, *A Psychiatric Study of Myths and Fairy Tales*, p. 363.

4 Karen E. Rowe, "Feminism and Fairy Tales," p. 252.

5 *Morgan's Passing* was honored with the National Book Critics Circle Award for 1981 as well as the Janet Heidinger Kafka Prize.

6 Alice Hall Petry, *Understanding Anne Tyler*, p. 8.

7 Frank Shelton, "The Necessary Balance: Distance and Sympathy in the Novels of Anne Tyler," p. 857; Joseph C. Voelker, *Art and the Accidental in Anne Tyler*, pp. 12, 87–88, 53.

8 Robert Towers, [Review of *Morgan's Passing*], *New Republic*, 22 March 1980, p. 31; reprinted in *Critical Essays on Anne Tyler*, pp. 103–106.

9 Jacques Lacan, in elaborating on the "other," discusses the *moi* as corresponding to the internalization of the other through identification, a

self of which we are aware, yet of whose origins we are unconscious. Although the "other" can refer to the recognition of the differences between the I and all others, one of the most often used definitions denotes members of a class or group with which a person does not identify. Another definition of the "Other" by both Jacques Lacan and Julia Kristeva differentiates the capitalized "Other" from the lowercase, locating it as a place or space that speaks or interacts with the I, with Lacan using the "Other" interchangeably with the unconscious. In my discussion of the puppets as the "Other," although I address both the lowercase and uppercase Other, I will principally be analyzing Emily and the puppets as the "Other"—a place she interacts with on an unconscious level. See Julia Kristeva, *Desire in Language*, ed. Leon S. Roudiez, transl. Thomas Gora, Alice Jardine, and Leon Roudiez (New York: Columbia University Press, 1980); and Jacques Lacan, *Speech and Language in Psychoanalysis*, transl. Anthony Wilden (Baltimore: Johns Hopkins University Press, 1968).

10 Marcia R. Lieberman, "'Some Day My Prince Will Come': Acculturation Through the Fairy Tale," *College English* 34 (1972): 394.

11 Karen E. Rowe, "Feminism and Fairy Tales," p. 239.

12 Ruth B. Bottigheimer, "Silenced Women in the Grimms' Tales: The 'Fit' Between Fairy Tales and Society in Their Historical Context," in Ruth B. Bottigheimer, ed., *Fairy Tales and Society: Illusion, Allusion, and Paradigm* (Philadelphia: University of Pennsylvania Press, 1986), p. 43.

13 Joseph C. Voelker, *Art and the Accidental in Anne Tyler*, p. 87.

14 Marcia R. Lieberman, "'Some Day My Prince Will Come': Acculturation Through the Fairy Tale," pp. 385–90.

15 John Updike, "Bellow, Vonnegut, Tyler, Le Guin, Cheever," in *Hugging the Shore* (New York: Knopf, 1983), pp. 273–83.

16 Bruno Bettelheim, *The Uses of Enchantment: The Meaning and Importance of Fairy Tales* (New York: Knopf, 1975), p. 308.

17 Ann L. T. Bergren, "Language and the Female in Early Greek Thought," *Arethusa* 16 (1983): 71.

18 Ruth B. Bottigheimer, "Silenced Women in the Grimm's Tales: The 'Fit' Between Fairy Tales and Society in Their Historical Context," p. 119. See also the following chapters in Ruth B. Bottigheimer's *Grimm's Bad Girls and Bold Boys* (New York: Yale University Press, 1987): "Bold Boys," "Patterns of Speech," "Paradigms for Powerlessness," "Spinning and Discontent," and Appendix B: "Patterns of Speech."

19 Maria M. Tatar, "Heroes in Grimm's Tales," in *Fairy Tales and Society: Illusion, Allusion, and Paradigm*, p. 100.

13. Everybody Speaks

1 Marguerite Michaels, "Anne Tyler, Writer 8:05 to 3:30," in *Critical Essays on Anne Tyler*, p. 43.

2 Wendy Lamb, "An Interview with Anne Tyler," ibid., p. 55.

3 Marguerite Michaels, "Anne Tyler, Writer 8:05 to 3:30," pp. 48–49.

4 Mary J. Elkins, "*Dinner at the Homesick Restaurant*: Anne Tyler and the Faulkner Connection," in *The Fiction of Anne Tyler*, p. 119.

5 Christopher Nash, "Literature's Assault on Narrative," in *Narrative in Culture* (London: Routledge, 1990), p. 200.

15. The Accidental Tourist *and* The Odyssey

1 Homer, *The Odyssey*, transl. Robert Fitzgerald (New York: Vintage, 1990), XIII, ll. 36–44.

2 Ibid., V, ll. 136, 142–43.

3 For an excellent discussion of Muriel as therapist, see Joseph C. Voelker, *Art and the Accidental in Anne Tyler*, pp. 147–64.

4 See G. E. Dimlock, Jr., "The Name of Odysseus," reprinted in Homer, *The Odyssey*, transl. and ed., Albert Cook (New York: Norton, 1967), pp. 406–24.

5 The second time I taught *The Accidental Tourist*, without *The Odyssey*, the novel still worked well. I tried a teaching technique this time that was too much fun not to tell someone about. After the students had discussed how "weird" the Leary family was, I asked them to "free-write" a list of everything about *their* families that would seem odd to outsiders. Then each of us read one item from our lists. Some of the funnier disclosures were that people had grandparents who saved used paper napkins, styrofoam plates, and the wax-paper bags from inside cereal boxes; that one student's family was partial to rhyming names— she had (I am not making this up) aunts named Novella, Rosella, and Sareyestella, and cousins named Purcesee, Earthedee, and Bularee; that one student heated her dog's food in the microwave and fed him by hand, and when her husband fed the dog, he used a fork. I hope this exercise showed students the essential humanity of the Learys. I am sure it was fun for its own sake.

6 Alice Hall Petry, *Understanding Anne Tyler*, pp. 231–32.

16. Breathing Lessons: *A Domestic Success Story*

1 See, for example, David Klinghoffer, "Ordinary People," *National Review*, 30 December 1988, p. 49; Robert Towers, "Roughing It," *New York Review of Books*, 10 November 1988, p. 40; Lee Lescaze, "Mid-Life Ups and Downs," *Wall Street Journal*, 6 September 1988, p. 28; Robert McPhillips, "The Baltimore Chop," *Nation*, 7 November 1988, pp. 464, 466; Alice Hall Petry, *Understanding Anne Tyler*, p. 234.

2 Ann Romines, *The Home Plot, Women, Writing and Domestic Ritual* (Amherst: University of Massachusetts Press, 1991), pp. 6–7.

3 Sandra Gilbert, "Private Lives and Public Issues: Anne Tyler's Prizewinning Novels," in *The Fiction of Anne Tyler*, pp. 141, 143.

4 Jay Parini, [Review of *Saint Maybe*], *New York Times Book Review*, 25 August 1991, p. 1.

5 Edward Hoagland, "About Maggie, Who Tried Too Hard," *New York Times Book Review*, 11 September 1988, p. 44. Joseph C. Voelker responds to what he sees as Tyler's wider ambition in *Breathing Lessons* to craft "more complicated emotions." Maggie "attains a serenity that Tyler suggests with the novel's title and sustains sadly through the rhythms of its sentences. Breathing, the involuntary act that ties us to the specific, physical moment, is also subject to calm, voluntary control" (see Joseph C. Voelker's *Art and the Accidental in Anne Tyler*, p. 166).

6 Peter Prescott, [Review of *Breathing Lessons*], *Newsweek*, 26 September 1988, p. 73.

7 Anne Tyler, "Olives Out of a Bottle," *Archive* 87 (1975): 81. Quoted by Joseph Voelker in *Art and the Accidental in Anne Tyler*, pp. 68–69.

17. Tyler's Literary Reputation

1 For a discussion of the pathologizing of the divergent critic, see Barbara Herrnstein Smith's *Contingencies of Value: Alternative Perspectives for Critical Theory* (Cambridge: Harvard University Press, 1988).

2 Barbara Herrnstein Smith uses the term "dynamics of endurance" to describe the many ways in which value is recreated in canonical works. It is not so much that value is "discovered" over a period of time as that it is "created" by those who praise, cite, reproduce, and in other ways increase the familiarity of a work.

3 See Richard Ohmann's "The Shaping of a Canon: U.S. Fiction, 1960–75" (*Critical Inquiry* 10 [1983]: 199–223; reprinted in his *Politics of Letters* [Middletown: Wesleyan University Press, 1987], pp. 68–91)

for a discussion of the role that readers play in the early stages of literary reputation. Ohmann says that the "early buyers of hardcover books exercised a crucial role in selecting the books that the rest of the country's readers would buy" (p. 201).

4 Carole Anne Taylor cites this remark in an unpublished essay, "Literary Theory, Critical Practice, and the Failure of 'Fit' for African Women Writers."

5 John Updike, "Family Ways," *New Yorker*, 29 March 1976, pp. 110–12, included in this volume.

6 For a list of her many reviews before 1984, see Mary F. Robertson's checklist in "Anne Tyler: Medusa Points and Contact Points," *Contemporary American Women Writers: Narrative Strategies*, eds. Catherine Rainwater and William J. Scheick (Lexington: University Press of Kentucky, 1985), pp. 119–42.

7 According to the Robertson checklist, Tyler reviewed exclusively for the *National Observer* from 1972 to 1976. See two substantial review articles by Clifford A. Ridley published during that time: "Anne Tyler: A Sense of Reticence Balanced by 'Oh, Well, Why Not?,'" *National Observer*, 22 July 1972, p. 23; and "Novels: A Hit Man, a Clown, a Genius," *National Observer*, 4 May 1974, p. 23.

8 See Richard Ohmann, "The Shaping of a Canon: U.S. Fiction, 1960–1975," pp. 199–223.

9 Hermione Lee ("Heart of Urban Darkness," *Observer*, 3 October 1982, p. 33) finds Tyler's writing "deliciously idiosyncratic" in *Dinner at the Homesick Restaurant*. John Fiction ("Food for Love," *Listener*, 21 October 1982, p. 24) says of the same novel that Tyler "writes with easy elegance and unmalicious humor." Carole Angier ("Small City America," *New Statesman and Society*, 20 January 1989, p. 34) describes an episode of *Breathing Lessons* as "high farce" but "also a painfully accurate picture of American tastelessness." Michael Wood ("Laughably Resilient," *Times Literary Supplement*, 20 January 1989, p. 57) says that Tyler conveys "a sense that comedy is a human constant, beyond any style or scenario, that we are all laughable creatures, as well as creatures who can laugh." Paul Binding has done favorable reviews in the *Listener* and also included Tyler in his book *A Separate Country: A Literary Journey Through the American South*.

10 See Mary F. Robertson, "Anne Tyler: Medusa Points and Contact Points."

11 Gail Godwin, [Review of *Celestial Navigation*], *New York Times Book Review*, 28 April 1974, p. 34.

12 See Alice Hall Petry, *Understanding Anne Tyler*, p. 98.

13 Clifford A. Ridley, "Novels: A Hit Man, a Clown, a Genius," *National Observer*, 4 May 1974, p. 23.

14 John Updike, "Family Ways," p. 110.

15 Katha Pollitt, [Review of *Searching for Caleb*], *New York Times Book Review*, 8 January 1976, p. 22.

16 Stella Nesanovich, "The Individual in the Family: Anne Tyler's *Searching for Caleb* and *Earthly Possessions*," p. 170.

17 See Nicholas Delbanco, [Review of *Earthly Possessions*], *New Republic*, 28 May 1977, p. 36; Katherine Bouton, [Review of *Earthly Possessions*], *Ms.*, August 1977, p. 36; Walter Sullivan, "The Insane and the Indifferent: Walker Percy and Others," *Sewanee Review* 86 (1978): 156–57; Angela Wigan, "Wilderness Course," *Time*, 9 May 1977, p. 86; John Updike, "Loosened Roots," *New Yorker*, 6 June 1977, p. 130.

18 David Evanier, "Song of Baltimore," *National Review*, 8 August 1980, p. 973; A. G. Mojtabai, "A State of Continual Crisis," *New York Times Book Review*, 23 March 1980, p. 14; James Wolcott, "Some Fun!," *New York Review of Books*, 3 April 1980, p. 34.

19 Francine du Plessix Gray, [Review of *Morgan's Passing*], *Commonweal*, 5 December 1980, p. 696; Paul Gray, "The Rich Are Different," *Time*, 17 March 1980, p. 91; Stella Nesanovich, "Anne Tyler's *Morgan's Passing*," *Southern Review* (1981): 619–21; Thomas M. Disch, "The Great Imposter," *Washington Post Book Review*, 16 March 1980, p. 2; John Updike, "Imagining Things," *New Yorker*, 23 June 1980, pp. 97–101.

20 Joseph Matthewson, "Taking the Anne Tyler Tour," *Horizon*, September 1985, p. 14.

21 Joseph Barbato, "'Breaking Out,'" *Publishers Weekly*, 31 May 1985, p. 30.

22 Pierre Bourdieu, *Distinction: A Social Critique of the Judgement of Taste*, transl. Richard Nice (Cambridge: Harvard University Press, 1984), pp. 411–17.

23 Benjamin DeMott, "Funny, Wise and True," *New York Times Book Review*, 15 March 1982, pp. 1, 14.

24 See R. Z. Sheppard, "Eat and Run," *Time*, 5 April 1982, pp. 77–78; Jean Strouse, "Family Arsenal," *Newsweek*, 5 April 1982, pp. 72–73; Andrea Barnet, [Review of *Dinner at the Homesick Restaurant*], *Saturday Review*, March 1982, p. 62. Very much the minority report were lukewarm reviews: by Cynthia Propper Seton ("Generations at Table," *Chicago Tribune Book World*, 4 April 1982, p. 7), in which she finds the characters uninteresting; and by James Wolcott ("Strange New World," *Esquire*,

April 1982, pp. 123–24), in which he describes the novel as "glum, low-plodding, and dogged."

25 John Updike, "More Substance Complexity of Family Relationships—Buried Horrors of Family Life," *New Yorker*, 5 April 1982, pp. 193–97.

26 Joseph Barbato, "'Breaking Out,'" *Publishers Weekly*, 31 May 1985, p. 31.

27 Larry McMurtry, "Life Is a Foreign Country," *New York Times Book Review*, 8 September 1985, pp. 1, 36.

28 Jonathan Yardley, "Anne Tyler's Family Circus," *Washington Post Book World*, 25 August 1985, p. 3.

29 Richard Eder, [Review of *The Accidental Tourist*], *Los Angeles Times Book Review*, 15 September 1985, p. 3.

30 Brigitte Weeks, [Review of *The Accidental Tourist*], *Ms.*, November 1985, pp. 28–29; Barbara Rich, "Class of 1985," *Women's Review of Books*, 19 April 1986, p. 11.

31 Diane Johnson, "Southern Comfort," *New York Review of Books*, 7 November 1985, pp. 15–17.

32 John Updike, "Leaving Home," *New Yorker*, 28 October 1985, pp. 106–12.

33 Peter Prescott, [Review of *Breathing Lessons*], *Newsweek*, 26 September 1988, p. 73.

34 The *New Yorker* (28 November 1988) gave *Breathing Lessons* a brief review: "This is a quieter book than others by Ms. Tyler, but it feels right" (p. 121).

35 Wallace Stegner, "The Meddler's Progress," *Washington Post Book World*, 4 September 1988, pp. 1, 6; Lee Lescaze, "Throwing Caution to the Winds," *Wall Street Journal*, 16 September 1985, p. 22; Barbara Rich, "Exquisite Eccentrics," *Women's Review of Books*, November 1988, pp. 20–21; Richard Eder, "Crazy for Sighing and Crazy for Loving You," *Los Angeles Times Book Review*, 11 September 1988, p. 3; R. Z. Sheppard, "Praise of Lives Without Life-Styles," *Time*, 5 September 1988, p. 75. Hilma Wolitzer, "Anne Tyler's Tender Ode to Married Life," *Chicago Tribune Book World*, 28 August 1988, pp. 1, 9.

36 Edward Hoagland, "About Maggie, Who Tried Too Hard," *New York Times Book Review*, 11 September 1988, pp. 1, 43–44; Robert Towers, "Roughing It," *New York Review of Books*, 10 November 1988, pp. 40–41.

37 See Bruce Bawer, "Anne Tyler: Gravity and Grace," *Washington Post Book World*, 18 August 1991, pp. 1–2; Ann-Janine Morey, "The Making

of *Saint Maybe*," *Christian Century*, 20 November, 1991, pp. 1090–92; Joyce Sister, "Road to Redemption," *Chicago Tribune Books*, 25 August 1991, p. 3; Crystal Gromer, "Never Far From Home," *Commonweal*, 8 November 1991, pp. 656–57; Paul Gray, "Looking for a Second Chance," *Time*, 9 September 1991, pp. 67–68; Richard Eder, "Quiescence as Art Form," *Los Angeles Times Book Review*, 8 September 1991, pp. 3, 17; Marilyn Gardner, "Ordinariness as Art," *Christian Science Monitor*, 25 September 1991, p. 13; Michiko Kakutani, "Love, Guilt, and Change in a Family," *New York Times*, 30 August 1991, p. C21; Brad Leithauser, "Just Folks," *New York Review of Books*, 16 January 1992, pp. 53–55; Jay Parini, "The Accidental Convert," *New York Times Book Review*, 25 August 1991, pp. 1, 26.

38 John Blades, "For NutraSweet Fiction, Tyler Takes the Cake," *Chicago Tribune Books*, 20 July 1986, p. 37.

39 Vivian Gornick, "Anne Tyler's Arrested Development," *Village Voice*, 30 March 1982, pp. 40–41.

40 Robert McPhillips, "The Baltimore Chop," *Nation*, 7 November 1988, pp. 464–66.

41 David Klinghofer, "Ordinary People," *National Review*, 30 December 1988, pp. 48–49.

42 Carol Iannone, "Novel Events," *National Review*, 1 September 1989, pp. 46–48.

43 Wallace Stegner, "The Meddler's Progress," p. 1.

44 R. Z. Sheppard, "Innocent with an Explanation," *Time*, 16 September 1985, p. 78.

45 Jonathan Yardley, "Anne Tyler's Family Circus," p. 3.

46 Stella Nesanovich, "The Individual in the Family: Anne Tyler's *Searching for Caleb* and *Earthly Possessions*, p. 173.

47 Joseph Matthewson, "Taking the Anne Tyler Tour," p. 14.

48 Richard Eder, [Review of *The Accidental Tourist*], p. 10.

49 Michiko Kakutani, "Love, Guilt, and Change in a Family," p. 21.

50 Let us note also that some of her reviewers are academics. Sometimes academic reviewers also write scholarly books and articles about an author.

51 Almost every critic mentions Welty. Voelker (in *Art and the Accidental in Anne Tyler*) especially makes much of Welty's influence, citing parallels in specific stories. See also Carol S. Manning's "Welty, Tyler, and Traveling Salesmen: The Wandering Hero Unhorsed," in *The Fiction of Anne Tyler*, pp. 110–18.

52 See Petry's comments in *Understanding Anne Tyler*, p. 19, n. 12, and "Anne Tyler, Writer 8:05 to 3:30" in the *New York Times Book Review*, 8 May 1977, pp. 13, 42–43.

53 Those who have written articles on the Faulkner connection are Adrienne Bond ("From Addie Burden to Pearl Tull: The Secularization of the South") and Mary J. Elkins ("Anne Tyler and the Faulkner Connection," in *The Fiction of Anne Tyler*, pp. 119–35).

54 Doris Betts, "The Fiction of Anne Tyler," p. 27.

55 Paul Binding, *Separate Country: A Literary Journey Through the American South*, p. 174.

56 Barbara Harrell Carson, "Art's Internal Necessity: Anne Tyler's *Celestial Navigation*," in *The Fiction of Anne Tyler*, pp. 16–27; Sue Lile Inman, "The Effects of the Artistic Process: A Study of Three Artist Figures in Anne Tyler's Fiction," in *The Fiction of Anne Tyler*, pp. 55–63.

57 Gordon O. Taylor, "Morgan's Passing," in *The Fiction of Anne Tyler*, pp. 64–72.

58 Mary F. Robertson, "Anne Tyler: Medusa Points and Contact Points," pp. 119–42.

59 Mary Ellen Gibson, "Family as Fate: The Novels of Anne Tyler," pp. 47–58.

60 Margaret Morganroth Gullette, *Safe at Last in the Middle Years: The Invention of the Mid-Life Process Novel: Margaret Drabble, Saul Bellow, Anne Tyler, and John Updike*, p. 119.

61 Joseph B. Wagner, "Beck Tull: 'The absence presence' in *Dinner at the Homesick Restaurant*," in *The Fiction of Anne Tyler*, pp. 73–83; Anne Ricketson Zahlen, "Traveling Through the Self: The Psychic Drama of Anne Tyler's *The Accidental Tourist*," in *The Fiction of Anne Tyler*, pp. 84–96; Virginia Schaeffer Carroll, "The Nature of Kinship in the Novels of Anne Tyler," in *The Fiction of Anne Tyler*, pp. 16–27.

62 John Updike, "More Substance Complexity of Family Relationships— Buried Horrors of Family Life," p. 197.

Selected Bibliography

Primary Sources

If Morning Ever Comes. New York: Knopf, 1964; London: Chatto &
    Windus, 1965, 1980.
The Tin Can Tree. New York: Knopf, 1965; London: Macmillan, 1966.
A Slipping-Down Life. New York: Knopf, 1970.
The Clock Winder. New York: Knopf, 1972; London: Chatto & Windus,
    1973.
Celestial Navigation. New York: Knopf, 1974; London: Chatto & Windus,
    1975.
Searching for Caleb. New York: Knopf; London: Chatto & Windus, 1976.
Earthly Possessions. New York: Knopf; London: Chatto & Windus, 1977.
Morgan's Passing. New York: Knopf, 1980.
Dinner at the Homesick Restaurant. New York: Knopf, 1982.
The Accidental Tourist. New York: Knopf, 1985.
Breathing Lessons. New York: Knopf, 1988.
Saint Maybe. New York: Knopf, 1991.

Secondary Sources

Betts, Doris. "The Fiction of Anne Tyler." *Southern Quarterly* 21 (1983):
    23–37; reprinted in *Women Writers of the Contemporary South*, ed.
    Peggy Whitman Prenshaw, Jackson: University of Mississippi Press,
    1984, pp. 23–37.
Binding, Paul. "Anne Tyler." *A Separate Country: A Literary
    JourneyThrough the American South*. New York and London:
    Paddington Press, 1979. 198–209.
Bond, Adrienne. "From Addie Burden to Pearl Tull: The Secularization
    of the South." *Southern Quarterly* 24 (1986): 64–73.
Bowers, Bradley R. "Anne Tyler's Insiders." *Mississippi Quarterly* 42
    (1988–89): 47–56.
Brock, Dorothy Faye Sala. "Anne Tyler's Treatment of Managing
    Women." Ph.D. dissertation, University of North Texas, 1985.
Brooks, Mary Ellen. "Anne Tyler." *The Dictionary of Literary Biography*.
    Vol. 6. American Novelists Since World War II. Ed. James E. Kibler, Jr.
    Detroit: Gale Research/Bruccoli Clark, 1980. 336–45.

Carson, Barbara Harrell. "Complicate, Complicate: Anne Tyler's Moral Imperative." *Southern Quarterly* 31 (1992): 24–34.

Crane, Gwen. "Anne Tyler." *Modern American Women Writers*. Eds. Lea Baechler and A. Walton Litz. New York: Charles Scribner's Sons, 1991. 499–510.

Elkins, Mary J. "*Dinner at the Homesick Restaurant* : Anne Tyler and the Faulkner Connection." *Atlantis: A Women's Studies Journal* 10 (1985): 93–105; reprt. *The Fiction of Anne Tyler*, pp. 119–35.

English, Sarah. "Anne Tyler." *The Dictionary of Literary Biography Yearbook: 1982*. Detroit: Gale Research, 1983. 187–94.

Evans, Elizabeth. *Anne Tyler*. New York: Twayne, 1993.

Ferry, Margaret. "Recommended: Anne Tyler." *English Journal* 76 (1987): 93–94.

Freiert, William K. "Anne Tyler's Accidental Ulysses." *Classical and Modern Literature* 10 (1989): 71–79.

Gardiner, Elaine, and Catherine Rainwater. "A Bibliography of Writings by Anne Tyler." *Contemporary American Women Writers: Narrative Strategies*. Ed. Catherine Rainwater and William J. Scheik. Lexington: University of Kentucky Press, 1985. 142–52.

Gibson, Mary Ellis. "Family as Fate: The Novels of Anne Tyler." *Southern Literary Journal* 15 (1983): 47–58.

Gullette, Margaret Morganroth. "Anne Tyler: The Tears (and Joys) Are in the Things." In her *Safe at Last in the Middle Years: The Invention of the Mid-Life Process Novel: Margaret Drabble, Saul Bellow, Anne Tyler, and John Updike*. Berkeley: University of California Press, 1988. 105–119.

Jones, Anne G. "Home at Last, and Homesick Again: The Ten Novels of Anne Tyler." *Hollins Critic* 23 (1986): 1–14.

Lamb, Wendy. "An Interview with Anne Tyler." *Iowa Journal of Literary Studies* 3 (1981): 59–64.

Linton, Karin. *The Temporal Horizon: A Study of the Theme of Time in Anne Tyler's Major Novels*. Uppsala, Sweden: Acta Universitatis Upsaliensis, 1989.

Nesanovich, Stella. "The Individual in the Family: A Critical Introduction to the Novels of Anne Tyler." Ph.D. dissertation. Louisiana State University, 1979.

———. "The Individual in the Family: Anne Tyler's *Searching for Caleb* and *Earthly Possessions*." *Southern Review* n.s. 14 (1978): 170–76.

Petry, Alice Hall. "Bright Books of Life: The Black Norm in Anne Tyler's Novels." *Southern Quarterly* 31 (1992): 7–13.

————, ed. *Critical Essays on Anne Tyler*. New York: G. K. Hall/ Macmillan, 1992.

————. *Understanding Anne Tyler*. Columbia: University of South Carolina Press, 1990.

Robertson, Mary F. "Anne Tyler: Medusa Points and Contact Points." *Contemporary American Women Writers: Narrative Strategies*. Eds. Catherine Rainwater and William J. Scheick. Lexington: University Press of Kentucky, 1985. 119–52.

Shelton, Frank. "The Necessary Balance: Distance and Sympathy in the Novels of Anne Tyler." *Southern Review* 20 (1984): 851–60.

Smith, Lucinda Irwin. *Women Who Write: From the Past and the Present to the Future*. Englewood Cliffs, N.J.: Prentice Hall, 1989.

Stephens, C. Ralph, ed. *The Fiction of Anne Tyler*. Jackson: University Press of Mississippi, 1990.

Town, Caren J. "Rewriting the Family during Dinner at the Homesick Restaurant." *Southern Quarterly* 31 (1992): 14–23.

Voelker, Joseph C. *Art and the Accidental in Anne Tyler*. Columbia, Mo.: University of Missouri Press, 1989.

Zahlan, Anne R. "Anne Tyler." *Fifty Southern Writers after 1900: A Bio-Bibliographical Sourcebook*. Eds. Joseph M. Flora and Robert Baines. Westport, Conn.: Greenwood, 1987. 491–504.

Index